Beyond the Tariff

Beyond the Tariff

Human rights and the release of life sentence prisoners

Nicola Padfield

Routledge
Taylor & Francis Group
LONDON AND NEW YORK

First Published by Willan Publishing 2002

This edition published by Taylor & Francis 2011

2 Park Square
Milton Park
Abingdon
OX14 4RN

Published simultaneously in the USA and Canada by

711 Third Avenue
New York
NY 10017

Routledge is an imprint of the Taylor & Francis Group, an informa business

First issued in paperback 2016

ISBN13: 978-1-903240-88-5 (hbk)
ISBN13: 978-1-138-96464-8 (pbk)

British Library Cataloguing-in-Publication Data

A catalogue record for this book is available from the British Library

Typeset by TW Typesetting, Plymouth, Devon

Contents

Preface

This book is a study of the history and evolution of a legal body which came into being in England and Wales in October 1992: the Discretionary Lifer Panel of the Parole Board (DLPs). DLPs have the task of deciding whether and when discretionary life sentence prisoners should be released. The term 'discretionary life sentence prisoner' is generally used to distinguish those on whom a judge has chosen to impose a life sentence, because of the risk that the offender poses to the public, his or her 'dangerousness', as opposed to those (murderers) for whom a life sentence is mandatory. However, as we shall see in Chapter 1, the distinction between the various forms of life sentence is anything but clear-cut. Nor is it only discretionary life sentence prisoners who are now entitled to an oral hearing before a DLP. The uncertainties and inconsistencies in both current law and current practice are explored in this book.

The roots of the DLP lie in Article 5(4) of the European Convention on Human Rights, which provides that:

> Everyone who is deprived of his liberty by arrest or detention shall be entitled to take proceedings by which the lawfulness of his detention shall be decided speedily by a court and his release ordered if the detention is not lawful.

As always with complex ideas expressed in simple words, the message of this Article can be interpreted in many ways. A book could be written on the meaning of Article 5(4), whether linguistic, legalistic or philosophical. This book simply attempts to explore how the words have been interpreted in the narrow context of the release of life sentence prisoners in England and Wales, by the European Court of Human Rights, by the Home Office, by Parliament and by the English courts between 1987 and the present day. In 1990–1 the Government was obliged ('forced'?) to act on the European Court of Human Right's decision in *Thynne, Wilson and Gunnell*[1] that the system of review available to discretionary life sentence prisoners fell below the standard required by the Convention. But the book starts with two chapters which provide the context for later

[1] (1991) 13 EHRR 666.

discussions – descriptions of the various life sentences available in English law and of the life sentence as served in English prisons. Chapter 3 then explores the background and reasoning applied in the *Thynne* case, as well as in the equally important case of *Weeks*[2] which preceded it and which the government successfully avoided acting upon until after the decision in *Thynne*. Other relevant decisions of the Court are also discussed in an attempt to analyse the arguments which lie behind the Court's reasoning that, once discretionary life sentence prisoners have served the period of their sentence imposed as 'punishment', the 'tariff'[3], and enter a stage of their sentence when they are detained simply for the protection of the public, they are entitled to an oral hearing before a 'court' to review the legality of their detention.

The government's response to the decision in *Thynne* is discussed in detail in Chapter 4. Active non-governmental organisations and a determined House of Lords forced on the government speedier change than the government would have chosen. Discretionary Lifer Panels of the Parole Board were thus created in late amendments to what became the Criminal Justice Act 1991, which took effect in October 1992. The law has been amended in Acts of Parliament in 1997 and in 2000. Chapter 5 reviews the operation of the Panels in the first eight years of their life, relying heavily on the research carried out in 1999 by the author and Dr Alison Liebling, with Helen Arnold, at the Institute of Criminology, University of Cambridge. The book then moves on to compare this system with other processes governing the release of those compulsorily detained in England and Wales: those detained in prison subject to long determinate sentences and as adult murderers (who receive a mandatory life sentence), and those detained against their wishes in mental hospitals. Mandatory life sentence prisoners also have their 'risk' assessed by the Parole Board, but they do not have the benefit of an oral hearing. The Home Secretary maintains the right to make the final decision on release. People detained compulsorily under mental health legislation may challenge the legality of the detention before a Mental Health Review Tribunal (MHRT). Although DLPs were closely modelled on MHRTs, we shall see in Chapter 6 that there are also important procedural differences. Recent challenges to the MHRT have implications for the DLP: most importantly, the first declaration of incompatibility issued under the Human Rights Act 1998 has resulted in a shift of

2 (1988) 10 EHRR 333.

3 The Lord Chief Justice has recently issued a Practice Statement As To Life Sentences (see the *Times* 4 June 2002) in which he explained that the term 'tariff' will no longer be used 'because it has commonly been misunderstood'. Instead judges should now use the term 'minimum term' to make it clearer that, even when released, the offender has not served his sentence which continues for the remainder of his life. The term 'tariff' is however used throughout this book, being the term employed during the period under review.

the burden of proof before the MHRT. It would have been easier to close the book at the end of the twentieth century, but an attempt has been made to include relevant changes in law and practice until July 2002. In a field which is moving fast, it is impossible to be quite up to date.

In one sense this book seeks to be a classic 'case study', well known to teachers of law: the decisions in *Weeks* and *Thynne* lie at the heart of the book, which seeks to interpret the law by traditional legal methods: the interpretation of statute and case law. But the book also seeks to do something more than this: to tell the stories of the lives of certain key prisoners and to put these stories in a wider legal and political context. The book seeks to take a 'law in action' perspective, looking at the actual meaning of sentences, as well as the theoretical background. By weaving together the personal, the legal and the political we may get closer to understanding the reality of what has been going on. Chapters 7 and 8 seek to draw this history together by exploring the underlying tensions and conceptual confusions. The book concludes by arguing that the European Court of Human Rights should not be seen as the only force driving change in this area: domestic judges have also been concerned. But the role of the judge is limited, and real change in this area depends not only on 'reform by judges' or on 'reform by Parliament' but on 'reform from within'. The decisions of individual prison staff and of probation officers, as well of prison and other criminal justice structures, may shape the outcome of decisions about release as much as the decisions of the Parole Board. I would like to pay tribute to the help and encouragement of numerous people within the Home Office and Prison Service, as well as those outside the corridors of power, who have helped me with this project. In an age preoccupied with protecting the public against the risk of serious crime, it is encouraging that real dialogue and debate is taking place. However, it is also important that the stories of the individuals, whose rights Article 5 was designed to protect, are also heard. The scales of justice are not always fairly balanced.

By the time the book had reached proof stage, the European Court of Human Rights had given its long awaited decision in *Stafford* v. *United Kingdom* (see pages 7, 59 and 118 below). Giving judgment on 28 May 2002, the Court stated:

> Since the Convention is first and foremost a system for the protection of human rights, the Court must . . . have regard to the changing conditions in Contracting States and respond, for example, to any emerging consensus as to the standards to be achieved . . . It is of crucial importance that the Convention is interpreted and applied in a manner which renders its rights practical and effective, not theoretical and illusory. A failure by the Court to maintain a dynamic and evolutive approach would risk rendering it a bar to reform or improvement. (para. 58)

Noting the steady erosion of the Secretary of State's decision-making power in this field, the Court went on to hold that

> it may now be regarded as established in domestic law that there is no distinction between mandatory life prisoners, discretionary life prisoners and juvenile murderers as regards the nature of tariff-fixing. It is a sentencing exercise. The mandatory life sentence does not impose imprisonment for life as a punishment. The tariff, which reflects the individual circumstances of the offence and the offender, represents the element of punishment. The Court concludes that the finding in *Wynne* (1994) 19 EHRR 333 that the mandatory life sentence constituted punishment for life can no longer be regarded as reflecting the real position in the domestic criminal justice system of the mandatory life prisoner. (para. 79)

Having found that the tariff comprises the punishment element of the mandatory life sentence and that the Secretary of State's role in fixing the tariff is a sentencing exercise, not the administrative implementation of the sentence of the court, the Court went on to hold unanimously that there had also been a violation of both Article 5(1) and Article 5(4) of the Convention since the lawfulness of the applicant's continued detention was not reviewed by a body with a power to release or with a procedure containing the necessary judicial safeguards, including, for example, the possibility of an oral hearing. The Home Secretary lost his power to detain post-tariff lifers against the recommendation of the Parole Board. But the Home Secretary's response was 'disappointment' that the effect of the judgment was that he would lose his power to decide the release of adult murderers whose tariff had expired. He was concerned that the judgment may be used as encouragement for those who would like to remove the Home Secretary's powers to set tariffs, and said that if the courts took this lead, he would use domestic legislation 'to enshrine the power of Parliament to provide adequate punishment for the guilty . . . It is crucial that jurisprudence does not interfere with [the] basic right on behalf of the elected government [to protect the public from dangerous offenders, while doing everything we can to assist and support victims and their families]'. It is perhaps romantic to hope that this book might play a small part in convincing the Home Secretary to change his stance.

Acknowledgments

Although singling out specific individuals for thanks is invidious, I would like to acknowledge the host of people who have helped me with this book in innumerable ways. The book arose out of research carried out with Alison Liebling and Helen Arnold in 1999, and my thanks to them are paramount. I would also like specifically to record my more recent debts to Trevor Allan, Joy Anderson, Hamish Arnott, Dan Bates, Tony Bottoms (particularly), Julian Broadhead, Simon Buck, Niall Campbell, Laura Davidson, Mark Elliott, Loraine Gelsthorpe, Gabrielle Garton Grimwood, Helen Griffiths, Ivan Hare, Philippa Helme, Roger Hood, Paul Jackson, Philippa Kauffman, Michael Rice, Terry Russel, Stephen Shute, Dirk van Zyl Smit, and Nigel Walker.

List of abbreviations

DCR	Discretionary Conditional Release
DLP	Discretionary Lifer Panel of the Parole Board
DSPD	dangerous severely personality disordered
ECHR	European Convention on Human Rights
ECtHR	European Court of Human Rights
HMIPP	Her Majesty's Inspectorates of Prisons and Probation
HMP	detention during Her Majesty's pleasure
LRC	Local Review Committee (of the Parole Board)
MHRT	Mental Health Review Tribunal
NDPB	Non-Departmental Public Body
OLR	Order of Life-long Restriction
PRES	Pre-Release Employment Scheme
RMA	Risk Management Authority
RMO	Responsible Medical Officer
SOTP	Sex Offender Treatment Programme

Table of cases

Table of statutes

1

Forms of life sentence

The basic rules of custodial sentencing in England and Wales are today found in sections 79 and 80 of the Powers of Criminal Courts (Sentencing) Act 2000, a codification of earlier legislation. Sections 79 and 80 replicate sections 1 and 2 of the Criminal Justice Act 1991,[1] which as we shall see, is the Act of Parliament which introduced Discretionary Lifer Panels of the Parole Board (DLPs). It was a controversial statute, in which the government chose to legislate the fundamentals of sentencing law. The heated debates in Parliament on these major changes in sentencing overshadowed the provisions of the Act which created DLPs. The essence of sections 1 and 2 of the 1991 Act were that, where a custodial sentence is imposed, the term imposed should be 'commensurate' with the gravity of the offence. However, where the offence was violent or sexual, a longer than commensurate sentence could be imposed, where in the opinion of the court 'this is necessary to protect the public from serious harm'.[2] The emphasis on 'commensurability' was an attempt to force judges to give proportionate sentences (and to resist the temptation to give deterrent sentences which might result in inconsistent practice).[3] However, this does not mean that life sentences were discouraged.

Thus a prisoner may be sentenced under section 79(2)(a) or (b):

> (2) Subject to subsection (3) below, the court shall not pass a custodial sentence on the offender unless it is of the opinion –
> (a) that the offence, or the combination of the offence and one or more offences associated with it, was so serious that only such a sentence can be justified for the offence; or
> (b) where the offence is a violent or sexual offence, that only such a sentence would be adequate to protect the public from serious harm from him.

The length of these sentences is governed by section 80(2):

[1] As amended by the Criminal Justice Act 1993.
[2] Sections 79 and 80 of the codifying Powers of Criminal Courts (Sentencing) Act 2000 reproduced sections 1 and 2 of the Criminal Justice Act 1991.
[3] See Home Office (1990).

(2) Subject to sections 110(2) and 111(2) below, the custodial sentence shall be –
   (a) for such term (not exceeding the permitted maximum) as in the opinion of the court is commensurate with the seriousness of the offence, or the combination of the offence and one or more offences associated with it; or
   (b) where the offence is a violent or sexual offence, for such longer term (not exceeding that maximum) as in the opinion of the court is necessary to protect the public from serious harm from the offender.

In essence, a prisoner should either be sentenced to a term commensurate with the seriousness of the offence (or the combination of the offence with other associated offences) or, in the case of violent or sexual offences, for a longer period which the court thinks is necessary to protect the public from serious harm from the offender. The relationship between these basic rules has been complicated by the introduction of minimum seven-year sentences for third-class A drug trafficking offences and minimum three-year sentences for third domestic burglaries by the Crime (Sentences) Act 1997[4] and of extended sentences by section 58 of the Crime and Disorder Act 1998,[5] which allows courts to extend sentences for the purposes of requiring offenders to undergo a longer period of post-release supervision. Within this framework, a sentence of 'life imprisonment' may be imposed in a wide variety of circumstances for numerous offences.

In this chapter, we will review the forms of life sentence imposed in England and Wales today, concentrating on the 'discretionary' life sentence which is the main focus of this book. The way the sentence is imposed at the sentencing stage and the way it is carried out within the prison system both provide keys to understanding release procedures: Chapter 2 moves the discussion on from the sentencing stage to prison practice. As we shall see, once the convicted life sentence prisoner finds himself serving the sentence in prison, he or she will find that the Prison Service makes little distinction between the different categories of life sentence. When it comes to the all-important question of release, however, the differences between the categories become once again vitally important. In this chapter, however, we concentrate on the role of the trial judge, who, on sentencing, is required to explain the nature of the specific sentence. The substance of what has to be explained in open court has varied over the years, and varies for the different forms of life sentence.

[4] Now sections 110 and 111 of the Powers of Criminal Courts (Sentencing) Act 2000.
[5] Now section 85 of the Powers of Criminal Courts (Sentencing) Act 2000.

Discretionary life sentences

Since at least 1861, a trial judge has been able to impose a sentence of life imprisonment, passed in the exercise of the court's discretion, on people convicted of any of the offences for which life imprisonment is provided by the relevant legislation as the maximum penalty for the offence.[6] It is usually imposed in practice on people who have committed a very grave crime, where it appears to the sentencing judge that the offender is a person of unstable character likely to commit such offences in the future, thus making him dangerous to the public in respect of his probable future behaviour unless there was a change in his condition. The criteria have been developed over the years by the Court of Appeal. Thus, in *Hodgson*[7] the criteria for a discretionary life sentence were said to be that:

1. the offence must in itself be grave enough to require a very long sentence;
2. the offender must be a person of mental instability who, if at liberty, will probably re-offend and present a grave risk to the public; and
3. it must appear that the offender will remain unstable and a potential danger for a long or uncertain time.

In *Wilkinson*,[8] Lord Lane LCJ said:

> It seems to us that the sentence of life imprisonment, other than where the sentence is obligatory, is really appropriate and must only be passed in the most exceptional circumstances. With few exceptions . . . it is reserved broadly speaking . . . for offenders who for one reason or another cannot be dealt with under the provisions of the Mental Health Act, yet are in a mental state which makes them dangerous to the life or limb of members of the public. It is sometimes impossible to say when that danger will subside, and therefore an indeterminate sentence is required, so that the prisoner's progress may be monitored by those who have him under their supervision in prison, and so that he will be kept in custody only so long as public safety may be jeopardised by his being let loose at large.

It was noted earlier that the general principle of determinate sentencing is that the length of the sentence should be 'commensurate' with the seriousness of the offence. But a discretionary life sentence is not a

[6] The list includes attempted murder, manslaughter, rape, robbery, arson, criminal damage with intent to endanger life, aggravated burglary, kidnapping, incest, infanticide and sexual intercourse with a girl under the age of 13.

[7] (1967) 52 Cr App R 113 (see also *Picker* (1970) 54 Cr App R 330).

[8] (1983) 5 Cr App R (S) 105, at pp. 108–9.

'commensurate' sentence: it is imposed as an exception to the general rule. In *Chapman*[9] the Court of Appeal made it clear that section 79(2)(b) of the Powers of Criminal Courts (Sentencing) Act 2000 is the source of the power to impose discretionary life sentences. In that case, the appellant had pleaded guilty to arson being reckless as to whether life was endangered and was sentenced by the trial judge to a discretionary life sentence, with a tariff of only 12 months. However, on appeal Lord Bingham CJ reduced the sentence to a determinate sentence of ten years: three years was the appropriate commensurate sentence but a further seven years were added for the purposes of public protection.

A reminder from the Court of Appeal that the offence must be serious before a discretionary life sentence is imposed was given in *Simmonds*.[10] A man had set fire to his ex-wife's home, when the house was unoccupied, completely destroying the contents. He had no previous convictions but was said to be suffering from a personality disorder. The Court of Appeal quashed a sentence of life imprisonment, substituting a term of six years' imprisonment. Although the offence was serious, it was not grave enough to require a very long sentence. The consequence of these decisions, as we shall see in Chapter 5, is that *Chapman* and *Simmonds* are subject to the Parole Board provisions relating to determinate sentences (Discretionary Conditional Release) rather than to an oral hearing before a Discretionary Lifer Panel. However, following the decision of the High Court in *R (Giles)* v. *Parole Board and the Secretary of State for the Home Department*,[11] this may now change and prisoners such as Chapman, serving a longer than commensurate sentence, may be entitled to an oral hearing.[12]

In this book we will trace how and why the courts have over the last forty years moved to the position whereby a period, often known as 'the tariff', is fixed by the sentencing judge in open court. The offender will serve this period before being considered for possible release. The Court of Appeal's recent guidance on the imposition of discretionary life sentences offered in *Marklew and Lambert*[13] serves as a good illustration of the current position. The case involved a 16-year-old and a 17-year-old, both convicted of arson with intent to endanger life and who had been sentenced to detention for life, under what is now section 90 of the Powers of Criminal Courts (Sentencing) Act 2000.[14] The Court of Appeal considered that it was important that the judge in all discretionary life

[9] [2000] 1 Cr App R 77.

[10] [2001] Crim LR 326.

[11] [2001] EWHC 834, 5 October 2001.

[12] Giles was overturned on appeal – see page 110 below.

[13] [1999] 1 Cr App R (S) 6.

[14] We shall see below (at p. 10) that detention for life is the equivalent for young people (those under 18) of a discretionary life sentence.

sentence cases should, when passing sentence, make clear to the defendant what the determinate (i.e. fixed term) sentence would have been had it not been necessary to impose a life sentence to protect the public. The judge should then exercise his discretion in fixing the specified period or tariff. In the case of a young person, that should be half the equivalent determinate period. In the case of adults, half the determinate period would also often be the appropriate tariff period, but circumstances might mean that in certain circumstances the period was more than half and up to two-thirds of the determinate sentence. The period of time that a defendant had spent in custody on remand has also to be taken into account in fixing the 'tariff' since this would have been taken into account in fixing the precise length of a determinate sentence.

Mandatory life sentences

The mandatory life sentence for murder dates back only to the Murder (Abolition of the Death Penalty) Act 1965. Until then, capital punishment was the penalty for murder, though in the early years of the twentieth century nearly half of those sentenced to death were reprieved. According to the Royal Commission on Capital Punishment in 1953,[15] between 1900 and 1949, the number reprieved was 45 per cent: 439 of the 1,080 men sentenced to death, 126 of the 130 women.[16] At this time too the life sentence tended to be much shorter than it is today.[17] During the passage of the Murder (Abolition of the Death Penalty) Act 1965, which abolished the death penalty for murder, there was considerable support for making the life sentence discretionary, but in order to achieve the passage of the Bill, a compromise was reached and the life sentence was made mandatory. Section 1 of the Act provides:

> (1) No person shall suffer death for murder, and a person convicted of murder shall, subject to subsection (5) below, be sentenced to imprisonment for life.
>
> (2) On sentencing any person convicted of murder to imprisonment for life the court may at the same time declare the period which it recommends to the Secretary of State as the minimum period which in its view should elapse before the Secretary of State orders the release of that person on licence under section 27 of the Prison Act 1952 or section 21 of the Prisons (Scotland) Act 1952.

[15] Royal Commission on Capital Punishment, Cm 8932, 1953. See also Padfield (2002) *Crim LR* 192.
[16] Royal Commission on Capital Punishment, Cm 8932, 1953) Appendix 2, Table 12.
[17] See p. 18 below.

There was nothing in the law at this stage which suggested a rigid 'tariff', the division of the life sentence into two parts. This has evolved more recently. The provision in section 1(2) empowering the sentencing judge to declare the minimum period which should elapse before the Home Secretary ordered release on licence was enacted to guard against excessive leniency by the Home Office. Indeed, the Home Secretary in 1965 did not want judges to set a minimum term since they would not have the benefit of the continual reports which could help him in the exercise of his discretionary powers to decide on release. The Home Secretary was at that stage more lenient than were Her Majesty's judges! However, the term 'tariff' started to be used informally within the Home Office to represent the period that the Home Office thought the lifer should serve by way of punishment. The system has evolved in the last thirty years whereby a 'tariff' is fixed in all cases (by the Home Secretary, having consulted the trial judge and Lord Chief Justice), and a case is not referred to the Parole Board until the tariff is due to expire.

Even today, the vast majority of mandatory lifers are not told their 'tariff' in court. Once the trial is over and the prisoner has been sentenced, the judge will be asked to complete a form in which both he and the Lord Chief Justice are consulted as to the period which the prisoner should serve before being considered for release. The Home Secretary may overrule this 'tariff' period, the penal element of the sentence. The opinion of the judges is 'no more than a component of the entire body of material' (per Lord Mustill in *Doody* v. *Secretary of State for the Home Department*).[18] In this case, Doody and three other applicants had been told the date of the first review of their cases by the Parole Board and considered that the Minister had increased the tariff periods recommended by the judiciary. They sought declarations that the Secretary of State was required to adopt the judicial view of the penal element of the sentence. While the House of Lords was not prepared to go that far, they were clear that prisoners were entitled to be treated fairly. As Lord Mustill put it, it was not the task of the court to say how it would choose to operate the scheme if it had a free hand: the only issue was whether the way in which the scheme was administered fell below the 'minimum standard of fairness'. These standards are not immutable, and depend on the context. The House of Lords granted the following declarations:

(1) The Secretary of State is required to afford to a prisoner serving a mandatory life sentence the opportunity to submit in writing representations as to the period he should serve for the purpose of retribution and deterrence before the Secretary of State sets the date of the first review of the prisoner's sentence.

[18] [1994] 1 AC 531; [1993] 3 All ER 92.

(2) Before giving the prisoner the opportunity to make such representations, the Secretary of State is required to inform him of the period recommended by the judiciary as the period he should serve for the purpose of retribution and deterrence, and of any other opinion expressed by the judiciary which is relevant to the Secretary of State's decision as to the appropriate period to be served for these purposes.

(3) The Secretary of State is obliged to give reasons for departing from the period recommended by the judiciary as the period which he should serve for the purpose of retribution and deterrence.

If a judge does mention a minimum in court, the prisoner may not appeal this recommendation, nor is it subject to judicial review. In *Leaney*,[19] the trial judge recommended that a man convicted of murder should serve a minimum period of twenty years. Although the Court of Appeal made it clear that they thought that the recommendation in the case was excessive, they considered themselves powerless to do anything about it, and the Lord Chief Justice urged that the matter 'ought to be reconsidered by Parliament as a matter of urgency'. It is an interesting question whether the Court of Appeal was truly powerless. The main authority (relied on in subsequent cases, admittedly) for not allowing an appeal in these circumstances is *Aitken*.[20] So much has changed since 1966, and it is arguable that this was a case where the Court of Appeal could have felt free to reconsider their previous decision.

The 'due process' improvements introduced by the courts in recent years have not affected the final discretion of the Home Secretary. Indeed, when in 1994 all mandatory lifers were told their minimum sentence, approximately twenty were told that the minimum period was their 'natural life'.[21] The government continues to argue that to allow judges to decide the length of a sentence for murder would weaken the public's confidence in the criminal justice system. This view seems to have been accepted unquestioningly in the European Court of Human Rights in *Wynne* v. *UK*.[22]

Little information is available about the way the tariff is fixed in murder cases. The Sentencing Advisory Panel (2001) reported that in February 2001 the Home Secretary considered tariffs in eleven murder cases, and that the trial judges in these cases had proposed tariffs of between 8 and 25 years. Frustratingly, the Sentencing Advisory Panel does not go on to describe the impact of the trial judge's, and the Lord

19 [1995] Crim LR 670.

20 (1966) 50 Cr App R 204.

21 See *R* v. *Secretary of State for the Home Department, ex p. Hindley* [2001] 1 AC 152.

22 [1994] 19 EHRR 333; now the *Stafford* v. *UK* (summarised in the Preface).

Chief Justice's, view on the final tariff. Justice (1996) suggested that a very significant consequence of the improvements in procedural safeguards introduced by Doody has been a decline in ministerial intervention in fixing the tariff. It would be useful to know more about current practice. We will return in Chapter 6 to the process which governs the release of mandatory life sentence prisoners.

Detention at Her Majesty's pleasure or for a specified period

The sentence imposed on children who are guilty of murder has been known as 'detention at Her Majesty's Pleasure' since the Children Act 1908. The Children and Young Persons Act 1933 then abolished the death penalty for murders committed by young people under the age of 18. Section 53(1) of that Act provided that offenders who committed murder when under 18 would be detained at Her Majesty's Pleasure; section 53(2) provided that those under 18 who were convicted of certain very serious offences (generally those for which a sentence of 14 years' imprisonment was available for adults) and for whom no other sentence was suitable, could be detained for any period not exceeding the adult maximum. The current law is to be found in sections 90 and 91 of the Powers of Criminal Courts (Sentencing) Act 2000. Section 90 provides that

> Where a person convicted of murder appears to the court to have been aged under 18 at the time the offence was committed, the court shall (not withstanding anything in this or any other Act) sentence him to be detained during Her Majesty's pleasure.

When Parliament in 1908 introduced a mandatory sentence for child murderers, it was clearly a sentence of indefinite duration and not a sentence of detention for life. The welfare of the child was even then an important consideration and this was underlined in section 44 of the Children and Young Person Act 1933, which remains in force:

> Every court in dealing with a child or young person who is brought before it, either as an offender or otherwise, shall have regard to the welfare of the child or young person and shall in a proper case take steps ... for securing that proper provision is made for his education and training.

In *R* v. *Secretary of State for the Home Department, ex parte Thompson and Venables*,[23] the House of Lords (by a majority of three to two) held (*inter*

[23] [1998] AC 407.

alia) that the decision of the Home Secretary in fixing the tariff was unlawful in that he had failed to take into account the progress and development of the children under review.[24] The European Court of Human Rights in *V* v. *United Kingdom; T* v. *United Kingdom*[25] went much further, holding that the fixing of the tariff by the Home Secretary gave rise to a breach of Article 6 as it was a sentencing exercise not by an independent and impartial tribunal. The Court also held that there was a breach of Article 5(4).

The government responded relatively promptly. On 13 March 2000 the Home Secretary made a statement in Parliament explaining that he would introduce legislation whereby in future the tariff for defendants under 18 would, as in the case of adults subject to a discretionary life sentence, be set in open court by the trial judge, subject to appeal by the defendant or, if it were unduly lenient, by the Attorney General. As to existing detainees, their tariffs would be reviewed by the Lord Chief Justice, and the Home Secretary announced that it would be open to them to make new representations to the Lord Chief Justice, whose recommendations as to tariff, he, the Home Secretary, would adopt. The Lord Chief Justice then issued a Practice Statement,[26] in which he explained that the usual tariff length would be 14 years. In October 2000, the Lord Chief Justice announced his recommendation and reasons for fixing the tariff of Thompson and Venables, then aged 18, at seven years and eight months.[27] He did so by starting with the ten years fixed by Lord Taylor, and reducing that figure to reflect the welfare and progress of the two young men.[28] Since then many HMP prisoners have had their tariffs reviewed, and the factors which have influenced the Lord Chief Justice to reduce tariffs include reports on the prisoner's positive development in prison.[29] This, of course, lies uncomfortably with the idea of the 'tariff' as a fixed term representing the period the prisoner should serve for retribution and deterrence: it reflects not only the requirement of the House of Lords in *Thompson and Venables* that the 'tariff' for juveniles should be something kept continually under review. It surely represents a continuing uncertainty about the nature and function of the 'tariff' part of the sentence.

[24] See Padfield, N, 'Fixing the tariff, and the Length of Her Majesty's Pleasure' (1997) 56 *Cambridge Law Journal* 477.
[25] (1999) 30 EHRR 121 (16 December 1999).
[26] [2000] 1 WLR 1656; [2000] 4 All ER 831.
[27] See [2001] 1 All ER 737.
[28] In *R* v. *Secretary of State for the Home Department, ex p. Bulger*, Rose LJ in the Divisional Court held that the victim's father could not challenge the tariff by way of judicial review: 'The invitation extended to him to make representations as to the impact of the offence on him was not an invitation to indicate views as to the appropriate tariff.'
[29] See, for example, *R* v. *PH* [2002] EWCA, 13 February 2002.

Section 60 of Criminal Justice and Court Services Act 2000 added a new section 82A to the Powers of the Criminal Courts (Sentencing) Act 2000 (determination of tariffs), which is applicable to sentences passed after 30 November 2000. The court when imposing a sentence of detention during Her Majesty's pleasure now orders that section 28(5)–(8) of the Crime (Sentences) Act 1997 shall apply as soon as he has served his tariff. Drafted in extraordinarily complex language, the section appears to say no more than that the court now fixes the tariff, and the Parole Board decides, as with discretionary life sentences, whether to direct release. The Secretary of State must act on such a direction from the Parole Board.[30]

Thus a sentence of detention during Her Majesty's pleasure has in many ways been drawn into line with the procedures applicable to discretionary life sentences, which we pursue through the pages of this book. This has certainly introduced better procedural safeguards from the point of view of the detainee. However, the changes ignore the important fact that the discretionary life sentence for adults is justified on very different grounds to the detention of child murderers: adults are subject to discretionary life sentences because they have committed a serious offence and are considered dangerous. Child murderers are detained indefinitely because of the nature of their offence: we shall consider further in Chapter 8 the varied and various justifications for indeterminate sentences.

At the beginning of this section it was noted that young people under the age of 18 may also be sentenced to detention for life, as a discretionary sentence (under what was section 53(2) of the Children and Young Persons Act 1933, now section 91 of the Powers of Criminal Courts (Sentencing) Act 2000). This was the case in *Marklew and Lambert* [1999],[31] where the Court of Appeal discussed the principles to be applied in fixing the tariff in all discretionary life sentence cases (discussed above).[32]

Custody for life

Custody for life is an indeterminate sentence reserved for young people aged between 18 and 21 when convicted. Section 93 of the Powers of Criminal Courts (Sentencing) Act 2000 (duty to impose custody for life in certain cases where offender is under 21) provides that:

[30] The current law is set out in Appendix 3.

[31] 1999 1 Cr App R (S) 6.

[32] Other key cases on section 91 (previously section 53(2)) are *Flemming* [1973] 57 Cr App R 524, *Bell* [1989] 11 Cr App R (S) 472, *Furber* [1998] 1 All ER 23.

Where a person aged under 21 is convicted of murder or any other offence the sentence for which is fixed by law as imprisonment for life, the court shall sentence him to custody for life unless he is liable to be detained under section 90 above.

Section 94 of the Powers of Criminal Courts (Sentencing) Act 2000 (duty to impose custody for life in certain cases where offender is under 21) provides that:

(1) Where a person aged at least 18 but under 21 is convicted of an offence – for which the sentence is not fixed by law, but for which a person aged 21 or over would be liable to imprisonment for life, the court shall, if it considers that a sentence for life would be appropriate, sentence him to custody for life.

(2) Subsection (1) above is subject to (in particular) sections 79 and 80 above, but this subsection does not apply in relation to a sentence which falls to be imposed under section 109(2) below.

This reflects the fact that until recently young adult male prisoners were held separately from older male prisoners. However, these sections will shortly become redundant. Section 61 of the Criminal Justice and Court Services Act 2000 abolishes custody for life. Until the section comes into force, custody for life may be imposed as a mandatory sentence or as a discretionary one. But young adult murderers will not get the benefit of an oral hearing before the Parole Board. For release purposes they are treated as 'ordinary' mandatory life sentence prisoners.

'Automatic' life sentences

Although not introduced until the Crime (Sentences) Act 1997, 'automatic' life sentences are now an important feature of the life sentence portfolio. First proposed in the White Paper *Protecting the Public – the Government's Strategy on Crime in England and Wales,*[33] these provisions require a court to impose a life sentence on all offenders who are convicted for a second time of a serious violent or sexual offence:

> The Government is determined that the public should receive proper protection from persistent violent or sex offenders. That means requiring the courts to impose an automatic indeterminate sentence, and releasing the offender if and only if it is safe to do so.[34]

[33] Cm 3190, presented to Parliament by the Home Secretary, Michael Howard in March 1996, Chapter 10.

[34] Para 10.11.

The White Paper maintained that the proposals were not designed or intended to increase the time that such offenders spent in prison as punishment. Indeed, it suggested that they might be more accurately described as 'automatic indeterminate sentences'. The White Paper noted that little use was made of the discretionary life sentence:

> In 1994, for example, 434 offenders were convicted of rape or attempted rape, but only 12 were sentenced to life imprisonment. In 1994, 217 offenders were convicted of a second serious violent or sexual offence, but only 10 received a discretionary life sentence.[35]

Thus the main argument for the introduction of the 'automatic' life sentence was that more use should be made of indeterminate sentences as a means of protecting the public. But the proposals were heavily criticised. It was argued that they would lead to injustice since judges would no longer to be able to look at the circumstances of an individual case or offender. And there were more practical concerns: would offenders plead guilty to such an offence if they knew they would be subject to an automatic sentence? Would partners or children be even less willing to give evidence in cases of domestic violence if they thought the case might result in an automatic life sentence? Would juries be more likely to acquit guilty people because they didn't like the automatic sentence?[36]

However, automatic life sentences were duly enacted in section 2 of the Crime (Sentences) Act 1997, now to be found in section 109 of the Powers of Criminal Courts (Sentencing) Act 2000, which provides that:

> (1) This section applies where –
> (a) a person is convicted of a serious offence committed after 30th September 1997; and
> (b) at the time when that offence was committed, he was 18 or over and had been convicted in any part of the United Kingdom of another serious offence.
>
> (2) The court shall impose a life sentence, that is to say –
> (a) where the offender is 21 or over when convicted of the offence mentioned in subsection (1)(a) above, a sentence of imprisonment for life,
> (b) where he is under 21 at that time, a sentence of custody for life under section 94 above, unless the court is of the opinion that there are exceptional circumstances relating to either of the offences or to the offender which justify its not doing so.

35 Para 10.4.

36 Indeed, this had been suggested by the Conservative government itself in 1990 when rejecting a system of mandatory sentences (see the White Paper (1990) *Crime, Justice and Protecting the Public*, Cm 965). See also Gale et al. (1997), at p. 17.

The list of 'serious offences' in section 109(5) includes attempted murder, manslaughter, causing grievous bodily harm with intent (contrary to section 18 of the Offences against the Person Act 1861), rape, attempted rape, intercourse with a girl under 13, robbery with a firearm or imitation firearm. The main question which has concerned the courts is when 'exceptional circumstances' exist which justify the court in not imposing a life sentence. To begin with, it seemed that 'exceptional circumstances' would be rarely recognised (see *Kelly*[37]), but in *Buckland*[38] the door started to swing open. The key case now is *Offen*[39] where the court construed the words in the light of the Human Rights Act 1998 so as not to contravene the prohibition on inhuman and degrading treatment (Article 3), or arbitrary and disproportionate punishment (Article 5). The court was also keen to interpret the legislation in a way which complied with its underlying purpose, not taking a narrowly literal approach to the interpretation of the statute. According to the Lord Chief Justice:

> The policy and intention of Parliament was to protect the public against a person who had committed two serious offences. It therefore can be assumed the section was not intended to apply to someone in relation to whom it was established there would be no need for protection in the future . . .[40]
>
> Section 2 establishes a norm. The norm is that those who commit two serious offences are a danger or a risk to the public. If in fact, taking into account all the circumstances relating to a particular offender, he does not create an unacceptable risk to the public, he is an exception to this norm . . . In our judgement, section 2 of the 1997 Act will not contravene Convention rights if courts apply the section so that it does not result in offenders being sentenced to life imprisonment when they do not constitute a significant risk to the public.[41]

The Lord Chief Justice stressed that the court was not saying that the automatic life sentence was no different to the discretionary life sentence. In cases coming within the 'automatic' category, the issue of dangerousness has to be addressed, and the sentencing judge has to give reasons if he decides not to impose a life sentence. The new test was applied in *Wallace*,[42] where the Court upheld an automatic life sentence on a woman who had made an unprovoked attack on her victim with a bottle causing

37 [1999] 2 Cr App R 36.
38 [2000] 1 Cr App R 471.
39 [2001] 1 WLR 253.
40 At para. 79.
41 At para. 97.
42 [2001] Crim LR 407; see also *Fletcher* [2002] 1 Cr App R (S) 82; *Kelly* No. 2 [2002] 1 Cr App R (S) 2002 and D. A. Thomas', Automatic Life Sentences after *Offen* (2002) 3 *Archbold News* 5.

serious injuries: there were no 'exceptional circumstances', given her earlier conviction for another section 18 offence in 1998 (for which she had been sentenced to a probation order). This case can be contrasted with *Frost*,[43] where the court had found 'exceptional circumstances' in the fact that the appellant had been made subject to a supervision order after his first section 18 conviction. There will doubtless continue to be many appeals in this area as the courts struggle to establish consistent policies.

Despite the legal uncertainties surrounding the automatic sentence, there has been a steady rise in the number of prisoners sentenced under this provision, often with very short tariff periods. In 2000, 57 offenders were sentenced under section 2 of the Crime (Sentences) Act 1997, of whom 28 were convicted of causing/inflicting grievous bodily harm.[44] By May 2001 there were already 298 automatic life sentence prisoners in custody.[45] It is not clear whether the decision in *Offen* will slow the growth in numbers.

We have already noted the difficulties surrounding the fixing of the 'tariff' in discretionary life sentence cases. These have been as problematic in the 'automatic' life sentence cases. Thus in *West*,[46] the Court of Appeal, accepting that a life sentence prisoner should be in no worse position when it came to an application for parole than a prisoner subject to a determinate sentence, explained that the period to be specified should be one half of the notional determinate sentence. Thus a man who might 'deserve' a determinate sentence for his second serious offence of eight years, but who qualifies for an 'automatic' life sentence, should have a four-year 'tariff' imposed. In *West* itself, a man was sentenced to an automatic life sentence following his conviction for attempted murder. He had been given a notional sentence by the trial judge of 13 years for the attempted murder, but the Court of Appeal reduced the 'specified period' from eight to six years. This book seeks to show that many life sentence prisoners spend long periods in custody unnecessarily post-tariff. The problem is much exacerbated when the tariff itself may well have been too long.

Conclusion

In this chapter we have looked briefly at the various forms of life sentence available in English law today. A variety of sentences may be

[43] [2001] Crim LR 143.
[44] *Source*: Crime and Criminal Justice Unit, IOS: 193-02.
[45] *Source*: Lifer Unit of the Prison Service.
[46] [2001] 1 Cr App R (S) 103.

imposed for a variety of different reasons. A judge may have a discretion whether to impose a life sentence (in the case of 'dangerous' rapists, arsonists, etc.), or he or she may have no discretion at all (in the case of those convicted of murder), or a little flexibility (in the case of those convicted of a second serious offence). We now turn to examine how these various sentences are served in prison.

2

Life sentences: in custody and approaching release

In the previous chapter, we explored the various forms of life sentence which may be imposed on an offender. However, once they are in prison custody, 'lifers' will find that the Prison Service makes little distinction between the different categories, except when it comes to questions of release and the preparation of cases for the consideration of the Parole Board.

Some statistics

Until 1948, life sentence prisoners could be, and were, released under the royal prerogative. Release appears to have been exercised generously. According to the Royal Commission on Capital Punishment which reported in 1953, most lifers were released on licence after 10–13 years' imprisonment. In the period between 1900 and 1949, 15 lifers served less than a year and 53 served only one to three years. One served 22 years, and no one served longer than that. By the end of 1948 only five of the 112 prisoners released in the previous twenty years had been reconvicted of another serious offence, and only one of them had been reconvicted of murder.[1] By 1953, it was exceptional for anyone to serve more than 15 years and the usual sentences were much shorter.[2]

Modern published statistics are not as helpful as they might be. The annual *Criminal Statistics* record the numbers of mandatory life sentences imposed for murder, and the number of discretionary life sentences imposed for other homicides, but not the number of life sentences imposed for other offences. Thus in both 1998/99 and 1999/00, 248 people were convicted of murder and were given a mandatory life sentence. In the same two years, the number of women convicted of murder was 16 and 10. In the same years, 15 and 12 people received discretionary life sentences for other homicides (2 each year were

[1] Royal Commission on Capital Punishment, Cm 8932, 1953, Appendix 2, Table 12.
[2] Ibid.

Table 2.1 Number of persons sentenced to life imprisonment and the offences for which they were sentenced, England and Wales, 1960, 70, 80, 90 and 2000[1] and offenders given mandatory sentences under the Crime (Sentences Act) 1997, England and Wales 2000

Offence description	1960	1970	1980	1990	2000	*Section 2* Mandatory life for 2nd serious offence
Violence against the person						
Murder	33	87	149	170	243	—
Attempted murder	—	3	2	9	8	—
Threat or conspiracy to murder	—	—	—	—	2	—
Manslaughter due to diminished responsibility	11	11	14	3	4	—
Other manslaughter	—	1	1	9	13	2
Wounding or other act endangering life	1	1	3	3	76	29
Malicious wounding and other like offences	—	—	—	—	21	12
Sexual Offences						
Buggery	—	3	2	2	3	—
Rape	—	6	4	11	*	—
Rape of a female	..	..	..	..	45	7
Rape of a male	..	..	..	..	4	1
Unlawful sexual intercourse with girl under 13	—	1	—	—	1	—
Robbery						
Robbery or assault with intent to rob	—	2	—	2	31	6
Criminal damage						
Arson	—	3	8	5	8	—
Criminal damage endangering life	—	—	—	—	1	—
Other indictable offences						
Kidnapping	..	..	—	—	6	—
Absconding from lawful custody	..	..	—	—	1	—
Total	45	118	183	214	467	57
Persons sentenced under sections 90–92 of the Powers of Criminal Courts (Sentencing) Act 2000, England and Wales, 1960, 70, 80, 90 and 2000[2]						
	1960	1970	1980	1990	2000[2]	
Murder	1	11	20	10	20	

[1] Staffordshire Police Force only able to submit sample data for persons proceeded against and convicted in the magistrates' courts for the year 2000. Although sufficient to estimate higher orders of data, these data are not robust enough at a detailed level and have been excluded from the table.
[2] Section 53 of the Children and Young Persons Act 1933 was repealed on 25 August 2000 and its provisions were transferred to sections 90–92 of the Powers of Criminal Courts (Sentencing) Act 2000.
.. = not available.
* = see below for breakdown of rape offences.
Source: Crime and Criminal Justice Unit, Home Office.
IOS 193—02

Table 2.2 Estimated population of life sentence prisoners 1970–1999

Year	*Lifer population in prison*	*Mandatory life prisoners*	*Discretionary life prisoners*
1970	566	415	151
1980	1,584	1,179	405
1990	2,795	2,230	565
1998	3,934	3,178	756
1999	4,206	3,308	898

Source: Padfield and Liebling (2000), table 2.1 and Home Office (2001).

women).[3] Thus the number of mandatory lifers much exceeds the number of discretionary lifers. In 2000, 57 people were given what the Home Office records as a 'mandatory' sentence under section 2 of the Crime Sentences Act 1997 for committing a second serious offence. In only two of these does it appear that the victim died.[4] Unfortunately the annual Prison Statistics do not differentiate between the various categories. Table 2.1 gives the number of people sentenced to life imprisonment and the offence for which they were sentenced in England and Wales in 1960, 1970, 1980, 1990, and 2000 (statistics were provided by the Home Office).

On 30 June 2000 there were 4,540 prisoners serving life sentences in prisons.[5] The numbers continue to grow, partly due to the increasing numbers of convicted murderers (all of whom get a mandatory life sentence) and to the increasing number of discretionary and automatic life sentences. To the published figure must be added the few children convicted of murder in the last few years, who remain in local authority accommodation until some time after their eighteenth birthday. According to the Sentencing Advisory Panel,[6] in the nine years between 1991 and 1999, a total of 170 young offenders were sentenced to Her Majesty's pleasure. Only five of them were aged under 15. Table 2.2 shows the estimated population of life sentence prisoners from 1970–2000.

Not only has there been this large rise in the total population, but the amount of time that prisoners have been serving in prison on a life sentence has also been rising. Of the 1,824 people received under sentence between 1965 and 1978, 200 (9 per cent) had not been released by the end of 1999 and had therefore served at least twenty years. The *Prison Statistics* explain this graphically by a figure (reproduced in Figure

3 See Table 4.9 of *Criminal Statistics*.
4 *Source*: Crime and Criminal Justice Unit, IOS: 193-02.
5 Prison Statistics 2000, p. 98, as corrected.
6 Sentencing Advisory Panel (2001), Consultation Paper on Tariffs in Murder Cases.

Figure 2.1 Population of Life Sentence prisoners 30 June 1975 and 30 June 2000 by time served under sentence

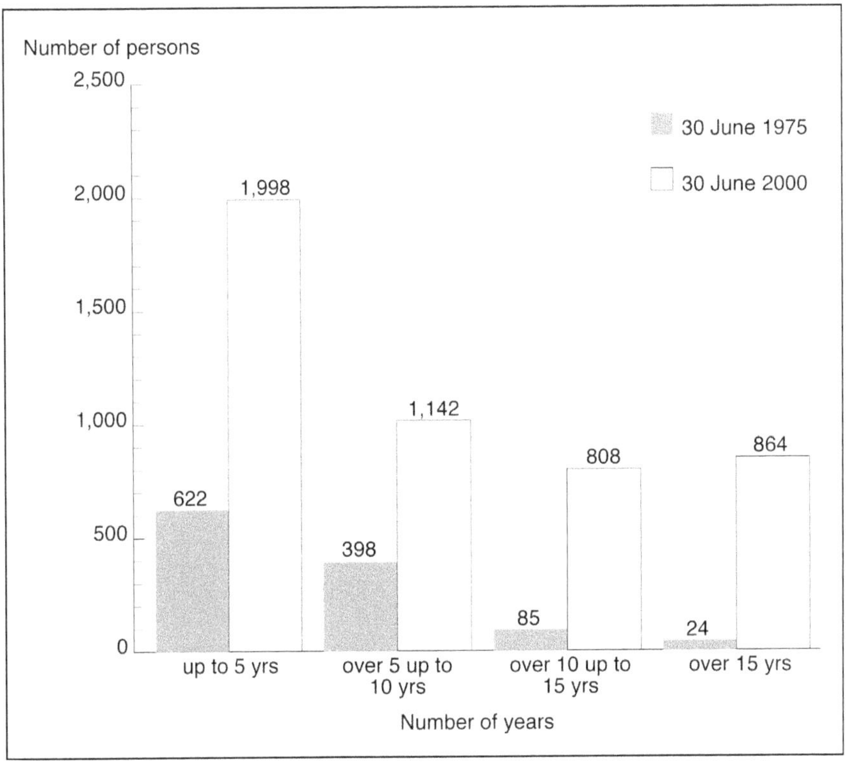

Source: *Prison Statistics* (2000), figure 5.3.

2.1) which shows the increased number of lifers who have served longer periods under sentence.

One would expect that the number of people released on life licence since 1967 would grow as the population as a whole has grown. Of course, release on licence is not the only route out of prison: the Prison Statistics 2000 state that about 15 a year are successful with their appeals, while about 15 a year die in prison (of what cause is not clear) and some move to and from psychiatric hospitals. Table 2.3 shows the numbers of discretionary lifers released in recent years. Note that the high number in 1993 is explained by the backlog of cases dealt with by Discretionary Lifer Panels, who first met only in October 1992.

Table 2.3 Releases of discretionary life sentence prisoners on life licence and average time served post-sentence*

Year of release	*Number released*	*Time served post-sentence (years)*
1990	17	15.5
1991	14	12.7
1992	23	15.3
1993	60	14.6
1994	29	13.6
1995	32	13.5
1996	14	17.3
1997	10	13.3
1998	8	13.6
1999	9	16.2
2000	14	13.5

*It is important to note that this figure excludes the significant amount of time spent on remand in custody pre-trial, or following any recall.
Source: *Prison Statistics* (2000), table 5.5.

Serving a life sentence[7]

Most people charged with an offence liable to a life sentence are of course remanded in custody pending trial. They will normally be held with other remand prisoners in a local prison. Some, those recognised as security risks, will be transferred to more secure prisons. The normal problems associated with the conditions for remand prisoners are likely to be exaggerated in the case of potential lifers, for example the difficulty of securing adequate legal advice. In a survey carried out for the Chief Inspector of Prisons, while governors in all but one prison holding remand prisoners stated that a set of legal reference books was available for the use of remand prisoners, only 11 per cent of male prisoners and 12 per cent of women prisoners said they had such access.[8] Fewer than half of the 63 per cent of prisoners who said that they had wanted to see a Bail Information or Legal Services Officer had been able to do so. It is not surprising that the Chief Inspector of Prisons suggested that preparing for trial should be a key part of the regime for unconvicted prisoners. Women suspects may well have a particularly difficult time since there are so few prisons for women: the Chief Inspector found that

[7] See for greater detail the Prison Service's Lifer Manual, the HM Inspectorates of Prison and Probation, *Lifers: A Joint Thematic Review* (1999), and Cullen and Newell (1999).
[8] See HM Chief Inspector of Prisons, *Unjust Deserts: A Thematic Review of Unsentenced Prisoners* (2000).

41 per cent of unsentenced women were held more than 50 miles from home.

Once sentenced, adult male lifers are likely to remain in their local prison for several months. Women will be taken to Durham or Bullwood Hall (see below). Children start their sentence in local authority secure accommodation and are usually transferred to the prison system at about the age of 18. To concentrate for the moment on adult males, conditions in local prisons for newly sentenced lifers were described in the Chief Inspectors of Prison and Probation Joint Thematic Review on Lifers (HMIPP, 1999) as 'generally unsatisfactory'.[9] The Review highlighted lengthy delays in the delivery of relevant paperwork from court to prison, poor induction and an absence of central policy. Sentence planning was reported to be poor, despite the introduction of Life Sentence Plans in 1993. Obviously the Prison Service is trying to confront these difficulties: an extra £0.5 m has been allocated to fund work in local prisons 'specifically with new and potential lifers, so that risk factors can be addressed at the earliest possible stage'.[10] A new Life Sentence Plan is being introduced which 'includes improved risk assessment procedures and ensures that a more systematic approach is taken to the management of lifers throughout their sentence'.[11] Perhaps the Chief Inspector of Prisons should carry out a useful follow-up Thematic Review to evaluate the success of these welcome initiatives.

After some time male lifers are transferred to one of five Main Centres, where they normally spend three or four years. There they should be able to undertake and complete a variety of courses. As we shall see, the Parole Board is influenced when assessing the risk of releasing an offender by the reports on the prisoner's completion of appropriate courses: the Sex Offender Treatment Programme (SOTP), offending behaviour courses, enhanced thinking courses, anger management courses, drug and alcohol misuse courses and so on. Yet not all prisons run all courses. There may be long waiting lists. In recent years the Prison Service has put great emphasis on 'accredited courses' and the Thematic Review on Lifers points out that 'courses such as relationship skills, gender awareness, coping with grief and loss, and violence against women had all become casualties of the diversion of resources into accredited programmes'.[12] The provision of relevant courses in different establishments seems poorly coordinated to the needs of individual

[9] At para. 1.6, p. 12.

[10] See Prison Service Annual Report and Accounts 2000–2001.

[11] Ibid, at p. 44.

[12] Her Majesty's Inspectorates of Prison and Probation (1999) *Lifers: A Joint Thematic Review*, at para. 6.37, p. 63.

prisoners. The Thematic Review was particularly critical of the absence of planning for different types of regime which might be required for females, young lifers and those from ethnic minorities.[13] But the problems in prison are related not only to lack of planning, but also to limited resources. The increased numbers of lifers has doubtless contributed to delays in moving prisoners through the system.

Those prisoners whose escape would be highly dangerous to the police, the public or to the security of the state, no matter how unlikely they are to escape, are categorised as 'Category A'.[14] The 'normal' route for other adult male lifers continues with a move from a Main Centre to a Category B trainer or dispersal prison. Cullen and Newell explain that many prisoners get into a 'log jam' at this stage, 'which often adds years to their imprisonment'.[15] They single out in particular those with (a) mental instability labels, (b) records of defiant, prison-based offending and/or (c) those who continue to protest their innocence. The prisoner should in due course move on to a Category C prison and eventually to an open (Category D) prison. The Parole Board is unlikely to consider release as a serious option before a prisoner has completed this journey through the system.[16] Indeed, the Parole Board may well be wise to consider that release into the community after a lengthy sentence can be achieved more smoothly from an open prison. The problem, as we shall see, is that prisoners get stuck in the system before they reach an open prison. And transfers are rarely smooth: while plodding along this route through the system, prisoners are likely to spend time in many different prisons, though it is probably true that the more compliant, the fewer moves he or she will suffer, but moves there will be. While the problem of adapting to transfers is a problem for all prisoners, especially as a result of the way the Incentive and Earned Privileges system is applied,[17] for a lifer the 'pains' of what seems like a retrograde step are particularly acute. Many lifers find it difficult to adjust to different regimes in different prisons. For example, a prisoner will find that when he or she moves to a new prison the 'privileges' available to a prisoner may be different to those in the previous prison; in particular, many suffer a loss of privileges on transfer to category C prisons. Others see the requirement to spend time in open conditions before having the opportunity of

13 Ibid., at para 1.12, p. 13.

14 For a fascinating review of the categorisation process, see Price (2000). Very recently in *Williams* v. *Secretary of State for the Home Department* [2002] EWCA Civ 498 (17 April 2002) the Court of Appeal has held that a prisoner may be entitled to an oral hearing before the Category A Committee: see p. 148 below.

15 Cullen and Newell (1999), at p. 26.

16 See Chapter 5, p. 94 below.

17 See Liebling *et al.* (1997).

what used to be known as a 'Pre-Release Employment Scheme' as a waste of time.[18]

The path of a woman lifer through the prison system will be different. Both young and adult women are allocated to one of only two main centres, one in the north of England (Durham) and one in the south (Bullwood Hall in Essex). Most are therefore imprisoned a substantial distance from their homes, and there is no separate regime for young women. Genders and Player, in one of the very few published studies of women lifers, point out that the assessment of women lifers at the beginning of their sentence has much less meaning than it does for their male equivalents because there is much less choice in future allocations: 'Facilities in the male system permit a degree of choice and flexibility in planning lifers' career paths'.[19] The women they describe (in H wing at Durham) 'felt trapped in a nightmare world of uncertainties'.[20] Because of the low numbers, many women suffer unnecessarily high security restrictions. According to the Chief Inspector of Prisons' Thematic Review of women in prison published in 1997, there were then no accredited programmes for women lifers,[21] and there remains a shortage today. We will return to some specific issues concerning the release of women lifers in Chapter 5.[22]

Release under the Criminal Justice Act 1967

The first statutory provisions governing the release of lifers were contained in the Criminal Justice Act 1948. Section 57 of the 1948 Act (replaced by section 27 of the Prisons Act 1952) provided for release on licence subject to such conditions as the Home Secretary might determine and subject to a right of recall. Release was largely unconditional, and few prisoners appear to have been recalled.

Parole was introduced by Part II of the Criminal Justice Act 1967. Determinate sentence prisoners became eligible to be considered by the Parole Board for release after they had served not less than one-third of their sentence or twelve months, whichever was longer. Local Review Committees were set up for every prison to discuss all cases in which the prisoner's parole eligibility date was imminent and their recommendations went to the Parole Unit of the Home Office. The system for lifers was much less precise. Under section 61 of the Criminal Justice Act 1967:

18 See Her Majesty's Inspectorates of Prison and Probation (2001) *Through the Prison Gate: A Joint Thematic Review* for a review of current resettlement provision and the need for a clearer strategy in this area.

19 Genders and Player (1987b), at p. 156.

20 Ibid., at p. 154.

21 See para. 6.55, p. 68.

22 See p. 103.

> (1) The Secretary of State may, if recommended to do so by the Parole Board, release on licence a person serving a sentence of imprisonment for life or a person detained under section 53 of the Children and Young Person's Act 1933, but shall not do so in the case of a person sentenced to imprisonment for life or to detention during Her Majesty's pleasure or for life except after consultation with the Lord Chief Justice of England together with the trial judge if available.

The Act continued the previous system which recognised that lifers might be released by executive discretion, but added another hurdle: the prisoner had to be recommended for release by the Parole Board before the Home Secretary could order release. The Home Secretary's power to recall was also maintained. At this time there was no differentiation between types of lifers when it came to release procedures. By virtue of section 62(1), where the Parole Board recommended the recall of any person who was subject to a licence, the Secretary of State could revoke the licence and recall him to prison. A prisoner recalled in such circumstances was entitled to be informed of the reasons for his recall and of his right to make representations. If he made representations the Secretary of State had to refer his case to the Board. Under section 62(2) the Secretary of State could himself revoke such a licence without consulting the Parole Board if 'it appeared expedient in the public interest to do so' before such consultation was practicable, but the case of a prisoner so recalled had to be referred to the Board. If the Board recommended the immediate release on licence of a recalled prisoner whose case was referred to it under section 62, the Secretary of State was bound to give effect to the recommendation. The Home Secretary kept the power to release life prisoners on licence on compassionate grounds at any stage (section 30).

The Act gave no guidance as to the precise procedures to be followed to decide questions on the release of lifers. Originally, when the Act came into operation, all life sentence cases were referred to the Parole Board when the prisoner had served not longer than seven years, irrespective of whether there was any likelihood of early release, and sometimes the referral was sooner. A prisoner's case would be referred to the Local Review Committee of the prison where he was held, and their recommendation would be passed to a Parole Board panel which would then consider the case, also taking into account the views of the judiciary. There appeared to have been no clear view as to when cases should be considered. Indeed, Lord Hunt commented in the House of Lords in 1991 on the 'pretty scandalous state of affairs' in the Home Office in 1967 with a 'great pile of dossiers relating to forgotten men'.[23]

[23] HL Debs, vol. 530, col. 1030.

In 1973 a Joint Parole Board-Home Office Committee was set up to recommend to the Home Secretary a date for the first formal review by the Local Review Committee as the first stage in a review by the Parole Board. They gave initial consideration to the timing of the first review usually after the prisoner had been detained for about three years, but this system proved ineffective: the Committee only recommended dates in about half the cases referred to it, simply remitting the remainder for reconsideration at a later date. Nor did they consult the judiciary at this stage, with the result that some reviews would be initiated before release was a realistic possibility.[24]

In 1983, the Joint Committee was disbanded[25] and new arrangements were made for fixing the date of the first formal review by the Local Review Committee. These arrangements were announced by the Home Secretary in the House of Commons on 30 November.[26] Under these arrangements the judiciary were consulted, usually, after a life prisoner had been detained for about three years, and asked for their views on the period necessary to meet the requirements of retribution and deterrence for the offence – what became known as 'the tariff period'. In the light of these views the Home Secretary would decide the date of the first reference of the case to the Local Review Committee, normally set for three years before the expiry of the tariff period.

The case of *Handscomb*,[27] sentenced to two discretionary life sentences in 1978, provides an example of practice at that time. In 1981 the Joint Committee of the Home Office and the Parole Board considered his case, and were unable to recommend a date for the first formal review for parole purposes. They asked for a reference back three years later. In the spring of 1984 (i.e. six years after sentence, some seven years after he had been arrested) the views of the Lord Chief Justice were obtained as to the period of detention necessary to meet the requirements of retribution and deterrence for Handscomb's offences. The Secretary of State then reviewed the case and decided that Handscomb's case should be reviewed by the Local Review Committee in 1991 (i.e. after some 14 years in custody). He could therefore expect at that stage to serve a minimum of 17 or 18 years in custody, the equivalent of a 27-year determinate sentence, with remission and without parole. In June 1985 a senior member of the Prison Service wrote to Handscomb to explain the system:

[24] See Padfield (2002) for more details.

[25] It is worth noting that Coker and Martin regretted its demise, seeing it as a downgrading of the importance of (and a vote of no confidence in) the Parole Board (see Coker and Martin (1985), pp. 241–2).

[26] 49 HC Official Report, 6th series, cols 505–7.

[27] (1988) 86 Cr App R 59.

> Your LRC review in 1991 is based on tariff (that is to say, what the judges and Ministers think you ought to serve as 'punishment' for your offence) . . . In the meantime, you should have interim 'reviews' at not longer than three-year intervals. The purpose of these is to let you know you are not forgotten, and to provide an opportunity for you and staff responsible for you to 'update' the situation, make any recommendations about a transfer etc . . . The interim review also allows staff to make recommendations about shortening your tariff, if they believe there are 'exceptional' grounds for it. This is the difficult bit, because I cannot tell you what these might be. The tariff was not lightly set, and is unlikely to be affected merely by 'good behaviour'. I think everyone would have to be convinced that something rather special had taken place in your attitude, outlook, personality or circumstances, and even then, it might not be sufficient to convince the higher authorities that any concession was justified.[28]

This letter illustrates the vague and imprecise criteria which were applied in deciding when and if to release lifers at this time. It is not surprising that prisoners started to turn increasingly to the courts, both domestic and European, to clarify their legal rights.

Judicial reviews of the process

English courts first recognised the importance of fixing the 'tariff' in three cases brought by three discretionary life sentence prisoners in the late 1980s.[29] The main focus of this book will be the changes introduced after the European Court of Human Rights had ruled in favour of four other discretionary lifers (Weeks, Thynne, Wilson and Gunnell). Interestingly, the domestic courts had by then already recognised the need to introduce some procedural safeguards into the treatment of discretionary lifers. But it is also worth noting that by the time these cases were decided, Weeks, and even Thynne, had already lodged their applications with the European Commission of Human Rights.[30]

In the first of the three, *Handscomb*,[31] four discretionary lifers had challenged the delay in the system which occurred before the Home Secretary consulted the trial judge and the Lord Chief Justice before fixing the tariff. The Divisional Court held that the existing policy was *Wednesbury*[32] unreasonable (and 'rather disquieting'[33]) and that the Home

[28] Cited at (1988) 86 Cr App R 59, at p. 62.

[29] *R* v. *Secretary of State for the Home Department, ex parte Handscomb and Others* (1988) 86 Cr App R 59; *R* v. *Secretary of State, ex parte Benson* (1988) *Times Law Reports*, 21 November and *R* v. *Parole Board, ex parte Bradley* (1991) 1 WLR 134.

[30] See Chapter 3.

[31] See note 29 above.

[32] That is, 'if a decision on a competent matter is so unreasonable that no reasonable authority could ever have come to it, then the courts can interfere . . .' as per Lord Greene MR in *Associated Provincial Houses Ltd* v. *Wednesbury Corporation* [1948] 1 KB 223, at p. 230.

[33] Per Watkins LJ, at p. 78.

Secretary should consult the judiciary immediately the sentence was passed. However, the court was happy to distinguish discretionary life sentences from mandatory ones, noting that different release procedures were essential to ensure that the purposes of the sentences were not frustrated. In *Benson*,[34] the court reviewed the Home Secretary's refusal to order the release of a discretionary life sentence prisoner who had been recommended for release by the Parole Board on three occasions. While the court did not hold that the Home Secretary had acted irrationally, his decision was quashed since he had taken into account irrelevant material. Lloyd LJ identified the kind of risk which justified detention:

> If risk to the public is the test, risk must mean risk of dangerousness. Nothing less will suffice. It must mean there is a risk of Mr. Benson repeating the sort of offence for which the life sentence was originally imposed; in other words risk to life or limb.

As Livingstone and Owen point out,[35] this was the first time that a lifer had successfully challenged the Home Secretary's exercise of his discretion to refuse to accept a Parole Board recommendation for release. In *Bradley*,[36] the Court went further in exploring the degree of risk which must exist to justify continued detention. Stuart-Smith LJ explained the discretionary life sentence thus:

> The rationale or justification for a discretionary life sentence must surely be this: that in exceptional cases the interests of public safety cannot be sufficiently protected by imposing a determinate sentence even to the maximum extent permissible – i.e. the tariff sentence merited in the way of punishment, uplifted to a limited extent allowed by established case-law for the protection of the public. Rather it is necessary to cater for the presently perceived risk that, upon completion of any lawful determinate sentence, the prisoner would, if freed, remain a grave danger to society. This is achieved by passing a life sentence so as to ensure that the public will be protected and the risk reassessed after the tariff period expires . . . the sentencing Court recognises that passing a life sentence may well cause the offender to serve longer, and sometimes substantially longer, than his just deserts. It must then not expose him to that peril unless there is compelling justification for such a course. That compelling justification is the perception of grave future risk amounting to an actual likelihood of dangerousness. But, of course, the Court's perception of that risk is inevitably imprecise. It is having to project its assessment many years forward and without the benefit of a constant process of monitoring and reporting such as will be enjoyed by the Parole Board.

34 See note 29 above.
35 Livingstone and Owen (1999), p. 405.
36 See note 29 above.

When at the post-tariff stage the assessment comes to be made by the Board they are thus much better placed to evaluate the true extent of the risk which will be posed by the prisoner's release.[37]

So what was the level of risk? Stuart-Smith LJ's advice to the Parole Board when evaluating the extent of the risk was that:

The Parole Board ... must clearly recognise the price which the prisoner personally is paying in order to give proper effect to the interests of public safety. They should recognise too that it is a progressively higher price. Accordingly, the longer the prisoner serves beyond the tariff period, the clearer should be the Parole Board's perception of public risk to justify continuing the deprivation of liberty involved.[38]

We will return to this analysis in Chapter 8 when discussing the theoretical justifications for post-tariff detention.[39] For the moment, it is important simply to note that these cases illustrate that at the time that the European Court of Human Rights made its first decision striking down the release process for discretionary lifers, domestic judges, in the context of applications for judicial review, were already beginning to become more active in protecting the rights of discretionary life sentence prisoners.

The government's position in the late 1980s

On 23 July 1987, in a parliamentary written answer to the House of Commons, the Home Secretary made the following statement in response to the Divisional Court judgment in *Handscomb*:[40]

I accept the conclusion of the Divisional Court that there are strong arguments for carrying out this consultation exercise [with the judiciary on the question of the period necessary to meet the requirements of retribution and deterrence] as soon as practicable following the imposition of a discretionary life sentence. Following consultation with the Lord Chief Justice it has been agreed that the most satisfactory way of obtaining the judicial view is to ask the trial judge to write to me, through him, in every case where a discretionary life sentence is passed giving his view on the period necessary to meet the requirements of retribution and deterrence. This view will be related to the determinate sentence that would have been passed but for the element of mental instability and/or public risk which led the judge to pass a life sentence and will also

[37] *R* v. *Parole Board, ex parte Bradley* (1991) 1 WLR 134, at p. 145.
[38] Ibid., at p. 146.
[39] See pp. 144 and 162 below.
[40] *R* v. *Secretary of State for the Home Department, ex parte Handscomb and Others* (1988) 86 Cr App R 59.

take account of the notional period of the sentence which a prisoner might expect to have been remitted for good behaviour had a determinate sentence been passed. The date of the first formal review by the Parole Board machinery will then be fixed in accordance with the judicial view on the requirements of retribution and deterrence, and the review will, as before, normally take place three years before the expiry of that period. I have agreed with the Lord Chief Justice that this new procedure will be introduced with effect from 1 October 1987 . . . I shall arrange for a review to be undertaken of all discretionary life sentence cases with a first formal review date of January 1988 or later. Where account has been taken of factors other than the judicial view on the requirements of retribution and deterrence in fixing the date, the date will be adjusted to bring it into line with the judicial view . . .

In cases of prisoners serving life sentences for murder, where the sentence is not at the discretion of the court, the question of the notional equivalent determinate sentence does not arise. I shall continue to take into account the view of the judiciary on the requirements of retribution and deterrence in such cases as a factor amongst others (including the need to maintain public confidence in the system of justice) to be weighed in the balance in setting the first review date. I shall ensure that the timing of the first formal review in such cases is fixed in accordance with my overall policy for ensuring that the time served by prisoners serving life sentences for the worst offences of violence fully reflects public concern about violent crime . . . no life sentence prisoner will be detained for more than 17 years without a formal review of his case even where the period thought necessary to meet the requirements of retribution and deterrence exceeds 20 years . . . However, as was made clear by the Divisional Court, the release of a life sentence prisoner is solely at my discretion and it is for me to decide, after receiving the Parole Board's recommendation and after consulting the judiciary as required by section 61(1) of the Criminal Justice Act 1967, when actual release should take place.[41]

So here we have, for the first time, a clear ministerial statement that fixing the tariff in mandatory and discretionary cases is different. In the case of mandatory life sentences 'the question of the notional equivalent determinate sentence' did not arise. The statement also made it clear that, in addition to his right to make representations to the Parole Board under the provisions of the Criminal Justice Act 1967, a discretionary lifer could seek judicial review of any decision of the Parole Board or of the Home Secretary on the ground that it was tainted by illegality, irrationality or procedural impropriety. As we shall see in the next chapter, the European Court of Human Rights was not convinced that this was an adequate response.

[41] 120 HC OR, 6th series, written answers, cols 347–9.

3

The view from Europe

Two cases decided by the European Court of Human Rights forced the British government to change the system of release, at least for discretionary life sentence prisoners. The first, *Weeks* v. *United Kingdom*,[1] did not have the impact of the second, *Thynne, Wilson and Gunnell* v. *United Kingdom*,[2] which is normally perceived as the 'key' case. Before examining these two cases, it is important to have a brief look at the European Convention of Human Rights (ECHR), as the backdrop against which the cases should be evaluated. When one looks at the Convention itself and the evolving European jurisprudence, it becomes evident that neither the decision in *Weeks* nor that of *Thynne* could have been a great surprise to the British government. Perhaps more interesting is why the government resisted these developments: but the government's response will be reserved largely for Chapter 4. In this Chapter we visit the decisions of the European Court of Human Rights.

The European Court of Human Rights

Many excellent books trace the history of the European Court of Human Rights.[3] It is sufficient here simply to rehearse an outline. The European Convention on Human Rights was signed on 4 November 1950 and came into force once ratified by ten of its signatories on 3 September 1953. As the Preamble states, it was framed to 'take the first steps for collective enforcement of certain rights stated in the Universal Declaration of Human Rights'. While the British took an active role in the drafting of the Convention, and indeed were the first country to ratify the Convention, it was not incorporated into domestic law until the Human Rights Act 1998. However, for present purposes, that should not distract us: applications can and could be made to the institutions of the

1 (1988) 10 EHRR 333.
2 (1991) 13 EHRR 666.
3 See, for example, Harris, O'Boyle and Warbrick (1995), Lester and Pannick (1999) and Emmerson and Ashworth (2001).

Convention by both individuals located in member states[4] and by member states against each other.

The European Convention on Human Rights was originally served by three institutions: the European Commission of Human Rights, the European Court of Human Rights and the Council of Ministers. Until 1998,[5] the Commission acted as a filter, the first point of contact for those who claimed their rights had been infringed. The Commission would investigate a complaint and decide if it was admissible. It would seek to reach a settlement between the parties, and if not successful would refer a case to the court, having itself expressed an opinion as to whether there had been a violation.

The right of an individual to petition the Commission was not an automatic right, but was dependent upon a declaration from a 'High Contracting Party' that it recognised the competence of the Commission to deal with petitions from its citizens. In the case of the UK, the government only accepted the right of individual petition in 1966 and this was renewed on a five-yearly basis.[6] For an application to be admissible, it must have exhausted domestic remedies and no more than six months must have passed from the date on which the final decision was taken. It must not be 'manifestly ill founded or an abuse of the right of application'.[7]

Substantive rights

The European Convention on Human Rights lists key rights and freedoms which the High Contracting Parties are required to guarantee to everyone within their jurisdiction. These include the right to life, freedom from slavery and forced labour, the right to a fair trial, the right to respect for private and family life, freedom of thought, conscience and religion and so on. For our purposes the key articles are:

> *Article 3: Prohibition of torture*
> No one shall be subjected to torture or to inhuman or degrading treatment or punishment.

[4] Citizenship of a member state is not a requirement.

[5] Lengthy and unacceptable delays, often of many years, led to major reforms and on 11 November 1998, Protocol 11 to the Convention came into force. The Convention is now served by only two institutions: the Committee of Ministers and the Court. The judicial business of the Court is now undertaken by committees, chambers and the Grand Chamber.

[6] See Lester (1998). Since 1998, individuals have had a mandatory right of access to the Court.

[7] See Article 34 of the ECHR.

Article 5: Right to liberty and security

1. Everyone has the right to liberty and security of person. No one shall be deprived of his liberty save in the following cases and in accordance with a procedure prescribed by law:
   (a) the lawful detention of a person after conviction by a competent court;
   (b) the lawful arrest or detention of a person for non-compliance with the lawful order of a court or in order to secure the fulfilment of any obligation prescribed by law;
   (c) the lawful arrest or detention of a person effected for the purpose of bringing him before the competent legal authority on reasonable suspicion of having committed an offence or when it is reasonably considered necessary to prevent his committing an offence or fleeing after having done so;
   (d) the detention of a minor by lawful order for the purpose of educational supervision or his lawful detention for the purpose of bringing him before the competent legal authority;
   (e) the lawful detention of persons for the prevention of the spreading of infectious diseases, of persons of unsound mind, alcoholics or drug addicts or vagrants;
   (f) the lawful arrest or detention of a person to prevent his effecting an unauthorised entry into the country or of a person against whom action is being taken with a view to deportation or extradition.
2. Everyone who is arrested shall be informed promptly, in a language which he understands, of the reasons for his arrest and of any charge against him.
3. Everyone arrested or detained in accordance with the provisions of paragraph 1(c) of this Article shall be brought promptly before a judge or other officer authorised by law to exercise judicial power and shall be entitled to trial within a reasonable time or to release pending trial. Release may be conditioned by guarantees to appear for trial.
4. Everyone who is deprived of his liberty by arrest or detention shall be entitled to take proceedings by which the lawfulness of his detention shall be decided speedily by a court and his release ordered if the detention is not lawful.
5. Everyone who has been the victim of arrest or detention in contravention of the provisions of this Article shall have an enforceable right to compensation.

Article 18: Limitation on use of restrictions on rights

The restrictions permitted under this Convention to the said rights and freedoms shall not be applied for any purpose other than those for which they have been prescribed.

The doctrine of a margin of appreciation

The function of the European Court of Human Rights can be seen essentially as 'fine-tuning'[8] legal systems which broadly respect human

[8] Livingstone and Owen (1999), at p. 111.

rights: the court allows a 'margin of appreciation' to national authorities to decide the appropriate boundaries of human rights protection. Thus in *Handyside* v. *UK*:[9]

> The Court points out that the machinery of protection established by the Convention is subsidiary to the national systems safeguarding human rights ... The Convention leaves to each Contracting State, in the first place, the task of securing the rights and liberties it enshrines. The institutions created by it make their own contribution to this task but they become involved only through contentious proceedings and once all domestic remedies have been exhausted ... Consequently, Article 10(2) leaves to the Contracting States a margin of appreciation. This margin is given both to the domestic legislator ('prescribed by law') and to the bodies, judicial amongst others, that are called upon to interpret and apply the laws in force. Nevertheless, Article 10(2) does not give the Contracting States an unlimited power of appreciation. The domestic margin of appreciation thus goes hand in hand with a European supervision. Such supervision concerns both the aim of the measure challenged and its 'necessity'; it covers not only the basic legislation but also the decision applying it, even one given by an independent court.

This view is echoed in many cases. The margin of appreciation permits domestic courts to play the primary role in the protection of human rights; the European Court of Human Rights provides simply a backstop.[10] Article 5(4), the vital paragraph for the discussion in this chapter, has been described as the 'habeas corpus provision of the Convention' and provides a person with a judicial remedy to test the validity of his or her detention. Thus the burden of proof lies on the state to show that the detention is lawful.[11] In *de Wilde, Ooms and Versyp* v. *Belgium*[12] the European Court of Human Rights held that Article 5(4) was infringed where three Belgians, each detained under national vagrancy laws, had no remedy before a domestic Court in which to challenge the decision of the magistrate to detain them. And in *Van Droogenbroeck* v. *Belgium*[13] the court had held that a man held as a recidivist by the Belgium Ministry of Justice and 'placed at the government's disposal' had also had his rights infringed. With a number of successful precedents, it is perhaps not surprising that a number of English discretionary life sentence prisoners challenged the legality of their detention and subsequent recall to prison. As we shall see, in the first of

9 (1976) 1 EHRR 737, para. 49.

10 We will, in Chapter 7, examine the extent to which domestic courts have heightened their level of scrutiny in judicial review cases.

11 *Zamir* v. *United Kingdom* (1996) 5 EHRR 533.

12 (1979) 1 EHRR 373.

13 (1982) 4 EHRR 433. Another example is provided by *X* v. *UK*, discussed in Chapter 6 (see p. 118).

these, in March 1987, the European Court of Human Rights held (by 13 votes to 4) there had been a violation of Article 5(4), though not of Article 5(1).

The case of *Weeks*[14]

Robert Weeks

In 1966, then aged 17, Robert Weeks had pleaded guilty to robbery and was sentenced to life imprisonment. He had entered a pet shop, threatened the owner with a starting pistol and had stolen 35 pence. At his trial, a prison medical officer testified that he could find no evidence of mental instability which would justify sending him to a mental institution. However, a probation report, prepared by a probation officer who had supervised him for a period of two years, characterised him as being susceptible to fluctuation of mood and emotionally immature, and as having a morbid interest in the literature of violence and a fascination for guns. The report also stated that he had taken to drinking heavily from time to time and that he had a high potential for aggression. No psychiatric report was available to the court. In passing sentence, Thesiger J said:

> . . . [T]he facts of the offence and the evidence of the character and disposition of the accused . . . satisfy me that . . . he is a very dangerous young man . . . I think an indeterminate sentence is the right sentence for somebody of this age, of this character and disposition, who is attracted to this form of conduct. That leaves the matter with the Secretary of State who can release him if and when those who have been watching him and examining him believe that with the passage of years he has become responsible. It may not take long. Or the change may not occur for a long time – I do not know how it will work out . . . [S]o far as the first count of the indictment is concerned, I think the right conclusion, terrible though it may seem, is that I pass the sentence that the law authorises me to pass for robbery and for assault with intent to rob with arms, that is life imprisonment. The Secretary of State can act if and when he thinks it is safe to act.

His appeal was dismissed by Salmon LJ:

> Now at the trial it appears that the prison doctor said that there was no evidence of any mental disorder then apparent which would have justified his detention in a mental institution. The learned judge, quite rightly in the view of this Court, took the view that this was not a case for borstal because borstal

14 See note 1 above. The facts are taken in large measure from the decision of the European Court of Human Rights.

> for one reason would not be a sufficiently secure place to send such a dangerous young man. The judge was therefore – since he could not send him to a mental institution for lack of evidence – faced with a difficult decision on whether he should give him what he did, namely life imprisonment, or sentence him to some long term, some definite term of imprisonment for a number of years. As he was at pains to point out, he in mercy really to the boy took the former course. Now life imprisonment in this case at any rate means an indeterminate sentence. If when he gets to prison it then appears after he has been there some time that there are grounds for transferring him to a mental institution for treatment, there are ample powers under the Act which will enable the Home Secretary to do so. Moreover, as soon as it becomes apparent, and it is to be hoped that it may not be long, but one cannot tell, that it is safe from the public point of view and from his own point of view to do so, this boy will be released. At first sight a sentence of life imprisonment, particularly having regard to his age, sounds terrible, but when the factors to which reference has been made are considered it will be seen that this is really in mercy to the boy and will perhaps enable him to be released much sooner than if a long term of imprisonment had been imposed, which was the only other alternative.

Thus the Court of Appeal upheld the life sentence as a mercy which would allow Weeks to be released much sooner than would have been the case had a long determinate sentence been imposed. In fact, he was first released in March 1976, a little over nine years later, which was the equivalent of at least a 12-year determinate sentence (taking into account remission and the period he spent in custody pre-sentence).

However, Weeks did not remain 'on the outside' for much more than a year. After being formally warned of a possible revocation of his licence, he was recalled to prison in June 1977 as a result of a various incidents involving minor violence while drunk, the use of an air pistol and a suicide attempt. The Parole Board confirmed the recall in December. Two years later he absconded from an open prison but gave himself up soon afterwards. In October 1981 he struggled with, and injured, a hostel warden at a pre-release hostel. He first lodged an application with the European Commission on 6 April 1982, arguing that his re-detention in June 1977 infringed his rights under both Article 5(1) and Article 5(4).

He was released on licence for a second time in October 1982, only to find that the Home Secretary revoked his licence once more in November 1984. The European Commission declared his application admissible on 7 December 1984, expressing the opinion (by 10 votes to 1) that there had been no breach of Article 5(1), but (by 7 votes to 4) that there had been a breach of Article 5(4). Weeks meanwhile was re-released, and then re-detained in April 1985. He was released once more on licence in September 1985. This licence was revoked in March 1986, though at the time of the hearing before the European Court, he was still at liberty, having fled to France. The oral hearing of the case was held on 17 March 1986, and the Court issued its judgment on 2 March 1987.

The Court's decision

In what it described as its central submission, the United Kingdom government argued that Weeks' recall to prison in 1977 had not deprived him of his liberty because both his liberty and his right to liberty had been taken away from him for the rest of his life by virtue of the original life sentence. The government drew a distinction between liberty, properly understood, and a life prisoner being permitted to live on licence outside prison. In the latter case, the government explained, the prisoner was still serving his sentence, albeit outside prison as a result of a privilege granted to him by the Home Secretary, but his right to liberty had not been restored to him. Thus it was one and the same deprivation of liberty in June 1977 as in December 1966, based on his original conviction and sentence, and no new issue arose under Article 5.

The Court was not convinced by this argument. Whether Weeks regained his 'liberty', for the purposes of Article 5 of the Convention, when he was released on licence in 1976 was a question of fact, depending upon the actual circumstances of the regime to which he was subject. He was lawfully 'at large', to use the terms of section 62(9) of the 1967 Act, when outside prison on licence. Admittedly, for persons sentenced to life imprisonment, any release under the 1967 Act was granted as an act of clemency and was always conditional. The freedom enjoyed by a life prisoner, such as Weeks, released on licence was thus more circumscribed in law and more precarious than the freedom enjoyed by the ordinary citizen. Nevertheless, the restrictions to which Weeks' freedom outside prison was subject under the law were not sufficient to prevent its being qualified as a state of 'liberty' for the purposes of Article 5. Hence, the European Court of Human Rights held that, when recalling Weeks to prison in 1977, the Home Secretary was ordering his removal from an actual state of liberty, albeit one enjoyed in law as a privilege and not as of right, to a state of custody.

A lengthy extract from the judgment is included as Appendix 1. In essence, the majority decided that Weeks' sentence was of a special character: a special security measure, but susceptible to change over time. (Without these 'special reasons' it might have infringed Article 3 (the prohibition on torture)[15]). There was no infringement of Article 5(1) as there was a sufficient connection between his sentence and his recall,

[15] See para. 47 of the judgment.

but there was an infringement of Article 5(4) because the Parole Board did not have the competence to decide:[16] the Home Secretary could veto their decisions. This seems to have been the Court's major misgiving about the procedure. It seemed less concerned whether the Parole Board constituted an 'independent' court, though it may be that the Court misunderstood the 'independence' of the Parole Board in an important respect: they accepted the government's statement that 'the functions of the Board do not bring it into contact with officials of the prisons or of the Home Office in such a way as to identify it with the administration of the prison or of the Home Office'.[17] While the expression 'in such a way as to identify it with' is extremely vague, it will be suggested in Chapters 5 and 7 that the independence of the Board can indeed be questioned. We will return to the Court's perception of the need for both subjective and objective independence. However, the issue has not been successfully challenged. The other area criticised by the European Court of Human Rights was the recall procedure, which they said showed 'a certain procedural weakness' in that it did not allow proper participation of the individual affected.

The two dissenting opinions are also included in Appendix 1. Judges Thór Vilhjálmsson, Lagergren, Sir Vincent Evans and Gersing held that there had been no violation of Weeks' rights. Judge De Meyer argued, at the other end of the scale, that there was a breach of both relevant paragraphs of Article 5.

The government's response

After this case, the government took time to consider its formal position. Some nine months after the Court gave its judgment, on 15 December 1987, Joan Ruddock MP asked the Home Secretary in the House of Commons what changes he intended to make. John Patten's answer on behalf of the Home Secretary was simply that the implications of the judgment were still under consideration.[18] When the cases of *Thynne, Wilson and Gunnell* were argued before the European Court of Human Rights, the government sought to argue that *Weeks* could be distinguished because of the highly unusual facts in that case. It will be remembered that Weeks' licence had been revoked in March 1986 and that at the time of the hearing of the case in the European Court of Human Rights, he was still unlawfully at large and living in France. Most surprisingly, two months after the decision of the Court, in May 1987, it was decided that the remainder of Weeks' life sentence should

[16] See para. 64.
[17] At para. 62.
[18] Hansard, vol. 124, col. 434.

be remitted by the exercise of the royal prerogative of mercy.[19] This meant that he was no longer subject to a life licence and the conditions in it. Does this imply a recognition that the various recalls and re-releases to which he had been subject were 'unfair'? Certainly they had gone on a long time. Perhaps there was some underlying recognition that, to quote the dissenting judgment of Judge de Meyer:

> Life imprisonment in its ordinary sense would indeed have been a punishment too 'terrible' for a somewhat aggressive young man of seventeen, guilty of robbing – after menacing his victim with a starting pistol loaded with blank cartridges – a sum of 35 old pence, which he did not even take away. It would have exceeded any reasonable relationship of proportionality with what actually happened. It would have been what the Eighth Amendment to the Constitution of the United States of America calls 'cruel and unusual punishment', and what Article 3 of the European Convention on Human Rights terms 'inhuman punishment'.

But the case did not end there. There was the question of compensation. The Divisional Court decided in early 1988 that Weeks was entitled to no compensation since he had been properly convicted.[20] Weeks' case returned to the European Court of Human Rights on 5 October 1988,[21] when the Court held unanimously that he should be paid £8,000. No compensation was payable in respect of the consequences attributable to his deprivation of liberty as such: the only prejudice to be taken into account was that caused by the violation found in the earlier judgment. The lack of the requisite remedy occasioned a loss of opportunities and a feeling of frustration and helplessness. Neither the remission of his sentence nor the finding of violation in the earlier judgment constituted adequate satisfaction in relation to the non-pecuniary damage. The Court also stated that 'in fixing the amount of compensation to be awarded, account should be taken of the special features of the case, notably the severity of the "indeterminate" life sentence in relation to the crime committed'[22]

Clearly Weeks' case continued to be seen by the UK government as an exception, a one-off. Otherwise they would not have argued as they did in the next case, that of *Thynne, Wilson and Gunnell*. As for Robert Weeks, he has been living back in this country ever since his licence was lifted and he has not been back to prison.[23]

19 Information given by the Prison Service.
20 Times LR, 15 March 1988.
21 See (1991) 13 EHRR 435.
22 At para. 15.
23 According to information given by the Prison Service.

The case of *Thynne, Wilson and Gunnell* v. *United Kingdom*

The Court heard these three cases together in the summer of 1990 (although the applications had been lodged even before the decision in *Weeks*). The Court gave its decision in October 1990. The facts behind the individual cases went back some years.

Michael Thynne

Michael Thynne's application was lodged with the European Commission on Human Rights back in 1985. Born in 1951, by 1975 he already had a long criminal record and had served various sentences of imprisonment for theft and burglary. In 1975, within 36 hours of being released from a prison sentence, he had entered a flat pretending that he was a policeman investigating a burglary that had just taken place there. The flat was occupied by a woman whom he threatened to kill if she made a noise. He raped and buggered her as well as inflicting minor wounds on her with a pair of scissors. He pleaded guilty at the Central Criminal Court, London, to rape and buggery and in November 1975 he was sentenced to life imprisonment on each count. In view of the nature of his personality disorder – described by a psychiatrist as 'a severe psychopathic character disorder' – the Recorder considered both a hospital order and a long determinate sentence to be inappropriate. The Recorder stated that an indeterminate life sentence was imposed to enable the Home Secretary to release Mr Thynne once his condition had sufficiently improved for it to be reasonably safe to do so. He went on:

> But for the psychiatric reports that I have seen I would impose on you a very long prison sentence. As it is, I am going to sentence you to life on each count in order that those in a position to observe any improvement in your personality disorder, those capable of carrying out any operative treatment which may [be] seen to be necessary, with your consent, on your frontal lobe, may judge the time when it is reasonably safe that you should be free.[24]

Thynne applied unsuccessfully for leave to appeal to the Court of Appeal (Criminal Division) against the life sentences on the ground that they were manifestly excessive and wrong in principle[25] as they resulted in custody for a longer time than the appropriate determinate sentence. He renewed his application to the full court. Refusing leave to appeal in March 1976, the Court stated as follows:

[24] Quoted in the European Court of Human Rights (1991) 13 EHRR 666, at para. 12.
[25] See section 2 of the Criminal Appeals Act 1968.

> Without going into any more detail as to the offences, it is quite clear and indeed is accepted . . . on the applicant's behalf, that this was a very serious and violent attack upon this lady which involved not merely violence but the indecency and indignities to which she was subjected . . . Life sentences are imposed in circumstances where the offence is so grave that even if there is little risk of repetition it merits such a severe, condign sentence and life sentences are also imposed where the public require protection and must have protection even though the gravity of the offence may not be so serious because there is a very real risk of repetition. This case falls within neither of those categories which express extreme situations but undoubtedly the offences here were very grave indeed and undoubtedly, in the light of the medical reports on this man, the Court cannot be sure by any means that he would, in society, not give way to outbursts of this nature which would very seriously affect other persons. In those circumstances the balancing exercise that the Court has to do is indeed a difficult one when presented with facts of this nature. We do not see the life sentence in this case as necessarily involving detention in custodial conditions for a very long period of time. It depends upon the regime to which he is subjected and the treatment that he can get. If a determinate sentence were to be substituted, then the Court would have to pass such a sentence as would ensure that he was kept in custody for a very long time indeed and, on the facts of this case as we see it, it will mean that probably the Court would err on the side of passing a sentence so long that it would result in his remaining in custody for a longer time than he probably will remain under a life sentence.[26]

In 1977 Thynne was accepted for treatment at the psychiatric prison, Grendon Underwood. However, he decided not to accept the place as, in the light of medical evidence that he was not amenable to surgery or psychiatric treatment, he was told that he would not automatically be given early release. Following representations made on his behalf, his case was referred to the Joint Parole Board-Home Office Committee, which was the body which at that stage would decide secretly whether the time had come to refer a prisoner's case to the Local Review Committee of the Parole Board.[27] In August 1980 the Committee recommended that Thynne's case should be referred to the Local Review Committee in September 1981, by which time he would have been detained for six years (the equivalent of a nine-year sentence). The Local Review Committee did not recommend release.

In May 1982 Thynne absconded from an open prison and committed various offences. He was arrested in July 1982 and was subsequently sentenced to six months' imprisonment on charges of theft, unlawful possession of drugs and criminal damage. The sentence was to run concurrently with the existing life sentence (as any determinate sentence

[26] Quoted in the European Court of Human Rights (1991) 13 EHRR 666, at para. 13.
[27] See p. 25 above.

must, when imposed on a lifer). In October 1982 the Parole Board recommended that his case be referred to the Local Review Committee nine months after his arrival at Maidstone Prison. In March 1983, however, he escaped when he was visiting his mother who was gravely ill. He was recaptured two days later and the date of referral to the Local Review Committee was put back to June 1984. In June 1983 he was transferred to Blundeston Prison where the prison psychiatrist found no evidence of mental illness and saw no need for psychiatric treatment. In 1984, the Local Review Committee again did not recommend release.

In 1985, when Thynne lodged his application to the European Commission, it was ten years since his original sentence. In January 1985 Ministers accepted that the punitive element of his sentence (the 'tariff') had been satisfied and that risk was the sole remaining consideration in his continued detention. In July 1985 his case was referred to the Parole Board which recommended a further review two years later. In July 1987 the Local Review Committee again recommended that he remain in custody, but in May 1989 it recommended his release. However, following its further consideration of his case in December 1989, the Parole Board again recommended that he remain in custody with no release date but that there should be a further review one year after his transfer to an open prison. Meanwhile, the European Court had in 1988 ordered the joinder of this application with that of Gunnell and Wilson and declared the cases admissible.

Benjamin Wilson

Benjamin Wilson was born in 1916. In May 1972 he pleaded guilty at the Central Criminal Court, London, *inter alia*, to one count of buggery, two counts of attempted buggery and seven counts of indecent assault on boys under 16. He had a long history of sexual offences and was sentenced to life imprisonment for the offence of buggery and seven years on each of the other nine counts, to be served concurrently. In passing sentence the judge said:

> I entirely accept that, to a large extent, you cannot help yourself. To that extent, your moral guilt is the less, but I have two duties to perform. One is a duty to find the correct sentence as far as you are concerned, having regard to your make-up, your physical and mental make-up. The other duty I have, and in the circumstances of the case I think it is the more important: I have a duty to the public, and in particular, to the young public, to protect them from people like you who, for one reason or another, can't control themselves. I hope that, in the course of time a method of treatment for your particular freakish affliction can be found. I think it will be in the best interest of society generally, and yourself in particular, if some form of treatment for you could be found. What I am going to do in your case may sound harsh from your point of view,

> but it will be explained to you, no doubt, by your counsel hereafter, that it may in fact hold out more hope to you than if I merely went up to perhaps 4, 5 or 6 years, or even 7 years in a particular case. The sentence of the court is that so far as the count of buggery is concerned, that is the eighth count on the indictment, you will go to prison for life. So far as the counts of attempted buggery and indecent assault are concerned, you will go to prison for a period of 7 years. All these sentences to be concurrent. Now I am sure that your counsel will have a word with you hereafter and will indicate what the situation is with regard to a life sentence, but as I say, I think my main duty in this particular case is to protect the public and the young public, in the light of what I have heard occurred in your case. I only hope that, in due course, some form of treatment, perhaps that to which the doctor refers in the medical report which I have seen, may help you.[28]

In 1972 Wilson's application for leave to appeal was refused. He renewed his application to the full court, but abandoned it in June 1973, a few days before it was to have been heard. In July 1976 he applied to the Court of Appeal to have his notice of abandonment set aside as a nullity. In November 1976, the Court of Appeal turned down his application. In the words of Lord Justice Shaw:

> ... the applicant has not established a situation in which this Court could properly allow him to withdraw the notice of abandonment. The Court has thought it right to go to some extent into the history of the matter in order to establish that even if such a withdrawal were permitted, it could not possibly be of advantage to the applicant, if we were to substitute for the life sentence a very long sentence that really would not be distinguishable from a life sentence. But if he wishes to take advantage of it, build himself up and strengthen his own character, he has far better prospects under an indeterminate sentence than under a long determinate sentence.[29]

Wilson's case was first referred to the Joint Parole Board-Home Office Committee three years after he was sentenced. They recommended that his case be reviewed by the Local Review Committee after he had served seven years. Accordingly, in 1979, the Local Review Committee heard his case and referred it to the Parole Board, who, in December 1981, recommended his release into a controlled protective environment with psychiatric supervision not later than December 1982 (i.e. ten years after he was sentenced). On 14 September 1982, pursuant to the Secretary of State's authorisation of 3 September 1982, he was released on licence on condition that he:

- live at a probation hostel;

[28] Quoted in the European Court of Human Rights (1991) 13 EHRR 666, at para. 22.
[29] Ibid., at para. 23.

- cooperate with his probation officer, attend appointments with his supervising consultant psychiatrist and take any prescribed treatment; and
- refrain from any activity involving young boys without the permission of his probation officer.

Five months after his release on licence, the Parole Board recommended his recall and on 14 February 1983 the Home Secretary revoked his licence. He was initially given no reasons, but was simply informed that he had been recalled because his conduct had given 'cause for concern' and he had failed to cooperate with his supervising officer. He exercised his right to make written representations against his recall, but on 16 September 1983, the Parole Board declined to change the decision.

In April 1984 Wilson initiated judicial review proceedings to have this decision quashed on the ground that he had not been provided with adequate details of the reason for his recall as required by section 62(3) of the Criminal Justice Act 1967 and that he had been unable to make effective representations. The Home Office conceded that the reasons given were inadequate and provided a one-page statement on 5 October 1984,[30] which included the allegations that:

1. Wilson had sought to get himself evicted from the probation hostel by refusing to pay his rent, by telling other residents of his offences and thus risking attack from them and by leaving a schoolboy's cap in the sitting-room of the hostel as a warning that he intended to reoffend;
2. he had protested against the probation officer's refusal to allow him to take part in activities at the local sports centre;
3. he had shown an interest in watching boys play football and his psychiatrist suspected that he was exploring ways of contacting boys again.

The Home Office agreed to allow Wilson to make further written representations to the Parole Board, which he did, denying the allegations made against him. In November 1984 his solicitors requested disclosure of a number of reports which had been before the Parole Board the previous September. In March 1985 the Divisional Court quashed the Parole Board's decision of 16 September 1983 on the ground that it was flawed by a procedural impropriety, in that Wilson had not been given sufficient reasons to enable him to make

[30] According to Coker and Martin (1985), this 450-word letter was the 'longest explanation so far provided for any recallee' (p. 247).

proper representations. By letter of 20 March 1985 his lawyer again requested disclosure of the probation report which alleged non-cooperation and asked for his client to be given an oral hearing with legal representation. However, the Parole Board did not answer this request and after a meeting on 22 March 1985 maintained the decision not to release Wilson.

In December 1986 the Local Review Committee reconsidered Wilson's case but did not recommend his release. In June 1987 the Parole Board recommended that his case should be referred to the Local Review Committee two years later. Again, in June 1989, the Local Review Committee re-examined his case but did not recommend release. In October 1989 the case was considered by the Parole Board which recommended a further review in two years' time, with the proviso that should his health deteriorate to such an extent that he was no longer considered to be a risk, the case should be reviewed at an earlier date. The Secretary of State accepted this recommendation. The next review date was fixed for October 1991, by which time it would be nearly 20 years since the original sentence (and Wilson would be 75 years old).

Meanwhile, Wilson's application to the European Commission on Human Rights had been lodged in September 1985, but as we have already noted, the European Court of Human Rights did not hear the case until June 1990.

Edward Gunnell

Edward Gunnell was born in 1930. In December 1965, he was convicted at the Central Criminal Court in London of four offences of rape and two offences of attempted rape. He was sentenced to life imprisonment on each of the four rapes. On the two counts of attempted rape he was sentenced to seven years' imprisonment, to run concurrently with each other and with the life sentences. He had entered houses, by some plausible excuse, when his victims were alone and by force (once at knifepoint) or by the threat of force had raped them. According to unchallenged medical evidence, he was suffering from a 'mental disorder' within the meaning of the Mental Health Act 1959 (namely psychopathy) and needed constant care and treatment in a maximum security medical setting. Nevertheless the sentencing judge concluded that, because of the gravity of the offences, punishment had to be an element in this case, and that punishment could only be achieved by imprisonment.

On 22 June 1966 the Court of Appeal (Criminal Division) refused leave to appeal. In the course of his judgment, Lord Parker CJ said:

> In regard to the application for leave to appeal against sentence in regard to the rapes and attempted rapes, the applicant is thirty-five and, though he has

> committed offences before, none of them have been offences of violence or of a sexual nature, but he has a long mental history. As long ago as 1946 he was committed to Manor Hospital, Epsom, from which he escaped eighteen times. In 1950 he was admitted to Farmfield Hospital, Horley. He absconded three times. In 1951 he was transferred to Rampton Hospital where he made no attempts to escape, possibly knowing that it is difficult to do so. In 1959, however, he was released on licence from Rampton and in 1960 he was discharged from the operation of the Mental Deficiency Act 1959. There was evidence, indeed it was uncontradicted, from the doctors that the applicant could be made the subject of a hospital order under the Mental Health Act 1959, in that he was a psychopath who needed constant care and treatment in a medical setting of maximum security such as Rampton and such a vacancy was then available. The learned judge refused to take that course and the ground of appeal here is that he was wrong in principle, when two doctors certified that the applicant was a fit subject for a hospital order and that treatment was warranted, not sending him to hospital but sending him to prison . . . This court would like it to be known that they agree with every word that the learned judge there said, indeed in an earlier case of Morris (1961) 2 QB 237, it was pointed out that there may be cases where although a court has powers to make a hospital order, yet where a punishment is required it would be right to send the offender to prison, it being recognised that the Home Secretary has ample powers under section 72 of the Mental Health Act 1959 to cause him to be treated in hospital when the need arises. This court would like to add one further reason justifying the judge's order in the present case. The applicant is obviously a dangerous psychopath. It is clear unless he is kept in circumstances of strict security he is liable to be a menace to the public. True, Rampton is said to be a secure hospital, but it does not mean that he would not get away from there. More important, it has to be observed that this dangerous psychopath has already been released on licence from Rampton. Bearing the interests of the public in mind, this court thinks it far safer that he should be kept in prison for as long as is necessary rather than he should be left to be dealt with as a hospital might deal with him, on a doctor and patient relationship under which it might be considered safe for him to be free, whereas from the public angle he remains a menace. This court is quite satisfied that the sentence was right and the application is refused.[31]

More than 14 years later, in December 1980, Gunnell's case was reviewed by the Parole Board. They recommended his release 15 months later, subject to his continued good conduct, the satisfactory completion of periods in open conditions and on the pre-release employment scheme, and suitable resettlement arrangements being made. After consulting the judiciary in accordance with section 61(1) of the 1967 Act, the Home Secretary accepted the Board's recommendation and in March 1982 he was released on licence on condition that he:

[31] Quoted in the European Court of Human Rights (1991) 13 EHRR 666, at para. 37.

1. cooperate with his supervisory probation officer;
2. attend Dr Field's Clinic at St Leonard's Hospital, London N1 for such care and treatment as recommended;
3. continue to take hormonal drug treatment, in tablet form, to control his sexual libido.

Gunnell was given no reason to believe that he had failed to keep the terms of his licence in any significant way. However, two incidents occurred in January and February 1983 in which it was alleged that he had been acting 'suspiciously'. His licence was revoked and he was recalled to prison. He protested that he had done nothing wrong but, in the words of the European Court of Human Rights, 'showed every indication'[32] that he fully realised why it was that the authorities had taken the decision which they did. He was interviewed on 1 March 1983 by a member of the Local Review Committee but was not shown his medical and other reports.

On 25 March the Parole Board rejected his representations but made a non-binding recommendation that, subject to satisfactory resettlement arrangements being made and to continuing psychiatric supervision, he should be released a month later. The Home Secretary did not accept the Board's recommendation, but decided that his case should be reviewed a year later. According to Gunnell, the first written explanations of the reasons for his recall and the first official account in any detail of the allegations made against him were made in a letter of 3 August. On 9 August 1983 he applied for judicial review of the decisions of the Parole Board and the Home Secretary confirming the revocation of the licence, but the application was dismissed on 2 November 1983.[33] His appeal to the Court of Appeal was dismissed on 30 October 1984.[34]

The Parole Board and the Home Secretary reviewed Gunnell's case again in 1984 but he was not released, at which point he lodged his application to the European Commission of Human Rights. Meanwhile, he was released on licence once more in September 1988, under the supervision of the Inner London Probation Service. However, on 24 September 1990 he pleaded guilty at the Central Criminal Court, London, to attempted rape, five charges of indecent assault and three charges of robbery. He was sentenced to life imprisonment, the life licence for his original offences having already been revoked.

[32] Ibid., at para. 43.
[33] Ibid., at para. 47.
[34] [1985] Crim LR 105.

The European Court of Human Rights' decision

As we have seen, Thynne, Wilson and Gunnell all lodged their applications with the Commission in 1985. The Commission declared the cases admissible in 1988. In its report adopted on 7 September 1989, the Commission's opinion was that, in relation to each applicant, there had been a violation of Article 5(4) (by 10 votes to 2) and additionally in the case of Wilson that there had been a violation of Article 5(5) (by 10 votes to 2). The hearing before the European Court of Human Rights did not take place until 25 June 1990. The Court was addressed by Alan Moses QC for the government, by Gaukur Jörundsson for the Commission, by P. Ashman, Legal Officer of Justice[35] for Thynne and by Edward Fitzgerald QC for Gunnell and Wilson. The Court delivered its judgment on 25 October 1990, holding by 18 votes to 1 that there had been a violation of Article 5(4) in the case of all three men, and by 18 votes to 1 that there had been a violation of Article 5(5)) in the case of Wilson.

The government had argued that these cases did not fall into the same category as *Weeks*, that in a normal discretionary life sentence no clear dividing line could be drawn by reference to the 'tariff' period between the punitive and security purposes for which the sentence was imposed. In their submission there was no clearly identifiable point after which the sole justification of the sentence was protective detention. The purpose of the tariff had been wrongly understood by both the applicants and the Commission as providing support for such a division: the 'tariff' was simply a notional period communicated by the judges to the Home Secretary in both mandatory and discretionary life sentences to enable him to fix the first review date by the Local Review Committee. It represented the judges' views as to the minimum period of detention necessary to satisfy the requirements of retribution and deterrence, and not necessarily the total such period. Thus the judges' recommendation was relevant only to the fixing of the date for the first review.[36] When considering release, the Home Secretary was not bound by the judicial view on 'tariff', but had to take into account a variety of factors which it was impossible to subject to finite analysis. Furthermore, the government also argued that the fact that the trial judge and the Lord Chief Justice were consulted a second time prior to a prisoner's release showed that consideration of the period necessary for punishment did not end at the expiry of the 'tariff' period. The government argued that the applicants'

35 The British section of the International Commission of Jurists.

36 It is curious that the government relied on this particular argument, given that it is difficult to reconcile with the Home Secretary's statement to the House of Commons of 23 July 1987 (i.e. three years earlier), discussed at p. 28 above, where he talked of the 'notional equivalent determinate sentence', the period necessary to meet the requirements of retribution and deterrence.

analysis confused the administrative procedures which governed the way the sentence is served with the nature of the sentence. The gravity of the offences was relevant at all times throughout the sentence, especially when the Secretary of State was called on to assess the risk factor when considering release. Gravity also remained the immutable justification in a discretionary life sentence – although not the sole justification – for the continued detention or recall of the life prisoner.

The Court was not convinced by these arguments. As in the case of *Weeks*, it considered the earlier cases of *De Wilde, Ooms and Versyp*,[37] *X* v. *the United Kingdom*,[38] and *Van Droogenbroeck*.[39] It also cited *Weeks* and *E.* v. *Norway*.[40] The following is an extract from the main judgment:

> 73. As regards the nature and purpose of the discretionary life sentence under English law, the government's main submission was that it is impossible to disentangle the punitive and security components of such sentences. The Court is not persuaded by this argument: the discretionary life sentence has clearly developed in English law as a measure to deal with mentally unstable and dangerous offenders; numerous judicial statements have recognised the protective purpose of this form of life sentence.[41] Although the dividing line may be difficult to draw in particular cases, it seems clear that the principles underlying such sentences, unlike mandatory life sentences, have developed in the sense that they are composed of a punitive element and subsequently of a security element designed to confer on the Secretary of State the responsibility for determining when the public interest permits the prisoner's release. This view is confirmed by the judicial description of the 'tariff' as denoting the period of detention considered necessary to meet the requirements of retribution and deterrence
>
> 74. The Court accepts the government's submissions that the 'tariff' is also communicated to the Secretary of State in cases of mandatory life imprisonment; that the Secretary of State in considering release may not be bound by the intimation of the 'tariff'; and that in the assessment of the risk factor in deciding on release the Secretary of State will also have regard to the gravity of the offences committed. However, in the Court's view this does not alter the fact that the objectives of the discretionary life sentence as seen above are distinct from the punitive purposes of the mandatory life sentence and have been so described by the courts in the relevant cases.
>
> 75. It is clear from the judgments of the sentencing courts that in their view the three applicants, unlike Mr Weeks, had committed offences of the utmost

37 (1979–80) 1 EHRR 373; 18 June 1971.

38 (1982) 4 EHRR 188; 5 November 1981, Series A no. 46, pp. 22–3, para. 52.

39 (1982) 4 EHRR 433; 24 June 1982, Series A no. 50.

40 (1994) 17 EHRR 30; 29 August 1990, Series A no. 181-A.

41 They referred, in particular, to the remarks by the Lord Chief Justice, Lord Lane, in *R* v. *Wilkinson* (1983) 5 Cr App R (S) 105 and Lord Justice Stuart-Smith in *R* v. *Parole Board, ex parte Bradley* [1991] 1 WLR 134.

> gravity meriting lengthy terms of imprisonment. Nevertheless, the Court is satisfied that in each case the punitive period of the discretionary life sentence has expired. In the case of Mr Thynne, it was accepted that by the end of 1984 risk was the sole remaining consideration in his continued detention. In addition to the life sentence imposed on him for the offence of buggery, Mr Wilson was sentenced in 1972 to seven years' imprisonment for each of the nine other counts to be served concurrently. In the circumstances of his case, it would seem reasonable to draw the conclusion that the punitive period of his life sentence had expired when he was released in 1982 and that thereafter his re-detention pursuant to that sentence depended solely on the risk factor. In Mr Gunnell's case too it may be taken that, notwithstanding the gravity of his offences on which the courts laid particular emphasis, the applicant had served the punitive period of his sentence by March 1982, the date fixed for his provisional release.
>
> 76. Having regard to the foregoing, the Court finds that the detention of the applicants after the expiry of the punitive periods of their life sentences is comparable to that at issue in the *Van Droogenbroeck* and *Weeks* cases: the factors of mental instability and dangerousness are susceptible to change over the passage of time and new issues of lawfulness may thus arise in the course of detention. It follows that at that phase in the execution of their sentences, the applicants were entitled under Article 5(4) to take proceedings to have the lawfulness of their continued detention decided by a court at reasonable intervals and to have the lawfulness of any re-detention determined by a court . . .

The Court then had to decide whether the available remedies satisfied the requirements of Article 5(4):

> 79. Article 5(4) does not guarantee a right to judicial control of such scope as to empower the 'court' on all aspects of the case, including questions of expediency, to substitute its own discretion for that of the decision-making authority; the review should, nevertheless, be wide enough to bear on those conditions which, according to the Convention, are essential for the lawful detention of a person subject to the special type of deprivation of liberty ordered against these three applicants.[42]
>
> 80. The Court sees no reason to depart from its finding in the Weeks judgment (paras. 60–69) that neither the Parole Board nor judicial review proceedings – no other remedy of a judicial character being available to the three applicants – satisfy the requirements of Article 5(4). Indeed, this was not disputed by the government.

On the question of compensation, the Court, referring to *Brogan and Others*[43] and *Fox, Campbell and Hartley*,[44] accepted Wilson's argument that

[42] See, *inter alia*, *Weeks*, para. 59, and *E* v. *Norway*, para. 50.
[43] (1989) 11 EHRR 117; 29 November 1988, Series A no. 145-B, p. 35, para. 67.
[44] (1991) 13 EHRR 157; 30 August 1990, Series A no. 182, p. 21, para. 46.

there had been a breach of Article 5(5) in that he did not have an enforceable right to compensation under the law of the United Kingdom in respect of the violation of Article 5(4). But even assuming that they have suffered certain feelings of 'helplessness and frustration', the Court shared the government's view that, in the circumstances, finding a violation of Article 5 in each of the cases constituted sufficient just satisfaction for the purposes of Article 50 and no order for compensation was made. They were awarded their lawyers' fees.

Dissenting opinion of Judge Vilhjálmsson

In *Weeks* three judges had dissented, holding that there had been no breach of Article 5(4), but this time Judge Thór Vilhjálmsson was alone. Because the Court was sitting in plenary, he considered himself free to examine the questions afresh and to reiterate his dissenting opinion in *Weeks*. The earlier case law 'could not . . . be taken to form a clear precedent for the case at hand'. He was particularly influenced by how the present judgment would influence the situation in other countries:

> I consider that the approach of the majority, which is difficult, if at all possible, to apply in the present case, would give rise to even greater difficulties if it were to be applied to sentences passed in other States. The words of the Convention do not require that our Court undertake the difficult task of breaking up sentences passed by courts in member States into their 'tariff' and 'security' components. This latter part of a sentence is said to be based on grounds 'susceptible of change with the passage of time'. I find that it is not possible to make this distinction under the Convention. It is also, in my opinion, relevant that the possibilities accorded to administrative authorities under national laws to shorten the time actually spent in prison is generally outside the control of our Court. The Convention has no clear rules on this point and it is, for the most part, left to the member States to regulate it . . . The Convention does not guarantee a right to be considered for parole nor does it contain rules as to the outcome of such procedures. I am of the opinion that the rights of the applicants Mr Wilson and Mr Gunnell are not changed by the fact that they were released on licence and then re-detained on the basis of their original sentences since these sentences were still in force. It goes without saying that the fact that the third applicant, Mr Thynne, escaped twice from detention, does not change his legal situation. Accordingly I have voted for no violation of Article 5(4). I therefore find no violation of Article 5(5) as claimed by the applicant Mr Wilson.

The outcome for Thynne, Wilson and Gunnell

We will see in the next chapter how the British government responded to this case by creating Discretionary Lifer Panels of the Parole Board. The first ones met in October 1992. Thynne was one of the first to benefit from an oral hearing and he was released on licence on 23 October 1992. However, his licence was revoked in January 1993 following concerns about his behaviour. He was subsequently sentenced in May 1993 to three years imprisonment for offences of burglary and assault which took the place the day before he was recalled in January. These offences resembled the offence for which he had received a life sentence: he had gained admittance by claiming to be a policeman investigating a burglary. Five years later, in April 1998, he was again released on licence but he died shortly afterwards, of a heroin overdose, aged 47.

Benjamin Wilson was eventually released in 1996 (aged 80), and has since died (aged 84). It will be remembered that Gunnell had pleaded guilty in 1990 to attempted rape and to several charges of indecent assault. He was sentenced once more to life imprisonment and the life licence for his original offences had already been revoked. He died, still in custody, in 2001, aged 71. The common belief that dangerous lifers leave prison after a short time and have an easy time of it are belied by the individual life stories mentioned here. But such stories create their own mythologies: during Padfield and Liebling's research carried out in 1999,[45] Thynne's apparent suicide from a drug overdose was mentioned several times by people on, or working for, the Parole Board as a reason for caution. There seemed to be a belief that the Parole Board should not 'set people up to fail' by releasing them inappropriately or on conditions that they were unlikely (or unwilling) to meet. This idea sits uncomfortably with the prisoner's right to be released if he is no longer considered dangerous. Paternalistic concerns about 'setting people up to fail' should surely result not in further detention, but in an insistence on greater support being made available in the community.

Wynne: murderers are different

Meanwhile, a mandatory life sentence prisoner also took his case to the European Court of Human Rights.[46] Wynne had been convicted of murder in 1964 and sentenced to life imprisonment. He was released on licence in May 1980 and killed another woman in June 1981. He was convicted of manslaughter and received a discretionary life sentence, and his licence was revoked. He later learnt that his tariff in relation to the second offence had expired in June 1991 and he sought to argue that the Court's ruling in *Thynne*[47] should also apply to those sentenced to a mandatory sentence. In a brief judgment, the European Court of Human

[45] See Chapter 5.
[46] (1994) 19 EHRR 333.
[47] (1991) 13 EHRR 666.

Rights accepted the 'essential distinction' between mandatory and discretionary life sentences. The Court said bluntly that

> the fact remains that the mandatory sentence belongs to a different category from the discretionary sentence in the sense that it is imposed automatically as the punishment for the offence of murder irrespective of considerations pertaining to the dangerousness of the offender. That mandatory life prisoners do not actually spend the rest of their lives in prison and that a notional tariff period is also established in such cases . . . does not alter this essential distinction between the two types of life sentence [at page 347].

Since Wynne was serving a mandatory life sentence, a review of the lawfulness of his discretionary life sentence would be devoid of purpose.

The European Commission, on the other hand, had not so readily accepted the government's position. They had been split 10–5, the dissenting opinion challenging the government's case in a way which was not examined at all by the Court. They pointed out (at page 343) that

> while the government contend that an additional factor, namely, the consideration of the maintenance of public confidence in the criminal justice system, is operative in mandatory cases, we note that in the 1987 policy statement,[48] this was relevant to the stage of deciding as to the appropriate length of the tariff and was not stated to be a factor which could require the continued detention of a person who had served his tariff and was no longer considered a risk. We further have doubts as to whether the criterion of maintaining public confidence is not merely a restatement of the risk principle.

The European Court of Human Rights' acceptance that the mandatory life sentence for murder is essentially different was successfully challenged in 2002 in the case of *Stafford* v. *UK*.[49]

The cases of *Hussain* and *Singh*[50]

The next important challenge to the way that indeterminate sentences are implemented in the United Kingdom to reach the European Court of Human Rights concerned young people under the aged of 18 convicted of murder. Hussain and Singh argued successfully that they, unlike those who are convicted of murder as adults, should be allowed the benefits of Article 5(4).

[48] Discussed at p. 28 above.

[49] See Preface.

[50] (1996) 22 EHRR 1.

Abed Hussain

Abed Hussain, a Pakistani national, was born in 1962 and was convicted in 1978, aged 16, of the murder of his brother, aged 2. He received the mandatory sentence of detention 'during Her Majesty's pleasure' pursuant to section 53(1) of the Children and Young Persons Act 1933.[51] In passing sentence, the judge stated:

> I regard you as someone who has demonstrated himself to be a cruel and unfeeling young man. I think you are – certainly for the time being – a dangerous person.

Later the trial judge wrote to the Secretary of State:

> Over the two or three days immediately preceding the baby's death, [Hussain] had undoubtedly treated him with very considerable violence by slapping, kicking and shaking. The baby was covered with over 60 bruises and his brain and spine were injured. Since [he] denied ever having laid hands on him, it was not possible to discover why he had acted with such violence.
>
> [Hussain] is unquestionably an unscrupulous young liar, but the most unusual feature of him was his impassivity. He demonstrated no feeling whatsoever for his brother's injuries and death.
>
> This gave me the impression that he is very probably a very dangerous young man who is quite unmoved by brutality. I am anxious that this aspect of his character should be borne fully in mind whenever the question of release arises. He still has three young siblings and their safety must be a predominant consideration. I am deeply concerned at the appearance of normality this young man gives; it is probably very misleading.
>
> I cannot recommend any period for his detention. It will have to continue until one can say with reasonable certainty that maturation has rendered him safe. The difficulty is that he is already 'old for his years', as one police officer described him. Maturation here involves much more than simply a young boy growing up.
>
> I can do no more than sound this sombre note of warning.[52]

He appealed against both his conviction and sentence. The Court of Appeal dismissed his appeal on 5 March 1980. He was first detained in the youth wing of Liverpool prison and then in a young offenders' institution before being transferred to an adult prison. It was not until 1986 that the Home Secretary (despite confidential judicial recommendations of ten years) set Hussain's tariff at 15 years. This was the equivalent of a determinate sentence of more than 20 years, imposed on a 16-year-old. Hussain first learnt of the judicial recommendations in a letter from the Home Office of 6 October 1994, sent in accordance with

[51] Now section 90 of the Powers of Criminal Courts (Sentencing) Act 2000; see p. 8 above.

[52] Quoted at (1996) 22 EHRR 1, para. 10.

the House of Lords' judgment in *Doody*.[53] By the time of the hearing before the European Court of Human Rights, the Parole Board had already considered Hussain's case on four occasions. The first Parole Board review took place in December 1986. The reports of progress were positive and, as Hussain learnt later, the Local Review Committee felt that he was suitable to be given a provisional release date. The Parole Board did not, however, recommend release, but only that he be transferred to a less restrictive Category C prison with a further review to commence in August 1990. In accordance with usual practice at that time, he did not see any of the reports before the Parole Board and had no opportunity to appear before it.

The second Parole Board review took place in 1990. Again he learnt later that the Local Review Committee had recommended that he should be given a provisional release date. But the Board did not recommend release, rather his transfer to open conditions with a further review to commence 18 months later. However, the Home Secretary rejected the Board's recommendation and directed that he should move to another Category C prison with a further review to commence in October 1992. Again he did not see any of the reports on him and had no oral hearing before the Parole Board. He was given no reasons for the decisions taken.

After the third review, in 1992, the Parole Board recommended that he be transferred to open conditions with a further review in six months' time. However, the Home Secretary again rejected this recommendation, directing that he remain in closed conditions with a further review to commence in March 1995. Hussain was informed in March 1993 that his release had not been recommended and about the date of his next review. He had by now served 15 years.

In June 1993, Hussain applied for judicial review of the decision communicated in March 1993 on the basis that he had not been shown the reports on him placed before the Board. He relied on the case of Prem Singh[54] as establishing that persons detained during Her Majesty's pleasure had a right at common law to disclosure of reports. On 13 October 1993, the Parole Board gave the High Court an undertaking to reconsider his case immediately and to disclose their case file to him so that he could make informed representations. He withdrew his application for judicial review.

In January 1994 Hussain was shown the reports on him that were before the Parole Board, but he was not given the opportunity to appear in person. Following this review, the Secretary of State accepted the Parole Board's recommendation to transfer him to open conditions. By

[53] *R* v. *Secretary of State ex parte Doody* [1994] 1 AC 531; see p. 6 above.

[54] *R* v. *Secretary of State for the Home Department, ex parte Prem Singh*, 20 April 1993, unreported (discussed below).

the time of the European Court of Human Rights' hearing Hussain was 33 years old, and had been detained for over 17 years.

Prem Singh

Prem Singh was born in 1957 and in 1973, aged 15, he was convicted of the murder of a 72-year-old woman, whom he strangled and had sex with at around the time of her death. He was released on licence in October 1990, 15 years later, but was arrested the next year in connection with alleged offences of deception and using threatening behaviour. His licence was revoked and the Parole Board did not recommend his release. The Parole Board considered his case again in December 1991 and in March 1992 the criminal charges against him were dismissed because the prosecution had presented the indictment out of time. Singh asked the Secretary of State to refer his case back to the Parole Board because of this development, but in July 1992 the Parole Board again decided not to recommend release. In April 1993 the Divisional Court quashed the Parole Board's decision of December 1991 on the ground that there had been a breach of natural justice because of the Board's failure to disclose the reports before it.[55] As a result, he was given his complete dossier and with the help of a solicitor made written representations to the Parole Board who reconsidered his case in June 1993. He was not present at the hearing. The Board did not recommend release.

In July 1994 a further hearing of the Parole Board recommended his release, subject to six months spent in a Pre-Release Employment Scheme (PRES). However, the Secretary of State did not accept this recommendation. This decision too was quashed by the Divisional Court in March 1995 on the grounds that the reasoning process followed by the Secretary of State had been flawed, because he had not explained how the findings he had made related to the test of dangerousness, defined as a danger to the 'life and limb' of the public.[56] In September 1995, Singh joined the PRES with a provisional release date in March 1996.

The Court's decision

Hussain applied to the Commission on 31 March 1993. The Commission declared the application admissible on 30 June 1994. The Court agreed unanimously that both Hussain and Singh were entitled under Article 5(4) to have the lawfulness of their detention decided by a court at reasonable intervals:

[55] *R* v. *Secretary of State for the Home Department, ex parte Prem Singh*, 20 April 1993, unreported; this was the case relied on by Hussain – see p. 54 above.

[56] *R* v. *Secretary of State for the Home Department, ex parte Prem Singh (No. 2)*, 16 March 1995, unreported.

50. The Court notes at the outset that, as has been commonly accepted, the central issue in the present case is whether detention during Her Majesty's pleasure, given its nature and purpose, should be assimilated, under the case-law on the Convention, to a mandatory sentence of life imprisonment or rather to a discretionary sentence of life imprisonment. In dealing with this issue the Court must therefore decide whether the substance of a sentence of detention under section 53 is more closely related to that at the heart of the cases of *Weeks* v. *the UK*[57] and *Thynne, Wilson and Gunnell*[58] or to that in the more recent case of *Wynne* v. *the United Kingdom*.[59]

51. It is true, as submitted by the government, that a sentence of detention during Her Majesty's pleasure is mandatory: it is fixed by law and is imposed automatically in all cases where persons under the age of 18 are convicted of murder, the trial judge having no discretion. It is also the case that the 1991 Act as well as recent policy statements treat the sentence at issue in the present case in an identical manner to mandatory life sentences as regards proceedings for release on licence and recall.

On the other hand, it is undisputed that, in its statutory origins, the expression 'during Her Majesty's pleasure' had a clearly preventive purpose and that – unlike sentences of life custody or life imprisonment – the word 'life' is not mentioned in the description of the sentence.

52. Nevertheless, important as these arguments may be for the understanding of the sentence of detention under section 53 in English law, the decisive issue in the present context is whether the nature and, above all, the purpose of that sentence are such as to require the lawfulness of the continued detention to be examined by a court satisfying the requirements of Article 5(4).

53. ... In the case of young persons convicted of serious crimes, the corresponding sentence undoubtedly contains a punitive element and accordingly a tariff is set to reflect the requirements of retribution and deterrence. However, an indeterminate term of detention for a convicted young person, which may be as long as that person's life, can only be justified by considerations based on the need to protect the public.

These considerations, centred on an assessment of the young offender's character and mental state and of his or her resulting dangerousness to society, must of necessity take into account any developments in the young offender's personality and attitude as he or she grows older. A failure to have regard to the changes that inevitably occur with maturation would mean that young persons detained under section 53 would be treated as having forfeited their liberty for the rest of their lives, a situation which, as the applicant and the Delegate of the Commission pointed out, might give rise to questions under Article 3 of the Convention.

54. Against this background the Court concludes that the applicant's sentence, after the expiration of his tariff, is more comparable to a discretion-

57 (1988) 10 EHRR 333.
58 (1991) 13 EHRR 666.
59 (1994) 19 EHRR 333.

> ary life sentence. This was, albeit in a different context, the view expressed by the Divisional Court in its judgment of 20 April 1993.[60] The decisive ground for the applicant's continued detention was and continues to be his dangerousness to society, a characteristic susceptible to change with the passage of time.

The Court went on to decide that judicial review did not provide an adequate remedy which satisfied the requirements of Article 5(4). Citing *Weeks*,[61] *E.* v. *Norway*,[62] and *Thynne, Wilson and Gunnell*,[63] the Court concluded that not only that the Parole Board did not satisfy the requirements of Article 5(4) because it could not order release, but also that 'the lack of adversarial proceedings before the Parole Board also prevents it from being regarded as a court or court-like body for the purposes of Article 5(4)'.[64] Finally:

> The Court is of the view that, in a situation such as that of the applicant, where a substantial term of imprisonment may be at stake and where characteristics pertaining to his personality and level of maturity are of importance in deciding on his dangerousness, Article 5(4) requires an oral hearing in the context of an adversarial procedure involving legal representation and the possibility of calling and questioning witnesses.
>
> It is not an answer to this requirement that the applicant might have been able to obtain an oral hearing by instituting proceedings for judicial review. In the first place, Article 5(4) presupposes the existence of a procedure in conformity with its requirements without the necessity of instituting separate legal proceedings in order to bring it about. In the second place, like the Delegate of the Commission, the Court is not convinced that the applicant's possibility of obtaining an oral hearing by way of proceedings for judicial review is sufficiently certain to be regarded as satisfying the requirements of Article 5(4) of the Convention.[65]

The Court gave no award for non-pecuniary damages, but awarded costs of £19,000, less 14,475 French francs already paid by way of legal aid, in respect of fees and travel and subsistence expenses.

Thus, the outcome of *Hussain and Singh* was that the European Court of Human Rights decided that young people convicted of murder (who of course like Hussain and Singh themselves are no longer young people by the time they come to be considered for release) should not be treated

60 *R.* v. *Secretary of State for the Home Department, ex parte Prem Singh*, see note 54 above.
61 (1988) 10 EHRR 333.
62 (1994) 17 EHRR 30.
63 (1991) 13 EHRR 666.
64 At para. 58. It may well be that all the Court meant by an adversarial procedure was an oral hearing.
65 At para. 61.

as adult murderers, despite the fact that they are by then adults who have been convicted of murder. Instead, they were entitled to the same due process rights as those who, for very different reasons, received discretionary life sentences. The Court gave its judgment on 21 February 1996, and the Crime (Sentences) Act 1997, as we shall see, extended the DLP process to those sentenced for Her Majesty's pleasure. For Singh this meant he was eventually released for the second time in March 1996 and at the time of writing, he remains on licence. Hussain was released on life licence in August 1997 and he too remains under the supervision of the Probation Service.

This leaves two indeterminate sentences we have not discussed in this Chapter: custody for life, the mandatory sentence from those aged over 18 and under 21 convicted of murder, and the more modern invention, 'automatic' life sentences. In *Bromfield* v. *United Kingdom*[66] and *Ryan* v. *United Kingdom*,[67] the European Commission held that those sentenced to custody for life were rightly treated as adult murderers for whom the sentence authorises life-long detention and thus they do not have the right to the benefit of Article 5(4). 'Automatic' life sentences are being treated for release purposes as discretionary life sentences.

Summary

This chapter has described certain key rulings of the European Court of Human Rights which led to the creation of the Discretionary Lifer Panels of the Parole Board. It started with the case of Robert Weeks, beneficiary of the prerogative of mercy after his success in the European Court of Human Rights. He won his argument that the procedure before the Parole Board, without an oral hearing and where the Parole Board had no power to decide the issue, infringed his rights under Article 5(4). Thynne, Gunnell and Wilson were equally successful before the Court (though less successful personally) and it was their cases which forced through the changes which led to the creation of Discretionary Lifer Panels of the Parole Board. These cases did not lead to a change for all lifers: the European Court of Human Rights held in *Wynne* that the sentence for murder was essentially different to the discretionary life sentence. Despite this, the Court subsequently held in *Hussain and Singh* that juvenile murderers should be entitled, like discretionary lifers, to the protection of Article 5(4).

This is not the end of the story. We shall see in Chapter 7 how two discretionary life sentence prisoners have more recently been successful

[66] (1988) 26 EHRR CD 138.
[67] (1999) 27 EHRR CD 204.

in the European Court of Human Rights in challenging the 'timeliness' of their DLP reviews. And now Stafford, a mandatory lifer who had been released on licence but later recalled, has taken his case to the European Court of Human Rights later in 2002 hoping to overrule the decision in *Wynne*. However, it is time to turn our attention to how the British government reacted to the decisions discussed so far. How the reasoning of the European Court of Human Rights has been interpreted by the United Kingdom Parliament is the subject of the next chapter. Later, in Chapter 7, we will analyse the arguments which lie behind the decisions in more depth.

4

Parliamentary and governmental responses

In this chapter we look at the response of the British government to the decisions of the European Court of Human Rights in the three key cases: *Weeks* decided in 1987, *Thynne Wilson and Gunnell* in 1990, and *Singh and Hussain* in 1996. In this chapter we trace the painful birth of Discretionary Lifer Panels of the Parole Board, concentrating on amendments added at a late stage to the Criminal Justice Bill 1990. It appears that the government was forced to act more swiftly than it wanted to, and produced a new 'court' to decide on the release of discretionary life sentence prisoners with some reluctance.

The Criminal Justice Bill 1990

The government was already committed to a substantial Criminal Justice Bill in 1990, long before the European Court of Human Rights gave its decision in *Thynne*. The roots of the Bill lay in the White Paper, *Crime Justice and Protecting the Public*,[1] and before that in a seminar convened by Douglas Hurd in 1987 at Leeds Castle. The White Paper had made no reference at all to life or indeterminate sentence prisoners. Its main proposals were directed towards the sentencing framework, although the government also intended to replace the existing system of parole to ensure that prisoners served at least half their sentences in custody and that 'prisoners serving sentences of 4 years or more would not get parole if this would put the public at risk'.[2] However, once the Bill reached the House of Commons life sentences were firmly on the agenda: a call for the reintroduction of the death penalty on the one hand, and, on the other, a call for the implementation of the recommendations of the

[1] Cm 965.

[2] The changes in the early release procedures for determinate sentence prisoners were based on the proposals of the Carlisle Committee (1988), which are discussed further in Chapter 6.

House of Lords Select Committee on Murder and Life Imprisonment, chaired by Lord Nathan.[3]

This Select Committee, which had been appointed on 21 July 1988 and had sat for the best part of a year before reporting in July 1989, included senior judicial figures as well as those with experience of the penal system: Lord Ackner, Lord Windlesham, Lord Harris, Lord Nathan.[4] The summary of their unanimous conclusions include the following:

> Murders differ so greatly from each other that it is wrong that they should attract the same punishment. The right way to deal with this matter is not to divide murder into categories, but to give the judge discretion to impose the sentence appropriate to the particular offence, taking into account all the relevant circumstances . . .
>
> Where a life sentence is awarded the judge should specify his reasons for imposing that sentence rather than a determinate sentence. In every case, the judge should specify in open court the period of years which he considers necessary to satisfy the requirements of retribution and deterrence. The Committee refer to the period as the 'penal sanction'. When the judge imposes a life sentence on the ground of risk, the penal sanction will be the period of years he would have imposed in the absence of this factor. Where he imposes a life sentence because of the heinousness of the offence, the penal sanction will be the period of years he would have imposed if the life sentence was not available. The penal sanction set by the judge should not be subject to revision by Ministers. It should, however, be open to appeal by either side . . .
>
> Up to the expiry of the penal sanction, parole arrangements should apply to life sentence prisoners as they do to prisoners on fixed term sentences.
>
> The decision to release should be an entirely judicial one. A judicial tribunal for considering life sentence release and recall decisions after the expiry of the penal sanction should be established.
>
> The tribunal should be composed of a High Court judge, a consultant psychiatrist and a chief probation officer. The prisoner should have the right to see all relevant documents. He should have the right of appearance and the right to be legally represented. The tribunal should have the characteristics of a court under the European Convention, and in particular, should be entirely independent of the executive.

3 HL Session 1988–89, Paper 78-I. For an analysis, see Morgan (1990), Richardson (1990), Windlesham (1990).

4 Lord Ackner was a senior judge, and Law Lord from 1986 to 1992; Lord Windlesham, a hereditary peer, had been a Conservative Home Office Minister and then Leader of the House of Lords in the early 1970s, and was Chairman of the Parole Board 1982–88; Lord Harris was Director of Publicity for the Labour Party in the 1960s and later joined the Liberal Democrats. He had chaired the Parole Board from 1979 to 1982; Lord Nathan, another hereditary peer and solicitor by training, had chaired the Committee.

> The decision of the tribunal should be final. However, if the tribunal ordered the release of a prisoner, this would be release on licence, and would afford the public the same degree of protection as the present licence system provides. The licence would entitle the tribunal, to whom the matter would be referred by the Home Office, to recall a licencee. Such a recall would immediately be referred to the tribunal for its decision.
>
> If the tribunal refused release on licence, it should state the time when the case should again be referred to the tribunal. The date of such re-consideration should be within three years . . .

It is worth considering the political context in which the Bill was being debated: perhaps two issues dominated the political consciousness. First, the resignation of Margaret Thatcher as Prime Minister on 28 November 1990. This resulted in important Cabinet reshuffles which must have had an impact on policy implementation.[5] Douglas Hurd had been the Home Secretary from 1985 until David Waddington[6] succeeded him in October 1990. Waddington lost this post after a very short time, in John Major's first reshuffle, when he became Leader of the House of Lords instead of Lord Belstead. Kenneth Baker took over as Home Secretary on 29 November 1990. Thus the Bill evolved under Douglas Hurd's stewardship, developed under David Waddington, and was steered through Parliament by Kenneth Baker. He held the post of Home Secretary only until succeeded by Kenneth Clarke in April 1992. The second major event dominating the political scene at the time was the Gulf War. Iraq had invaded Kuwait on 2 August 1990, and failed to leave by the 15 January deadline. 'Operation Desert Storm' took place in January/ February 1991. Other events which attracted political attention included a mortar bomb launched at Downing Street from a van in Whitehall on 7 February 1991 and the release of the Birmingham Six on 14 March.

The Bill in the House of Commons

The Criminal Justice Bill 1990 (Bill 6) had its first reading in the House of Commons on 8 November 1990, some three weeks after the decision of the European Court of Human Rights in *Thynne*. There was at this stage absolutely no reference to release procedures for life sentence prisoners. The Second Reading took place on 20 November.[7] The Bill was introduced by the then Home Secretary, David Waddington. There was

[5] See, for example, the political memoirs of Kenneth Baker (1993).

[6] Interestingly, David Waddington was the only Conservative Home Secretary since the 1960s to favour the return of capital punishment.

[7] Hansard, vol. 181, cols 139–236.

a lively debate, including strident calls for the reintroduction of the death penalty, led by Ivan Lawrence (a Conservative MP). Since a vote on the death penalty always takes place on the floor of the House (although technically in the Committee stage), a debate on new clauses on the death penalty took place on 17 December 1990. The proposal that the penalty for murder of a police officer should be death was defeated by 350 votes to 215,[8] and a more general death penalty clause was defeated by 367 votes to 182. A clause, which would have abolished the death penalty for treason etc, was defeated by 289 votes to 257,[9] and another clause which would have introduced the death penalty for certain murders, subject to a judicial discretion, was defeated by 349 votes to 186.

Committee Stage: the Sheerman proposals[10]

By the time that the Bill reached Committee Stage, Kenneth Baker had replaced David Waddington as Home Secretary. The Bill was considered in Committee from 29 November 1990 until 7 February. The first issue raised by the Opposition was whether draft Rules would be available before the Bill completed its consideration in Committee. The Act which eventually reached the statute book had 18 sections granting enabling powers to the Home Secretary (described variously as rules, regulations, orders, directions) and it is not surprising that members of the Opposition felt that to get the real 'flavour' of the Act they needed to see the draft Rules. John Patten, a Home Office Minister, argued that since any Rules would be subject to the negative resolution procedure, they would be subject to debate in the House of Commons later. Mr Andrew Bennett responded that this was 'nonsense': 'in an hour and a half's debate on regulations, we have very little control and no power to amend . . . On the floor of the House one has to take regulations or reject them'.[11] This discussion is important, given the subsequent history of the Parole Board Rules made under section 32(5). Unlike the powers granted to the Home Secretary under Part I of the Act, these powers were not exercisable only by statutory instrument. They were simply placed in the House of Commons library, and only after the new procedures had come into force. They have not been discussed in Parliament.

There was also considerable concern expressed that the Bill was being discussed in Committee shortly before the publication of the Woolf

[8] Hansard, vol. 183, col. 113.

[9] The death penalty for treason and piracy was finally abolished by section 36 of the Crime and Disorder Act 1998. This section was introduced at a late stage (on Report in the House of Lords) by Lord Archer of Sandwell, a Labour peer and senior lawyer, and was not opposed by the new Labour government.

[10] Session 1990–1991, Official Report, Standing Committee A.

[11] Session 1990–1991, Official Report, Standing Committee A, col. 8.

Report,[12] which had been commissioned to report fully into the causes of the unrest and riots in a number of English prisons in the spring of 1990 and was led by a senior judge.[13] The Report was published on 25 February 1991 and the Opposition argued that the findings of the Report could usefully have informed their own debate. The failure to wait for the findings of the Report was presumably also of some irritation too to those working on it.

It was in Committee on 15 January that the European Court's decision in *Thynne* was first raised. Barry Sheerman (Labour MP for Huddersfield) introduced amendments and new clauses to implement the European Court of Human Rights' judgment. These new clauses had the support of the civil rights organisations Justice and Liberty and would have:

- given all life sentence prisoners (mandatory and discretionary) the right to have their cases reviewed by the Parole Board every 12 months;
- given the Parole Board the power to release lifers on licence or unconditionally;
- once a prisoner was on licence, it would have given the Parole Board the duty to review licence conditions every five years;
- given the Lord Chancellor authority to institute rules to enable the Parole Board to become a 'court' for the purposes of the Convention;
- enabled the Parole Board to dispose of an application without a formal hearing where such a hearing was not requested by the applicant.

It is interesting to note how different these proposals are from those eventually enacted: for example, the provisions which Mr Sheerman proposed would have applied to all life sentence prisoners, unlike the provisions which were eventually enacted, which apply only to discretionary life sentence prisoners. Nor did the government accept that it should be possible to release prisoners unconditionally. Importantly for the question of 'independence', the power to draft Rules was in the end given to the Home Secretary and not to the Lord Chancellor.[14]

John Patten, a Home Office Minister, responded that, since it was only three months since the decision in *Thynne* and two months since the appointment of a new Home Secretary, the government needed more time to consider 'the issues'. These issues included the views of the

[12] Cm 1456; published on 25 February (see below).

[13] Lord Woolf was then a judge of the Court of Appeal, and became a Law Lord in 1992. He was later to become Master of the Rolls and then Lord Chief Justice.

[14] This is discussed in detail at pp. 134–5 below.

House of Lords Select Committee (the Nathan Committee) on tariff setting. He also argued, somewhat disingenuously, that the discussion was also untimely as certain key issues relating to tariff-setting were *sub iudice* (Pegg, Pierson, Smart, Doody were seeking judicial review)[15], concluding that 'I am inclined neither to accept the amendments nor to say at this stage when or how we shall implement the Strasbourg judgment'.[16] Mr Sheerman, although he was 'flabbergasted' by the Minister's remarks on 'unright time' (*sic*), agreed not to push the matter to a vote if the Minister agreed in principle to amend the Bill either in the House of Lords or in the House of Commons on Report. Mr Sheerman also proposed a clause to abolish the mandatory life sentence for murder but he withdrew it on 7 February.

Report Stage

At the Report Stage, on 20 February, Barry Sheerman reintroduced his new clauses.[17] One of his main arguments for applying the provisions to all lifers was the government's own argument before the European Court of Human Rights in *Thynne* that it would be wrong in principle and impractical in operation for two sets of rules to be operated by Parole Board depending on whether it was a mandatory or a discretionary case. He criticised the delay in introducing the changes, since this had been necessitated not just by *Thynne* but since the decision in *Weeks*, decided two years earlier. He also insisted that the Parole Board should have the power to set a period for the licence that was less than life. Mrs Rumbold, for the government, replied simply that the Home Secretary would put proposals before the House when he had completed his considerations. On a division, Mr Sheerman's clauses were defeated by 279 votes to 195. There followed some debate on a clause which would have abolished the mandatory life sentence for murder, proposed by the Labour MP Mr Archer, but this was withdrawn without a vote. The Report Stage of the Bill was concluded on 25 February (the day the Woolf Report was published and also debated in the House of Commons), and the Bill was read a third time.[18]

The House of Lords

It was in the House of Lords that the most significant campaign for reform of the law was launched. But the campaign was spearheaded

[15] See [1993] 3 All ER 92 and p. 6 above.
[16] Official Report, Standing Committee A, 15 January 1991, col. 337.
[17] Hansard, vol. 186, col. 350.
[18] Hansard, vol. 186, col. 748–54.

more by the Nathan Committee recommendations than by the decisions of the European Court of Human Rights. The initial emphasis was on the proposal to abolish the mandatory sentence for murderers, not on the rights of discretionary lifers (indeed all lifers) to a fair release process. The Criminal Justice Bill received its Second Reading in the House of Lords on 12 March 1991. A number of peers[19] hoped that during the passage of the Bill the law would be changed in line with the Select Committee report generally, and the decision in *Thynne* was mentioned. For Lord Campbell of Alloway, the failure to implement the Select Committee Report almost beggared belief.[20] Winding up the debate for the government, Earl Ferrers made clear that the government had no intention to abolish the mandatory life sentence. However, they were now 'looking for' an alternative release procedure which would both meet the requirements of the European Court of Human Rights and which would be acceptable to public opinion.

Committee Stage: Lord Nathan's 'Life Sentences Review Tribunal'

The House of Lords moved on to the Committee Stage of the Bill on 26 March 1991, where the House of Lords passed a number of amendments to give effect to the Nathan Committee recommendations. On 18 April, the Committee agreed by 177 votes to 79 on Lord Nathan's amendment to abolish the mandatory life sentence.[21] The arguments relied overwhelmingly on the report of the Select Committee, those who disagreed largely relying on the argument that abolition was not acceptable to the public. The next amendment was a clause to force the trial judge to state in open court 'the penal term', which was defined as 'the sentence of imprisonment the court would have passed if it had not been open to it to pass a sentence of imprisonment for life and it had not taken into account the risk of serious harm to the public if the offender were to be released after a determinate number of years' imprisonment'. This was agreed to by 120 votes to 68.

Lord Nathan proposed the next amendment introducing a 'Life Sentences Review Tribunal'. He explained:

> The Select Committee considered that the decision should be an entirely judicial one in which the Home Secretary and the Parole Board should not be involved. We considered that the court system is not well adapted to consider those matters and therefore recommended that a judicial tribunal should be established to consider life sentence release and recall decisions after the

[19] Including Lord Lane, the Lord Chief Justice, and Lord Windlesham.
[20] Hansard, vol. 527, col. 112.
[21] Hansard, vol. 527, col. 1583.

> expiry of the penal term. The tribunal should be composed of a High Court judge, a consultant psychiatrist and a chief probation officer.[22]

This body would have dealt with all life sentence prisoners. Lord Nathan made clear that in the context of life prisoners convicted of an offence other than murder, the Tribunal would be able to release the prisoner on licence or unconditionally. When releasing on licence, the Tribunal would be able to direct the length of time that the licence remained in force. If the Tribunal gave no direction as to the length of the licence it would be reviewed at three-yearly intervals. In the case of murderers, the licence would continue for life.

David Waddington (recently created a life peer and now Leader of the House of Lords) was cautious:

> The idea that the judiciary should take responsibility for decisions about offenders after they have been sentenced is completely new in the law of this country and we must think through its implications.[23]

He also pointed out that most of the criticisms in the Nathan Report about ministerial involvement concerned the power of ministers to lengthen tariffs. He raised two important questions at this early stage: would there be any role for the Secretary of State in the making of the representations to the Tribunal? And would there be an appeal? However, once the government undertook to consider the issues raised and to come back to the matter, no vote was taken on this amendment.

The Report Stage started on 14 May[24] and continued on 20 May.[25] The government appeared to have done nothing at all following the earlier discussion, and so Lord Windlesham moved an amendment to insert a clause introducing the Life Sentences Review Tribunal. This was, he explained, closely modelled on the Mental Health Review Tribunal and would transfer the decision on the release of a lifer to 'an independent tribunal with the characteristics of a court'.[26] Again the emphasis of his speech was on the Select Committee's report, with secondary support gained from the European Court of Human Rights' decision in *Thynne*. In his response, the Lord Privy Seal and Leader of the House (Lord Waddington) accepted that the law would have to be amended because the European Court had held that 'it is appropriate for the prisoner's release to be considered by a body having the status of a court' once the tariff period had expired:

22 Hansard, vol. 527, col. 1588–9.
23 Hansard, vol. 527, col. 1598.
24 Hansard, vol. 528, col. 1480.
25 Hansard, vol. 529, col. 9.
26 Hansard, vol. 529, col. 61.

> Clearly, the body should operate in a judicial manner, giving the prisoner the opportunity to appear before it and to be legally represented.[27]

He announced that the government had decided to introduce amendments to the Bill during its later stages but these would differ from the Nathan Committee proposals:

> We believe, for instance, that it may be preferable for the tribunal function to be carried out by the Parole Board, operating under a special procedure in the cases concerned rather than that a completely new tribunal should be set up. The relevant panel of the Parole Board would, however, be constituted under the chairmanship of a judicial member of the board, which reflects the proposal in the amendments we are considering.

He also made clear that the government would not be accepting the proposal that some life sentence prisoners might be released unconditionally or that the licence might at some future stage be lifted. The life sentence would not then, he said, be a life sentence.

The first to speak after the Leader of the House was Viscount Colville (who had become chairman of the Parole Board in 1988) who stated that:

> There will have to be a proper tribunal because, otherwise the procedure will not comply with Article 5 of the European Convention. If it is a proper tribunal, it is likely that the Mental Health Review Tribunals will be a good model. They involve a substantial body of statutory procedure and hearings with witnesses and representation. There is therefore a considerable commitment of time and personnel in any such procedure.[28]

He acknowledged that the Parole Board could do it in terms of personnel, but not at that moment in terms of resources.

Lord Richard for the Opposition cautiously welcomed the Leader of the House's statement but made it clear that the Opposition would not support the introduction of a panel for discretionary cases and not for mandatory cases. Lord Harris, for the Liberal Democrats, agreed that nothing could be stranger than this division. He hoped that

> the government would persist in their intention to have a High Court judge as chairman, a consultant psychiatrist (who in my view will be absolutely essential) and a chief probation officer, and I emphasise the word 'chief'. In my view, those three must be members of the tribunal. I do not have a view as to whether there should be other members.[29]

27 Hansard, vol. 529, col. 64.
28 Hansard, vol. 529, col. 66.
29 Hansard, vol. 529, col. 70.

Lord Nathan also welcomed the statement but pressed the amendments which were agreed to without a vote. The Report Stage continued the next day (21 May) with his amendments agreed to.

The Third Reading took place on 4 June, when the Bill was passed and returned to the Commons with amendments. The debate had concentrated exclusively on the need for procedural change, the need for a new judicial body. There was no discussion at all of the criteria for release.

Back in the Commons: the government reacts

On 25 June 1991, the House of Commons considered the Lords' amendments. First, they voted down the amendments to abolish the mandatory life sentence for murder. The debate was led by Kenneth Baker, the Home Secretary, with Roy Hattersley, Shadow Home Secretary, leading for the Opposition. The amendment was rejected by 236 votes to 158.[30] From there, the House moved on to consider the Lords' amendment to provide that the sentencing court should state the 'penal term' in open court, and MPs then had their first opportunity to discuss the government's own proposals. Perhaps the death knell of the Lords' proposals was sounded by the Speaker who had ruled that the amendments which sought to set up a Life Sentence Tribunal were out of order on the ground that they were outside the money resolution.[31]

At last, Mrs Rumbold presented the government's proposals, commenting that the Home Secretary would have preferred a little longer to 'digest all the implications of the judgment'. However, she announced, the government now proposed that the Parole Board should be required to sit as an

> independent body having the status of a court . . . operating under a special set of procedures which would be laid down in rules made by the Secretary of State under clause 26(5). We intend that the panel of the Parole Board which will consider discretionary life sentence cases will be chaired by a judge who is a member of the board, and one of its members will be a psychiatrist. The prisoner will be entitled to appear before the panel and be legally represented. If the panel concludes that the prisoner's continued detention is no longer necessary to protect the public, the Parole Board will direct the Secretary of State to release him. The Secretary of State will then be obliged to release the prisoner on licence, subject only to a power, exceptionally, to delay release for up to six months if it is in the public interest to do so – for example, because

30 Hansard, vol. 193, col. 894.

31 Viewed in this way the money resolution, decided on Second Reading, is a useful device for stifling dissent from government proposals. Once it is agreed that a Bill will not cost more than a certain amount of money, more expensive proposals can easily be ruled out.

> the release of a terrorist prisoner would otherwise coincide with some sensitive terrorist incident.[32]

She confirmed that prisoners appearing before the Parole Board in such cases would be eligible for legal aid. The Opposition's response, given by Mr Sheerman, was that since the proposals from the Lords were superior to the government's reaction, the Opposition would be opposing the government's amendments. First, he believed that the Secretary of State's proposed power to defer release by six months flew in the face of the European Court which would not accept such executive interference. The Parole Board could and should be given the appropriate power. He was also, once again, concerned that the Home Secretary was to be given the power to make Rules, insisting that the basic rights of the prisoner should be on the face of the Bill. Thus, for example,

> the burden of proof as to whether a prisoner is safe seems to have been reversed. Now, the prisoner must satisfy the Board that he or she is safe, rather than the board having to demonstrate that the prisoner's incarceration is necessary. The Minister did not make that clear.[33]

Here Mr Sheerman is raising for the first time an important evidential point. But there was no further debate on the objects and policies behind these new powers. The spokesman for the Liberal Democrats (Mr Maclennan) supported Mr Sheerman, but the government's proposals were quickly accepted by 219 votes to 147.[34] The House then returned to debate other Lords amendments unrelated to life sentences.

Back to the House of Lords

The Bill returned from the Commons on 27 June 1991 and amendments were considered in the Lords on 3 July. At this stage the Lords decided not to persist in their attempts to abolish the mandatory life sentence for murder, despite widespread acceptance that the House of Commons' approach was 'nonsense'. Lord Hailsham in characteristic language stated that:

> One day people will see sense, even in another place, and the hairy heel of populism which they have followed will ultimately disappear.[35]

[32] Hansard, vol. 193, col. 904.
[33] Hansard, vol. 193 col. 906.
[34] Hansard, vol. 193, col. 911.
[35] Hansard, vol. 530, col. 993.

Lord Nathan perhaps summed up the mood of the House by suggesting that it was worth avoiding a confrontation with the Commons on this issue, since other Commons amendments were more constructive. This was a time of considerable dispute between the two Houses, and feelings were raw in the House of Lords in relation to the War Crimes Bill and the Court and Legal Services Bill, as well as the Criminal Justice Bill. There was a sense in which it was agreed that the House of Lords could not win all of their battles all of the time, and that some battles were better not fought and lost.

The House of Commons' proposals were presented to the House by Lord Waddington who explained:

> It would, under the government's proposals, be open to the trial judge, exceptionally, not to set a term. This would be an indication that the crime which had been committed was so wicked that detention for life was justified according to the seriousness of the offence alone, irrespective of the risk to the public. Such a life sentence prisoner would therefore be in the same position as a mandatory life sentence prisoner. The question of his eventual release would be a matter for the Secretary of State.[36]

He argued that it would be incompatible with the reasoning of the European Court to apply the new procedure to mandatory life sentence cases. Nor should the judge have to declare a tariff: he chose the example of a terrorist who is discovered to have placed a bomb on a plane just before it takes off and is convicted of the attempted murder of hundreds of people. In such a case, although the life sentence was discretionary, the judge should not fix a tariff (the unstated implication presumably being that a 'whole life' tariff would be appropriate).[37] The Parole Board had been chosen as the appropriate body because of 'its great expertise and knowledge in matters relevant to assessing the early release of prisoners'. Acknowledging the need for the Board to have the power and status of a court, a judicial member would chair panels, and one of its members would be a psychiatrist. The Secretary of State would be obliged to follow 'directions' of the Parole Board subject to a power exceptionally to delay release for up to six months if it was in the public interest to do so. The European Court of Human Rights had recognised that a power to delay might in some circumstances be justified on the grounds of 'expediency':

[36] Hansard, vol. 530, col. 1009.

[37] We shall see in the next chapter that the judiciary did not accept this: the Lord Chief Justice issued a Practice Statement soon after the new law came into effect which stated that judges should, save in exceptional circumstances, fix a tariff. Even if he thought that detention for life was justified by the seriousness of the offence alone, he should so state in open court when passing sentence: see [1993] 1 WLR 223.

> We would fail in our duty to protect the public from offenders of that kind if we did not retain that ability to supervise their activities and prevent their committing further offences for the rest of their days.[38]

Lord Nathan made his disappointment clear:

> It is rare, if not unique, for a substantive amendment to be introduced after Third Reading in both Houses, especially when the subject has for long been known and under discussion.[39]

He invoked the support of the House as a revising Chamber to improve the drafting and to ensure compliance with the European Convention on Human Rights. He had three main improvements to suggest: the Home Secretary should have no power to defer release; the new court should have the power to bring the licence to an end; the trial judge should have a duty to fix the tariff.

> Approving our amendments in your Lordships' House will enable them to be considered by another place. To do so does not create conflict or confrontation but would, I hope and believe, promote the substantial step forward represented by the Commons amendment.[40]

Many others criticised the government's proposals. Lord Richard condemned the government's 'half-way house'. Lord Campbell of Alloway pointed out that:

> Superimposed on the text of the Bill is a four-tier drafting process which tends to obscure the nature of the essence of the disagreement as it now arises between the two Houses. There are the Lords' amendments; there are the Commons proposed amendments and new clauses; there are the Lords proposed amendments and the Commons proposed new clauses; and there is a Lords amendment to a Lords proposed amendment . . . That interesting, if somewhat perplexing process of law making, is worthy of the pen of A.P. Herbert and the satirical revelries of the honourable Mr Justice Cocklecarrot.[41]

Lord Morton and Lord Ackner concentrated on what they saw as the wrongful exclusion of mandatory lifers from the new process. Lord Longford argued that the Commons should be resisted since a matter of principle was at stake: whether those serving mandatory life sentences are treated humanely. Lord Hailsham announced that if he had been a betting man, which he was not, he would have been prepared to wager

[38] Hansard, vol. 530, col. 1012.
[39] Hansard, vol. 530, col. 1013.
[40] Hansard, vol. 530, col. 1015.
[41] Hansard, vol. 530, col. 1017.

20–1 that the European Court of Human Rights would shortly decide that that the same principle should be applied to mandatory as discretionary life sentence prisoners.[42] He argued passionately against any rigid distinction between the sentence for murder and that for manslaughter. Lord Hutchinson spoke of 'Thynne the human being', pointing out with some indignation that some four months after the European Court's decision, the Home Office had simply written that

> this judgement does not have any immediate effect on Mr Thynne's case . . . his case will continue to be dealt with under the existing arrangements. It has been decided that his case should be referred to the local review committee at his local prison in February 1992.[43]

Lord Harris, a former Chairman of the Parole Board, did not 'begin to understand' how one could possibly differentiate between mandatory and discretionary life sentence prisoners.

Lord Waddington replied. In relation to Lord Campbell's point that High Court judges should chair the tribunals, he said he had discussed the matter with the Lord Chancellor who felt strongly that experienced people on the Parole Board could carry out the function and that

> he believes that he would find it very difficult to operate the system if it had to be operated entirely by High Court judges.[44]

Lord Hunt intervened by reminding the House that within a matter of months of the Parole Board being set up

> we found a pretty scandalous state of affairs in the Home Office. We found a great pile of dossiers relating to forgotten men in the room of the then Under-Secretary. It was two High Court judges – indeed, the only two whom we had on the Board – who cleared the log jam.[45]

The government was defeated when the House voted 134–83 in favour of Lord Nathan's amendment to make the new procedure applicable to mandatory as well as discretionary lifers. There was a series of similar votes to remove the word 'discretionary' from the clauses and to create a flexible licence period. Again, the emphasis throughout was on the determination of a majority of peers to introduce a 'fairer' release procedure for all life sentence prisoners. The criteria for release were not in issue.

[42] He would of course have lost the bet: we saw in the previous chapter how the European Court of Human Rights four years later in *Wynne* v. *United Kingdom* upheld the distinction.

[43] Hansard, vol. 530, col. 1026.

[44] Hansard, vol. 530, col. 1030.

[45] Hansard, vol. 530, col. 1030.

Lord Harris's amendment that a judge of the High Court, sitting with a psychiatrist and chief probation officer, should chair the tribunal was the next to be debated. There was support for the suggestion that if more High Court judges were needed, more should be appointed. In a brief discussion on whether the Parole Board was 'independent', the Lord Chancellor stated that he believed that the qualification for being the chairman of a Panel should be that of a judge of the High Court or of a circuit judge. He felt that a circuit judge approved to try murder cases might be perfectly suitable. Lord Ackner, a Law Lord, protested that there was all the difference in the world between the function of a judge presiding in the trial of a murder case – not usually the most difficult of cases – where the decision is made by the jury, and that of the judge presiding over such a tribunal where he must take a leading part in making what may often be a difficult decision.[46]

Lord Waddington agreed with the Lord Chancellor about the practical problems of insisting upon a High Court judge:

> The panel that we propose will, in addition to the judge, include a medical member with a psychiatric qualification. The third member might well be a chief probation officer. However, it is not desirable to make an inflexible rule about that because many wise and distinguished members of the Parole Board are not chief probation officers and they may be equally suitable to undertake these duties. I should not like to rule them out.
>
> I am satisfied that taken together the provisions set out in the Commons amendments will ensure that the European Court of Human Rights will regard the Parole Board as a court in Strasbourg terms. The European Court will not be concerned about whether provisions appear in the Bill, in the rules, or in a mixture of both; it will look at the substance of our arrangements. The government have no doubt that it will find our arrangements adequate.

Lord Harris continued to insist that a High Court judge should chair Panels, but this amendment was lost by 73 votes to 65.

Lord Harris then repeated a question he had asked earlier, whether the Council on Tribunals would oversee the Parole Board. This Council was created after the Committee on Administrative Tribunals and Inquiries under the Chairmanship of Sir Oliver Franks (later Lord Franks) reported in 1957.[47] The Committee had concluded famously that the general characteristics which should make for the good administration of the growing number of tribunals was 'openness, fairness and impartiality'. The Council on Tribunals was created to act as a watchdog, and as an advisory body reporting to the Lord Chancellor. While many

[46] Hansard, vol. 530 1046-7.
[47] (1957), Cmnd 218.

have commented on the relative powerlessness of the Council,[48] its annual reports reveal that it provides useful advice. Thus Lord Harris insisted that the Council on Tribunals should be fully involved, pointing out that in their annual reports they had criticised the substantial delays which occur in hearing cases in Mental Health Review Tribunals. Since criticisms of precisely that character had been made of the parole system, it was therefore highly desirable that the Council on Tribunals had the right to look into the matter. To this Lord Waddington replied:

> We have not made statutory provisions for that but we shall explore the possibility of the Council providing advice on an informal basis about the procedures which the Parole Board will adopt in discretionary life sentence cases. I also give an undertaking that we shall consult the Council on the draft rules to be made for that purpose under Clause 26(5).[49]

We will return to the significance of the exclusion of the DLP from the supervision of the Council on Tribunals in Chapter 7.

Back to the Commons again

The Bill returned briefly to the Commons on 16 July 1991.[50] Angela Rumbold defended the government's position, facing a spirited, last-ditch attack from Barry Sheerman. She insisted that the mandatory life sentence was different to a discretionary life sentence because the element of risk was not decisive in handing down the mandatory life sentence. The reason the government wanted the trial judge not to have to specify the period in court was because sometimes then court would be imposing a discretionary sentence based on the seriousness of the offence, not on risk:

> In such cases, it would be inappropriate and illogical to require the court to state a term within the sentence which was appropriate to the seriousness of the offence. In those circumstances, the whole of the life sentence is there to punish the offence, not just part of it.[51]

The government also rejected the amendment that the Parole Board should be able to direct that a licence should be lifted after a certain period on the ground that it made nonsense of the whole concept of a life sentence: it would be wrong 'to deny the public protection for the

48 See, for example, Williams (1984).
49 Hansard, vol. 530, col. 1047.
50 Hansard, vol. 195, col. 307.
51 Hansard, vol. 195, col. 312. This stands oddly with the purposes of discretionary life sentences as explained in the case law: see Chapter 1 above.

remainder of the offender's life'. The government's one concession was to the Lords' amendment to remove the Home Secretary's power to keep a discretionary life sentence prisoner in custody for up to six months after his release had been ordered by the Parole Board. Although the government believed that such a limited residual power for the Home Secretary accorded with the European Court's agreement that the executive should be able to detain a prisoner on grounds of expediency, they withdrew: the Home Secretary

> has come to the conclusion that the kind of situation which this power is intended to cover could be handled without recourse to the exercise of that kind of reserve power.[52].

This appears to mean that the Home Secretary did not need this statutory power since he had it anyhow! In Chapter 5 we will note the considerable delays to which the new process has been subject: could it be argued that the government is manipulating a 'power' to delay?

Mr Sheerman, for the Opposition, carefully went through all four of the amendments made in the House of Lords with the warning that 'when the Executive nakedly interferes with the judiciary it can only be at the cost of justice'.[53] The four amendments were:

- to extend the proposed panels to mandatory lifers;
- to remove the power of the courts to determine that new release procedures for discretionary lifers should not apply to the case before them;
- to give the Parole Board the option of ending the licence after a period of time:

  > The *Thynne* judgment made it clear that when it comes to a discretionary life prisoner, a court or the Parole Board must have the power to bring the licence to an end.[54]

- to remove the power of the Home Secretary to defer release for up to six months.

Since the government was prepared to accept the last one, he ruefully accepted a success rate of 25 per cent.

Yet again he asked when MPs would see the regulations:

> It seems odd that we are reaching the end of the Bill's passage through the House without knowing the context of the regulations that are to flow from it.

[52] Hansard, vol. 195, col. 313.
[53] Hansard, vol. 195, col. 313.
[54] Hansard, vol. 195, col. 316.

> It is impossible to judge whether or not they are acceptable without having sight of them.[55]

John Greenway and Ivan Lawrence justified treating mandatory lifers differently and said presciently that the European Court would not be striking them down. Gerald Birmingham added a final impassioned plea for the House of Lords' amendments but the remaining three amendments were defeated 153–52.[56]

Finally the Bill returned to the Commons on 23 July to agree a drafting change that resulted from the House of Commons' acceptance of the removal of the Home Secretary's power to defer for six months, and the Bill received Royal Assent on 25 July 1991. The final text of sections 32 and 34 of the Act are to be found in Appendix 2.

Drafting the regulations

Section 32(5) permitted the Home Secretary to make 'rules' and section 32(6) to give 'directions' to the Parole Board. The Rules were to be procedural and the 'directions' on matters which should be taken into account by the Parole Board when discharging its function. It would seem that Opposition fears about the drafting of rules were well placed. There was nothing in the Act which said that these rules had to be subject to Parliamentary control, or indeed to be in the form of a statutory instrument. The Parole Board Rules were not made until 31 August 1992. It was in response to a question from Sir John Wheeler that the Home Secretary announced in a written answer on 27 October 1992 that a copy of the Rules had been placed in the Libraries of both Houses.[57] They were not debated on the floor of the House. The Rules had in any case already come into effect on 1 October 1992. They are attached, as amended in 1997,[58] at Appendix 4. The only other information that the Home Secretary reported to the House was that he had written to the Chairman of the Parole Board asking him to bear in mind the following criteria when selecting panel members:

> Chairman
> Panels should be chaired by a High Court judge member of the Board where cases involve: terrorist offences; the attempted murder or wounding of a police or prison officer; the sexual assault or mutilation and killing of a child (i.e. in

[55] Hansard, vol. 195, col. 316.
[56] Hansard, vol. 195, col. 322.
[57] HC Deb 27 Oct. 1992, col. 580W. See also HL Deb of the same day, cols 99–100WA.
[58] See below, p. 80.

the same incident); serial rape; manslaughter following release from prison on a previous manslaughter sentence; offences giving rise to multiple life sentences. Otherwise, a circuit judge or recorder may take the chair.

Second member
The second member should generally be a psychiatrist. But, if there is conclusive medical evidence that no serious concern exists about the prisoner's state of mind at the time of the offence or subsequently during imprisonment, a psychologist or probation officer may be appointed.

Third member
The third member of the panel should be a lay member, a criminologist, or a psychologist or probation officer (where he or she is not already the second member).[59]

Despite the power granted to the Home Secretary in section 32(6),[60] directions have never been issued.[61] The Home Secretary has issued directions (and training guidance) to the Parole Board on the release of determinate sentence prisoners, on the release of mandatory life sentence prisoners, on the transfer of life sentence prisoners to open conditions and on the recall of mandatory life sentence prisoners. There is no guidance on the matters to be taken into account by the DLP in deciding on the release of discretionary life sentence prisoners – presumably because the Home Secretary believes that it would be inappropriate for him to give directions to an 'independent court'. While this may be constitutionally correct, it does not mean that Parliament itself should not have laid down further guidance. It is hard not to agree with Genevra Richardson's comments on the 'poverty of legislative involvement'[62] in this area: Parliament has left the policies on release unspecified, which make it particularly difficult for the any 'court' to review the legality of decisions taken. Parliament's interest in creating the DLP was purely procedural: the government eventually decided to comply with the procedural requirements of the European Court of Human Rights, and even other proponents of change, the supporters of the Nathan Committee proposals, were pushing for procedural improvements. (We shall look in the next chapter at how the DLP actually discharges its functions under the Criminal Justice Act 1991 (as amended), and whether the DLP has enough guidance on the factors which it should take into account when deciding on the release of discretionary life sentence prisoners.)

[59] The letter, dated 1 September 1992, ends: 'I recognise these criteria will reduce your flexibility in scheduling panels. If they cause too much difficulty in scheduling panels, I hope you will let me know'.

[60] See Appendix 2.

[61] This is confirmed in the Annual Report of the Parole Board 1999–2000, at p. 9.

[62] Richardson (1993), at p. 324.

Meanwhile, the Lord Chief Justice issued a Practice Direction[63] explaining that despite the wording of section 34 of the Criminal Justice Act 1991, which merely permitted the judge to specify the 'relevant part' of the sentence, in fact the judge should do this whenever imposing a discretionary life sentence, giving reasons. The relevant part specified would consist of 'the period of detention imposed for punishment and deterrence, taking into account the seriousness of the offence'. The Court of Appeal made it clear that only in very exceptional cases should a judge not specify a period.[64]

The Crime (Sentences) Act 1997: extending the procedure

After the decision of the European Court of Human Rights in *Hussein and Singh* v. *United Kingdom*,[65] the government accepted that those detained during Her Majesty's pleasure should also be able to put their case before a Discretionary Lifer Panel of the Parole Board. The change was introduced during the Committee Stage of the Crime (Sentences) Bill in the House of Lords.[66] However, the government specifically did not change the procedure for setting the tariff at the beginning of the sentence (see section 28(4)). Baroness Blatch in the House of Lords defended this:

> Our well established position is that the Home Secretary has a legitimate and valuable role in the sentence imposed on those convicted of the unique and heinous crime of murder, whether they be adults or juveniles. This role is essential in establishing the distinctive nature of the penalty for murder. To remove the role of the Home Secretary would downgrade the unique seriousness of the offence. It would mean that the penalty for murder committed by juveniles would operate exactly the same way as the life sentence for those offences where it is the maximum rather than the only penalty.[67]

In complex language, the new Act simply brought HMP prisoners within the existing DLP procedure: sections 28–32 of the Crime (Sentences) Act 1997.[68] Since 1997, the law has changed several times. First, section 119

[63] Practice Direction (Imposition of Life Sentence) (1993) 1 WLR 223.

[64] See, for example, *Hollies* (1994) 16 Cr App R (S) 463; [1995] Crim LR 171; D (1994) 16 Cr App R 564.

[65] *Hussain and Singh* v. *UK* (1996) 22 EHRR 1; see Chapter 3.

[66] HL Cttee, 20 Feb. 1997.

[67] HL Cttee, 20 Feb. 1997, col. 819.

[68] See Appendix 3.

of the Crime and Disorder Act 1998 introduced minor amendments, as did the Powers of Criminal Courts (Sentencing) Act 2000. This Act was enacted as an attempt to codify the law of sentencing, but unfortunately, Parliament did not recognise the difficulties of codifying the law on imposing sentences of imprisonment without dealing at the same time with the law on release from sentences. Nor did it deal with the question of fixing the tariff in life sentence cases. Secondly, a more substantial change was made by section 60 of the Criminal Justice and Court Services Act 2000. This section reflects the government's acceptance of the decisions of the European Court of Human Rights in *T* v. *UK* and *V* v. *UK*,[69] that it was not compatible with Article 6 of the Convention for the Home Secretary to set the tariff in cases of detention during Her Majesty's Pleasure. Section 60 creates a new section 82A of the Powers of Criminal Courts (Sentencing) Act 2000. Section 82A, again in extraordinarily complex language, makes provision for the sentencing court to set the tariff in all discretionary life sentence cases and in any life sentence passed on an offender under the age of 18 when the offence was committed. Appendix 3 contains the current version of sections 28–32 of the Crime (Sentences) Act 1997, and section 82A of the Powers of the Criminal Courts (Sentencing) Act 2000.

The Parole Board Rules 1997

The inclusion of those sentenced to detention at Her Majesty's pleasure into the Discretionary Lifer Panel of the Parole Board process necessitated some minor amendments to the Parole Rules. These amendments were made and announced in a similar way to the 1992 Rules, by way of a written answer to a Parliamentary question after the new Rules had come into force:

> Fiona Mactaggart: To ask the Secretary of State for the Home Department if he has made provision for those detained during Her Majesty's pleasure to have their cases considered by the Parole Board at oral hearings.
>
> Mr. Straw: The Parole Board Rules 1997, which were made on 6 October 1997 under section 32(5) of the Criminal Justice Act 1991, came into force on 6 October. A copy of the Rules has been placed in the library.
>
> The rules apply to those detained during Her Majesty's pleasure and to all discretionary lifers, including those sentenced under section 2 of the Crime (Sentences) Act 1997.
>
> Apart from minor changes to statutory references and interpretation, the rules are identical to their predecessors, the Parole Board Rules 1992.[70]

[69] (1999) 30 EHRR 121; see p. 9 above.
[70] HC Deb 28 Oct. 1997, col. 774W.

The Parole Board Rules 1997, which remain the current Rules, are found in Appendix 4.

Summary

Following the decisions of the European Court of Human Rights in *Weeks* v. *U.K.* and *Thynne, Wilson and Gunnell* v. *UK*, discussed in the previous chapter, three different proposals for reform emerged during the passage of the Criminal Justice Bill 1990. The Labour Party in opposition in the House of Commons adopted the proposals of Liberty and Justice which would have given the Parole Board the power to review all life sentences every 12 months and the power to release unconditionally or conditionally. The Nathan Proposals, successfully adopted in the House of Lords but rejected in the Commons, would have created a much stronger and more obviously 'independent' Life Sentences Review Tribunal. However, neither of these proposals was accepted by the government. They were pushed into creating a more modest reform of the Parole Board, the Discretionary Lifer Panel. In subsequent chapters we will consider whether these 'minimalist' proposals have satisfied the requirements of the European Convention on Human Rights, as interpreted by the European Court of Human Rights. Both the Court and Parliament were concerned simply with procedural reform. Parliament, in particular, failed to discuss at all the substantive grounds for release to be applied by the DLP. Genevra Richardson, commenting on the options facing the government in late 1990, stated somewhat presciently that 'whatever the precise composition of the decision-making body, however, its ability to provide a real means of testing the substantive lawfulness of a prisoner's continued detention will depend, in large part, on the nature of the criteria that it is required to apply'.[71] How DLPs have worked in practice is the subject of the next chapter.

[71] Richardson (1991), at p. 38.

5

DLPs in practice

In this chapter we review how Panels have worked in practice. Doubtless there was much activity in the Parole Board as they worked to get the new Panels up and running by October 1992. These preparations included visits to Mental Health Review Tribunals as a precursor to the drafting of the Parole Board Rules 1992. In 1999, the Home Office commissioned the first observational study of the nature and quality of decision-making at Discretionary Lifer Panels,[1] and this research is the source of much of the information contained in this chapter.

An average of over 200 DLP cases have been considered each year: more than 1,500 hearings in total (see Table 5.1). About 17 per cent of hearings have resulted in a direction for release, although over the years this figure has varied, from 20 per cent in 1993 to 9 per cent in 1998–9 to 16 per cent in 2000/01. Approximately 20 per cent of prisoners whose cases have been heard every year have been recommended for transfer to open conditions. The number of prisoners who have been recalled has also increased: eleven released discretionary life sentence prisoners were recalled to prison in 1998–9, nine each in 1999–2000 and 2000–1, compared with only four in 1993.

The first review

We have already noted that although the Criminal Justice Act 1991 did not compel a judge to specify a 'tariff' period, this has since the Lord Chief Justice's Practice Statement[2] been normal practice. Section 34 of the 1991 Act has now been repealed and replaced by section 28 of the Crime (Sentences) Act 1997, which itself has been repealed in part and replaced by section 82A of the Powers of Criminal Courts (Sentencing) Act 2000.[3] In practice, all lifers whose cases fall to be considered by a DLP will now have a tariff period specified in open court by the sentencing judge.[4]

[1] See Padfield and Liebling (2000). The research was carried out between March and December 1999. After a period of pilot work, information was collected on a total of 69 cases. Fifty-two cases were observed (49 including the deliberations, normally held in private). These hearings took place in 22 different prisons. Eight of the observed cases were recalled prisoners.

[2] [1993] 1 WLR 223 – see p. 79 above.

[3] See Appendix 3.

Table 5.1 Outcomes of DLP hearings 1992–9

DLP Decisions 1992–9	
Directed for release	216 (17%)
Recommended for transfer to open conditions	254 (20%)
Recommended for transfer to PRES/Resettlement	20 (1.6%)
Recommended for transfer to other prisons	150 (11.8%)
Recommended for consideration of specialist treatment	222 (17.5%)
No recommendation or remain in current location	407 (32%)
Recommended for release for deportation	2 (0.2%)
67 prisoners released by DLPs have been recalled to prison; a recall rate of 31 per cent (excluding deportees)	
Total	*1,271*

Source: Padfield and Liebling (2000), table 2.3.

Three years (or three and a half years) before tariff expiry, a 'paper' review of the case will take place. This is not a full DLP, but has important implications for the prisoner. The purpose of this review is to allow the Parole Board to recommend suitable prisoners for open conditions at this stage so that they may be considered for release when they reach the point of 'tariff': it is therefore a key but invisible stage in the DLP process. Prisoners do not have the right to be heard at this hearing. It is only on completion of the 'tariff' part of the sentence that the prisoner is entitled to a full DLP hearing. No research or published data exists which comments on the efficacy of this early review. However, few lifers are released as soon as they complete their tariff, suggesting that more could be done to speed especially the non-dangerous through the prison system. Thus the increasing number of 'automatic' life sentence prisoners with short tariffs potentially face a particular disadvantage: clearly there is a need to monitor the speed of their progress through the system.

Preparing for the DLP

A discretionary life sentence prisoner who has completed his 'tariff' is entitled to a new hearing before a DLP at least every two years. The DLP itself may recommend an earlier review, and indeed there have now been decisions of the European Court of Human Rights, which declare

[4] The continuing uncertainties which surround the appropriate length of such 'tariff' periods were noted in Chapter 1.

the need for a more flexible approach to the timing of hearings.[5] Contrary to what might be expected from the wording of Article 5(4) of the European Convention on Human Rights, it is not the prisoner who initiates the DLP process but the Home Secretary (or in practice the Prison Service). Referrals are made on a quarterly basis: seven months before the beginning of a particular quarter, the Lifer Unit of the Sentence Management Group[6] of the Prison Service provides the Parole Board secretariat with a list of prisoners whose DLP should be heard during that quarter. The Parole Board secretariat then compile a skeleton Panel programme for the quarter. Parole Board members who have been selected and trained to do DLP work are notified of the date and location of each proposed Panel and are asked about their availability. A final programme is then drawn up by the Parole Board secretariat and a copy sent to the members who will form the Panels and to the Lifer Unit. 'As soon as practicable thereafter'[7] the prisoner receives a standard letter informing him that the Home Secretary has referred his or her case to the Parole Board (as required by section 28(6) of the Crime Sentences Act 1997) and the letter informs him where and when the case has been listed for hearing. The oral hearing is not always held, but only the prisoner can waive it: the letter states that 'You have the right to insist on an oral hearing at which you can be present . . . You are required within five weeks of the date of this notice to notify the Board and the Secretary of State whether or not you wish to attend'. The prisoner is also informed of his right to be represented and his duty to inform the Board and the Secretary of State within five weeks of the name, address and occupation of his representative. The process then follows a strict timetable, following the prescriptions of the Rules.

The dossier

Within eight weeks of listing, the Home Secretary (again, in reality the Lifer Unit of the Prison Service) serves on the Parole Board and on the prisoner all the information and reports required by Schedule 1 of the Parole Board Rules. This is the Parole Board dossier, a large bundle of documents. A typical dossier is somewhere between fifty and a hundred pages long. It starts with an index and a summary of the relevant legal provisions. A useful summary of the latest reports and recommendations is followed by a thick bundle of documents which includes particulars

[5] See page 139 below.
[6] Before the reorganisation of 2000, it would have been the Lifer Review Unit of the Prison Service.
[7] See Parole Rules 1997, Rule 4 (see Appendix 4).

of the original crime and sentence, prison history, a summary of previous parole reports as well as those prepared for this occasion. The dossier ends with the documents submitted by the prisoner himself. The dossier is not always easy to negotiate: reports are not always clearly dated, and it can be difficult to work out whether a report was written for this hearing, a previous hearing or some other sentence planning purpose.

The dossier is not simply a collection of documents, but has been constructed from various sources. The main body of the dossier is made up of reports written by prison staff, often on standard forms not necessarily designed for the parole process. Reports tend to be subjective and judgmental, and negative labels stick.[8] One report writer may well have read the reports of others.[9] There is a useful literature highlighting the dangers inherent in relying on such reports,[10] and much research remains to be done. Hawkins, in a paper which stresses the moral character of criminal justice decision-making, points out that 'the act of defining what is "relevant" or "significant" enough to warrant inclusion in the records – quite apart from the actual language employed in the account – is an opportunity for the supplier of "facts" and "descriptions" to absorb the ultimate decision-maker into his or her own moral universe'.[11] The material is likely to be organised in such a way that the case is 'constructed' according to the Prison Service's perspective.[12] There is a danger that opinions formed early in a prisoner's career are reinforced and built on as the years go by and that out-of-date material is reused. A 'fact' repeated over and over again can develop a significance it does not merit.[13]

There is very often a time lag between the preparation of the reports and the hearing itself. In Chapter 6 we will examine the procedures followed at Mental Health Review Tribunals. There, it is the Tribunal secretariat who prepare the paperwork, not the hospital staff. Perhaps a similar procedure might improve the quality and timeliness of DLP dossiers.

[8] See Coker and Martin (1985), at p. 47.

[9] In their study of Discretionary Conditional Release (see Chapter 5), Hood and Shute found that prison staff and probation officers, asked how they collected the information for their reports, said they relied on prison and probation records as well as their interview with the prisoner. Seconded and home probation officers liaised with each other on at least 80 per cent of prisoners before writing their individual reports (Hood and Shute (2000), at p. 13).

[10] See, for example, Hawkins (1983a and b), McConville, Saunders and Leng (1991), Liebling (1992).

[11] Hawkins (1983b), at p. 114.

[12] McConville, Saunders and Leng (1991) argue similarly in relation to the way police files are 'constructed' for the Crown Prosecution Service.

[13] See Padfield and Liebling (2000), at p. 83, for a graphic example of how a prisoner's lies can get repeated in the dossier and 'come back and haunt him'.

The final contribution to the dossier is the 'Secretary of State's view'. In the early years of the DLP this was not presented in written form but orally by the presenting officer at the hearing. However, in order to help the presenting officer, who as we shall see is usually a member of the governor grade personnel in the prison, this view has evolved into a brief written statement of the Home Secretary's view of a satisfactory outcome or decision at the hearing. In reality, it is prepared by a senior civil servant in the Lifer Unit: only if the Lifer Unit wish to recommend that the prisoner should be released or transferred to open conditions is a Minister actually consulted. It would be interesting to explore the extent to which the need to seek Ministerial approval for these positive recommendations encourages the Lifer Unit to propose more cautious outcomes. In six of Padfield and Liebling's 52 observed hearings, the Secretary of State's view disagreed with a majority of the report writers: in each of these cases, he took a more cautious approach.[14] Sometimes 'the Secretary of State's view' offers no view: this is usually because of the late arrival of key reports. We will return to consider the impact of this document later in this chapter.

The prisoners

The review of the statistics[15] in Chapter 2 showed that the vast majority of lifers (73 per cent in 2000) are murderers subject to the mandatory life sentence. These people, as we shall see in Chapter 6, do not have an oral hearing before a panel. Discretionary lifers make up a small proportion of the whole lifer population. Although the tribunals under review are called Discretionary Lifer Panels, a surprisingly large proportion of the prisoners whose cases are considered are in fact murderers: those detained during Her Majesty's pleasure because they were convicted when children. In Padfield and Liebling's study, 14 (27 per cent) of the 52 prisoners whose cases were observed were convicted of murder, 13 (25 per cent) of manslaughter, 9 (17 per cent) of arson, 7 of rape (13 per cent), 6 (12 per cent) of other violent offences and 3 (6 per cent) of other sexual offences. Of the 11 recalled lifers, 6 were HMPs.

There is no reason to believe that the prisoners in this study were untypical. The average length of their 'tariffs' was eight years, with a range of two to 17 years. The total length of time served by discretionary life sentence prisoners is often much longer than this. The average length of time already served post-tariff by the prisoners in the sample was five years, with the longest time served since tariff expiry being already more than 15 years. Many of these people were of course nowhere near

[14] See Padfield and Liebling (2000), at p. 107.

[15] See Chapter 2, p. 18.

release. In one case, a man with a tariff of two years, had already served four years and as a Category B prisoner, was unlikely to be released for some years. As we have seen, a prisoner can expect to progress through the prison estate from Category B (or A) to Category C and then on to an open (Category D) prison, where he will normally spend some time before release. A key finding of the study was that while the Parole Board may direct the release of a discretionary lifer, the reality was that no prisoner in the study was released unless he was already in open (Category D) conditions.[16] Only 23 per cent of prisoners in the study were in open conditions, even though they had all completed their 'tariffs', some many years earlier. Padfield and Liebling therefore concluded that the spotlight should not be focused only on the DLP process, the release process narrowly construed, but also on the wider process that leads towards release, the entire life sentence process.[17]

In preparing for a DLP, a prisoner has to decide on what he or she hopes to achieve from the hearing: perhaps release or simply a recommendation which will help speed his or her progress through the prison system. A prisoner facing a DLP in a closed prison may realistically have a different 'agenda' to that of a prisoner hoping that his release will be ordered by a DLP held in an open prison. The letter telling the prisoner of the date of his hearing does not inform him of his legal aid eligibility. Yet it hardly needs to be said that the quality of legal representation may have a significant impact, not only on the way the case is presented at the DLP but also in the thoroughness of the preparation. Effective legal representation can also help a prisoner develop realistic expectations of the DLP. In Padfield and Liebling's study, all the prisoners were represented by lawyers, or employees of firms of solicitors. It was not possible within the confines of that study to explore the amount of pre-hearing research and preparation solicitors were able to do for the case. But it was clear that there was considerable concern amongst lawyers that legal aid funding restrictions prevented them for preparing the prisoner's case as fully as they felt that they should be able to do. A number of firms have developed reputations in this area and are recommended by prisoners to each other. It was rare for a prisoner to be represented by the firm of solicitors who had represented him at trial, and so the new firm has to undertake considerable research preparing for the hearing. Legal representation, recognised as an essential by the European Court,[18] especially good

[16] This is not to say that release from closed conditions never happens, simply that it is relatively rare.

[17] See also the recommendations of Her Majesty's Inspectorates of Prison and Probation (2001) *Through the Prison Gate: A Joint Thematic Review* (London: Home Office).

[18] *Golder* v. *United Kingdom* (1975) 1 EHRR 524, *Campbell* v. *United Kingdom* (1992) 15 EHRR 137.

quality representation, is not cheap and it is important that it be made more secure for those challenging their fundamental right to liberty against the state.

The Panel

The Parole Board currently has over 100 members, but not all members sit on Discretionary Lifer Panels. Judges and psychiatrists will certainly do so. After they have served on the Board for a number of years, other members of the Board may, or may not, be invited to sit on DLPs, as 'independent members', i.e. the third member of the Panel. A DLP is always chaired by a judge[19] and Panels also always include a psychiatrist (despite the letter of 1 September 1992 which had suggested only that psychiatrists should 'generally' be appointed[20]) , though the psychiatrist is not always a forensic psychiatrist. The third member of the Panel is a 'lay' or 'independent' member, perhaps a senior probation officer or a criminologist, or a full-time member of the Parole Board, or a part-time member, who come from a wide variety of backgrounds: teachers, businesspeople and so on. The Panel will receive the dossier perhaps two weeks before the hearing. The size of the dossiers means that a considerable amount of time is needed to read the papers. Only the judge is likely to be involved in pre-hearing directions.

Pre-hearing directions

From the time the case is listed until the hearing, there will be frequent informal contact between the Lifer Unit of the Prison Service, the Parole Board secretariat and perhaps the prisoner's legal representative. The Parole Board Rules are clear: within 12 weeks of the case being listed for hearing, any party wishing to call witnesses must apply to the Board giving the substance of the evidence he or she proposes to adduce (Rule 7). The Chairman of the Panel may grant or refuse an application, and must give reasons in writing in the case of a refusal (Rule 7(2)). The Rules provide that the Chairman of the Panel may 'give, vary or revoke directions for the conduct of the case'. An appeal from such directions lies to the Chairman of the Parole Board within 14 days (Rule 9). In practice, the judge as Chairman receives the dossier before the other Panel members and any directions which he or she may give are dealt with very informally. Most often the judge simply agrees requests over the telephone to the Parole Board secretariat, who deal with the paperwork. By 1999, there had been only one oral pre-hearing applica-

[19] The judge is more often a circuit judge than a High Court judge. Judges do not necessarily chair mandatory lifer Panels: see Chapter 6.

[20] See p. 77 above.

tion, heard by the judge in the County Court where he normally sat. This was a recall case, which involved challenges to factual evidence. There has not yet been an appeal to the Chairman of the Parole Board. Greater formalisation of the pre-hearing directions stage might reduce the frequency of delays and deferrals.

The DLP in practice

The second review, which should take place on (but frequently in practice shortly after) tariff expiry, is the first to take place at the prisoner's prison, and the first at which he or she appears in person. It is, as we have seen, the Lifer Unit of the Prison Service who initiate the process: not the prisoner, nor indeed the Parole Board itself. But it is the Parole Board secretariat who conduct the practical arrangements for hearings, in liaison with the prison where the hearing is to take place. There is a clear attempt to plan hearings efficiently: normally two, occasionally three, cases are scheduled for one day.[21]

On arrival, Panel members are seen to the room allocated for the hearing. They are primarily looked after by a Panel secretary, a member of the Parole Board secretariat, whose role seems to extend from coffee maker to legal adviser. The extent to which this person involves themselves in the decision-making process varies. Padfield and Liebling cite the wording of the Panel secretary's job description in order to highlight some of the ambiguities in their role, which seems partly that of administrative assistant and partly that of professional/legal adviser:[22]

- Ensure that all Panels are conducted effectively by the due date, in accordance with internal instructions, and provide sound, considered and thorough advice and guidance to the Panel members, particularly in respect of drafting their decisions and recommendations.
- Ensure the efficient preparation of cases due to be considered by lifer Panels including the issue of prompt and accurate responses to all written and telephone enquiries from solicitors and the Prison Service, and offering sound advice to Panel chairmen in the preparation of their directions.
- Ensure the practical arrangements for the oral hearings are efficient, and take proper account of budget implications and that details of arrangements are conveyed to all parties.

[21] It is this administrative efficiency which led the High Court to uphold the three-monthly listing system in *Noorkoiv,* holding that a delay of up to three months did not breach Article 5: see p. 140 below.

[22] These ambiguities are discussed further at p. 99 below.

- Ensure Panel decisions adhere to current guidelines and directions and are circulated within the required time scale. Deal effectively and as promptly as possible with any enquiries resulting from those decisions.[23]

A hearing can be divided into four stages: the pre-hearing discussion; the hearing itself; the deliberation; and the drafting of the reasons for the decision. The pre-hearing discussion, often informal and held over coffee, sometimes more structured, is an important part of the process during which the Panel explore the key issues and exchange provisional views on the likely outcome. Late papers, most frequently the Secretary of State's opinion, may well be received on the morning of the hearing or shortly before the Panel meet and these have to be read swiftly before the parties are brought in.

Once the Panel is ready to start, the Panel Secretary invites all those waiting outside to come in. The main parties normally sit around a table: see Figure 5.1.

Figure 5.1 Plan of a typical DLP hearing

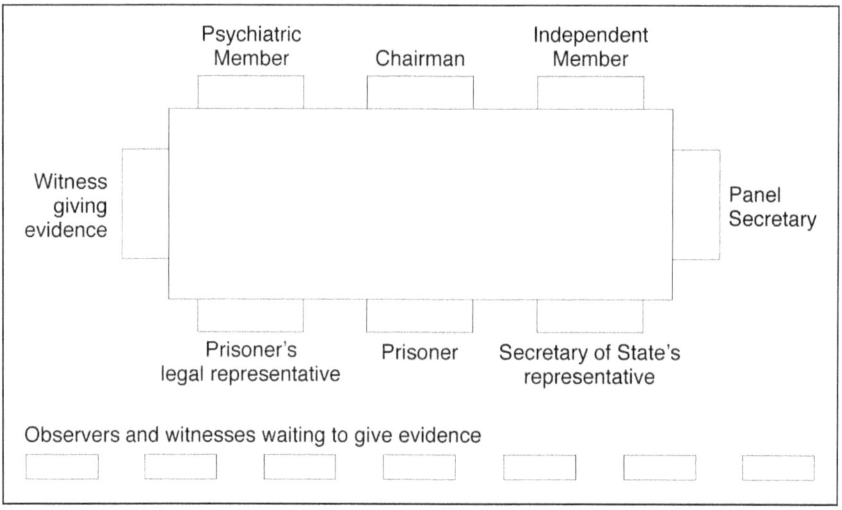

Source: Parole Board, *The DLP Panel Hearing – A Guide for Participants*, available from the Parole Board website and reproduced here with permission.

All participants, including possible witnesses, are invited into the hearing at the same time. After a few words by way of introduction, the judge will invite the 'Secretary of State's representative' to present the Secretary of State's view. The Secretary of State's representative is usually the lifer governor or lifer liaison officer in the prison. Clearly the

[23] See Padfield and Liebling (2000), at p. 99.

original expectation was that this role would be minimal. The original written Guidance stated that:

> The role of the presenting governor is not to act as a lawyer might in court. It is not for him or her to seek to underline the prisoner's case or to try to argue the Panel round to a particular decision for or against release . . . It may of course be the case that the presenter can use his or her expertise and knowledge of the system to challenge the prisoner's side on any claims which might be made regarding suitability for release. But, generally speaking, this will be a matter for the Panel.[24]

In Padfield and Liebling's study many representatives were clearly uncomfortable with their role, and wished to follow this 'minimalist' advice. They were prepared to help the Panel where necessary, but they preferred to be generally detached from the questioning. We will return to the position of the Secretary of State's representative in Chapter 7: given the huge importance of this decision to keep someone in prison beyond tariff, it is curious that no one is there strongly putting the case for detention. The absence of any strong representative of the state means that the Panel can be forced to take on that role themselves.[25]

As we have noted, all the prisoners in Padfield and Liebling's study were legally represented, sometimes by a barrister but more often by a solicitor or an unqualified practitioner who specialised in DLP or prison work. The more successful seemed to be those who were able to support the prisoner, perhaps acting as friend and 'translator' of complex questions. As elsewhere in the criminal justice process, prisoners can sometimes be significantly disadvantaged by the negative effect of their advocate. Those who let the prisoner himself do the talking seemed to be the most effective: the prisoner himself has a key role in persuading the Panel that he can be released, or moved on to open conditions.

The evidence at a DLP is tested through the questioning of witnesses, who normally all sit in the room throughout the hearing. The order in which the witnesses are heard will be agreed at the beginning of the hearing. The Policy and Procedures Manual of the Parole Board says that 'it is customary but not obligatory to take the prisoner's evidence first, assuming of course that he wishes to give evidence'.[26] Although the order of witnesses is not prescribed, once a witness is called, he or she is likely to be questioned as in a traditional court hearing: witnesses will be asked questions first by the representative who called them, then by the representative of the other party and finally by the Panel themselves.

24 See Page (1998).
25 See below pp. 140–2.
26 Para. 13.A18.

The psychiatrist normally takes the lead, especially when mental health issues are important. When psychiatric issues are less relevant, psychiatrists vary in the extent to which they get involved in questioning. However, there is no binding formality here: some Panel members interrupt and ask questions much more than others, some judges preside with much greater formality than others. The level of informality largely depends on the personal style of the judge as Chair.

For any prisoner seeking release, the key witness is his home probation officer: without the strong support of the home probation officer, release is totally improbable. In the Padfield and Liebling study, only one prisoner was released without the home probation officer having been personally quizzed by the Panel. But experts such as a psychologist or psychiatrist are also frequently called, as are family members, prison staff or even friends. Rule 12 of the Parole Board Rules specify that the hearings should be in private, but that 'the Chairman of the Panel may admit to the hearing such persons on such terms and conditions as he considers appropriate'. Not everyone who attends a hearing necessarily knows at the beginning of the hearing whether or not they will be called as a witness, and in Padfield and Liebling's study, some prison staff would intervene even when they were not formally witnesses. Because the onus[27] appears to be on the prisoner to prove that he is safe to be released (and indeed it is certainly the prisoner who has the primary interest in changing the status quo), witnesses are more often called by the prisoner or his legal representative. The Secretary of State's representative is more likely to rely on the dossier, except when refuting arguments raised by the prisoner. Padfield and Liebling concluded that witnesses 'played a very influential role but their appearance seemed somewhat haphazard'.[28]

After all the witnesses have been questioned, the representatives of both parties are invited by the judge as Chairman to make their concluding remarks, with the prisoner's representative having the final word. The Chairman then asks everyone to leave so that the Panel can deliberate in private (though the Panel Secretary remains present throughout). The prisoner is informed that he or she will receive the Panel's decision in writing within seven days. The Chairman advises the parties that they may be called back for further questions, but after a few minutes they will be told that they are no longer required to wait.

Evidence of risk

The Parole Board may not give a direction for release unless it is satisfied that it is no longer 'necessary for the protection of the public' that the

[27] The burden of proof at DLPs is discussed further at p. 143 below.
[28] Padfield and Liebling (2000), at p. 103.

prisoner should be confined.[29] Risk to the public is, in the words of the Parole Board Manual, 'the determinative consideration'. Panel members are advised by the Manual to take into account the evidence in the dossier; the evidence heard on the day; the Secretary of State's view and the last Parole Board decision letter. But what is this evidence? The discretionary life sentence prisoner should only be detained post-tariff if they are a 'grave danger to society'.[30] We noted in Chapter 4 that Parliament has failed to clarify the criteria which justify detention, and that the DLP has no formal guidelines. What evidence do they take into account? Panels in Padfield and Liebling's study took into account the obvious factors, which included the offender's index offence, his current security classification and location in the prison system, his attitude and behaviour in prison, his insight into his offending (largely measured by the completion of offending behaviour courses), his release plan, his attitude to his victim. They also noted his relationships with his family and other 'risk factors' such as medical treatment. Some validated risk factors, such as age, experience of local authority care, number of convictions at an early age, were not discussed. 'Whether what panels did during a hearing could accurately be called 'risk assessment' without more standardised and validated techniques at their disposal was a question which troubled us throughout the research process'.[31] This gap at the heart of the process raises important questions about the fairness of the DLP process. Are the 'right' prisoners detained?

It is widely agreed that predicting risk in this population of prisoners is highly problematic. The literature on risk assessment is vast.[32] It shows that even the most sophisticated actuarial tools have limitations: 'the propensity for violence is the result of the accumulation of risk factors, no one of which is either necessary or sufficient for a person to behave aggressively toward others. People will be violent by virtue of the presence of different sets of risk factors'.[33] Not everyone accurately categorised to be in a high-risk group will commit a violent act. As Buchanan and Leese[34] show, the danger of 'false positives' is likely to result in the detention of many people who are not likely in fact to commit a violent act. By doing a detailed analysis of existing studies using current predictors, Buchanan and Leese demonstrated that at least six people diagnosed as 'dangerous severely personality disordered'

[29] See section 34(4) of the Criminal Justice Act 1991; now section 28(6) of the Crime (Sentences) Act 1997.

[30] See, for example, *R* v. *Parole Board, ex parte Bradley* (1991) 1 WLR 134.

[31] Padfield and Liebling (2000), at p. 140.

[32] For example, Clarke *et al.* (1993), Nash (1999), Monahan *et al.* (2001), Buchanan and Leese (2001).

[33] Monaghan (2001), at p. 142.

[34] See note 32 above.

(DSPD) would have to be detained for a year to prevent one violent act. Their overall 'estimate for sensitivity' suggests that for every ten people with DSPD who would be violent, five would be identified and detained and five would be missed. Even with a cautious approach to risk, some people who are released will 'unpredictably' reoffend ('false negatives'). Many will be detained unnecessarily ('false positives'). Risk assessment in this population of offenders is a 'rough and ready' clinical, not an actuarial, process.

Decisions and outcomes

Padfield and Liebling were surprised by the speed with which Panels reached their decisions: while hearings ranged from eight minutes to four hours in length, the deliberation itself never lasted for more than 20 minutes.[35] It was the drafting of the letter to the prisoner, which contains the reasons for the decision, which took longer: up to 50 minutes. There was often considerable consensus. Even while they were drafting the reasons, Panels continued to comment on the strength of the evidence and the factors which influenced their decision. While the Board's sole statutory function is to decide whether or not to direct his release (and on what licence conditions), they often recommend other progressive moves or an early review. The Panel also often used the decision letter to fulfil many functions including relaying a message to the Prison Service, for example, that they felt it was time a prisoner was moved nearer to his home.[36]

Decisions to release[37]

In Padfield and Liebling's study, nine (out of 52) prisoners were released (see Figure 5.2). All the prisoners whose release was directed were released within 29 days of receiving the decision letter. All of those whose release was directed were in an open prison at the time of the DLP, and in terms of status, three were HMPs, five were discretionary lifers and one was a recalled prisoner on his third review post-recall. Two of the prisoners were released after their first oral hearing. The average time served of those released was 14 years and 7 months

35 See Padfield and Liebling (2000) p. 64.

36 Jowell's review of the impact of recent developments in judicial review suggests that a practical implication of 'the new constitutional litigation' is that 'in order to demonstrate that the decision pursued the least restrictive alternative, the decision-maker will have to consider alternative courses of action' (see Jowell, 2000, at p. 681). The implications of this for the DLP process could be significant.

37 Taken from Padfield and Liebling (2000), p. 78.

Figure 5.2 Decisions made at hearings observed by Padfield and Liebling

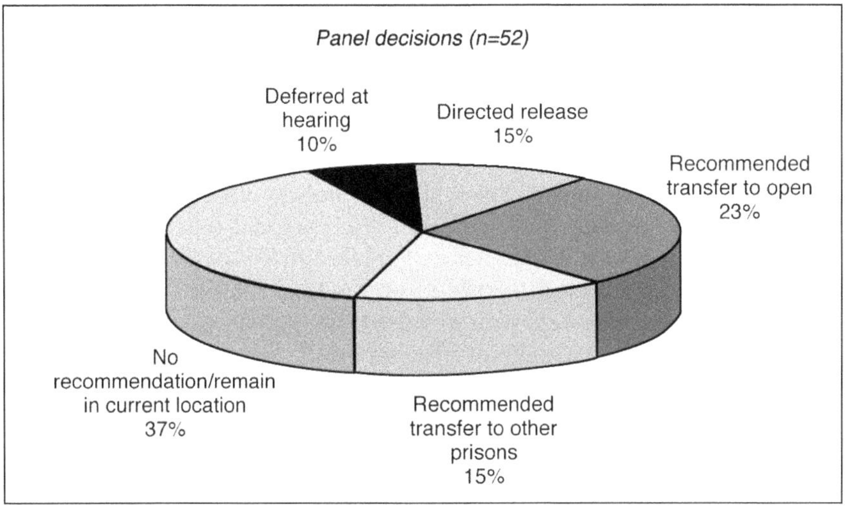

Source: Padfield and Liebling (2000), figure 4.1.

(ranging from 8 years 4 months to 21 years) and they had served an average of 4 years 10 months beyond tariff (with a range from 0 to 14 years). In terms of index offences, the three HMPs had been convicted of murder; the others of rape (3), manslaughter (2) and wounding with intent to cause actual bodily harm (1). In every case witnesses had been called (a psychologist in four cases and a home probation officer in all cases but one).

Of those prisoners whose release was directed, the Secretary of State's view in three cases had been that the prisoner presented an acceptable risk and had suggested licence conditions. In another four cases the Secretary of State's view had been that they were not suitable for release, but the Panel had decided against the Secretary of State's view. In two further cases the Secretary of State had not been 'in a position to provide a view on suitability for release'.

Padfield and Liebling only witnessed one full hearing at an open prison at which the Panel made the decision not to release. In this case both the prison probation officer and the home probation officer were witnesses at the hearing and all the reports were in support of release to a hostel. However, the Secretary of State had stated that he was 'not in a position to provide a view on suitability for release due to the continued uncertainty regarding the release plan'. (Suitable accommodation had not been found for the prisoner.) The Panel recommended a further review in 12 months and stated in the decision letter that this 'would allow time for those responsible for the preparation of a release plan to find out whether a specialist housing association or charity could provide accommodation and intensive support, which would provide adequate protection for the public'.

In every case where release was directed, the home probation officer had recommended release. In all seven of the release cases where a psychiatrist had made recommendations, their reports too had supported release on licence. A prison psychologist had recommended release in five of the release cases, the lifer liaison officer had recommended release in eight of the cases, and the personal officers and prison probation officers had recommended release in six cases each. In three of the release cases all the reports recommended release. In seven of the nine cases where prisoners were released, the Panel's decision to release accorded with the majority of the reports.[38] Some prisoners sought release from closed conditions, all unsuccessfully.

The importance of this analysis is to underline the key point that it is vital for a prisoner seeking release to have moved through the prison system to open conditions. Successful negotiation of the categorisation and allocation hurdles earlier in his prison sentence is an essential prerequisite to release.

Recommendations for open conditions

As we have seen, a key hurdle for a lifer is to reach open conditions. Panels may only recommend this, not decide it, and the Secretary of State then decides whether or not to accept the recommendation. He controls the decision. In Padfield and Liebling's study, of the 12 prisoners whom the Panel recommended for transfer to open conditions, several months later only two prisoners had actually been transferred and in five further cases the Secretary of State had agreed to the move, but the prisoner had not yet been transferred. The other cases were still under consideration by the Secretary of State.

In all but two of these 12 cases the prisoner had been located in a Category C prison at the time of the DLP (one was in a Category B prison and the other was a recalled prisoner in a local prison). In half of the 12 cases, the Secretary of State's view had been that the prisoner should not be moved to open conditions. In another four cases he had had no view. Thus in only two cases where transfer to open conditions was recommended by the Panel had the Secretary of State supported this move at the time of the Panel hearing. In two of the four cases where the Secretary of State had expressed no view, but where the Panel had

[38] Perhaps therefore it is fair to conclude that Panels do not acquiesce or endorse recommendations made to them quite as 'routinely' as did Peay's Mental Health Review Tribunals (see Peay (1989) at p. 202). She concluded that the MHRT's decision amounted largely to a ratification of a decision which had been structured by earlier choices.

recommended transfer to open, the prisoners had moved to open conditions.

There was no discernible pattern in the cases in which the Panels recommended transfer to open conditions in terms of which report writers' recommendations were followed. In three of the 12 cases the majority of reports had not recommended open and in these three cases the Secretary of State's view had been against transfer to open. In four cases where transfer to open had been recommended, it had been the prisoner's first oral hearing.

In total 12 prisoners had sought a recommendation for transfer to open conditions (some of those who were recommended for transfer to open conditions had asked for release). Of these only two were unsuccessful, and in both cases the Secretary of State had not supported transfer to an open prison. In both cases the Panel had felt that more work on sexual offending was required, despite the fact that in one case the prisoner had been in open conditions for two years but had been transferred back to closed conditions in order to undertake the SOTP (which he did).

It is difficult (and perhaps dangerous) to attempt to draw conclusions from this small study, but it might be possible to conclude that the Panel is less cautious than the Secretary of State at the time of the DLP hearing, but that the Secretary of State is sometimes persuaded to act after a Panel recommendation. However, because the Secretary of State is ultimately not obliged to take any notice of a DLP recommendation, in such cases, the prisoner is very unlikely to be released even at his next hearing since he will not have spent time in open conditions.

Other recommendations

Panels sometimes make other recommendations in order to try to help move the prisoner through the system. Of the nine cases where the Panel recommended transfer to another prison other than to open conditions, five were recommendations by the Panel to transfer the prisoner from a Category B to a Category C prison, two were recommendations for transfer for purposes of specifically identified offending behaviour work and one was in support of transfer from one Category C prison to another.[39] All these recommendations built on suggestions which emerged either in the reports, or at the hearing. One prisoner moved within a month of the recommendation, and another was transferred

[39] The Panel's view was often worded in the decision letter in such a way as to encourage the Prison Service to take a particular action but without wording it too strongly, for example, 'the Panel recommend that serious consideration be given to your transfer to a Category C prison', and 'the Panel believes that consideration should be given by the Prison Service to assessing you for a move to a Category C prison'. Sometimes they added a reminder that the decision did not fall within the remit of the Panel.

after three months. In one case a recalled prisoner was transferred from a local prison to a resettlement prison 16 days after the Panel hearing (which was held some eight months after his recall). In three cases the prisoner was actually transferred to another Category B establishment (despite the recommendation by the Panel of transfer to Category C) and three recommendations for transfers were simply rejected. Thus the Prison Service rejected the Panel's recommendation in two-thirds of the nine cases, in effect confirming the limited role the Panel performs at this stage. In 12 cases the Panel recommended further offending behaviour work in the form of specific accredited programmes and in seven cases they suggested further assessment. Padfield and Liebling concluded that, given the importance of such recommendations to the prisoner, they should create a 'legitimate expectation' for the prisoner unless rejected by the Home Secretary within a fixed time-frame and with written reasons.[40]

In 13 cases, Panels had recommended an early review, the majority for 12 months' time (three for 18 months' time), though it is not known whether these recommendations were accepted. We return to the thorny question of 'early reviews' in Chapter 7.[41]

Key issues

The Panel's function

The assessment of risk lies at the heart of the DLP's function, yet we have already seen how the Panel has remarkably little guidance on how to assess risk, and even on how much risk is acceptable. Although Panels need to weigh both seriousness and certainty of risk, Padfield and Liebling were struck by the extent to which Panels seemed to avoid discussing levels of risk. Again, there was little distinction between the management of risk and the assessment of risk: a prisoner may remain in prison simply because the facilities do not exist in the community which allow the Probation Service confidently to manage the (small or large) risk that he continues to present adequately. Some prisoners stayed in prison simply because courses from which they would benefit were available in prison and not in the community.

[40] Padfield and Liebling (2000), at p. 143. The doctrine of 'legitimate expectations' is used in administrative law to put a certain limit on the executive's discretion to change its mind by affording the claimant some procedural protection and (more controversially) substantive protection: 'it is ... the court's duty to protect the interest of those individuals whose expectation of different treatment has a legitimacy which in fairness outtops the policy choice which threatens to frustrate it' (per Sedley J in *R* v. *Ministry of Agriculture, Fisheries and Food, ex parte Hamble (Offshore) Fisheries Ltd* [1995] 2 All ER 714, at p. 731.

[41] See p. 139.

The extent to which the risk factors considered really are indicators of risk was not explored by Padfield and Liebling: it may be that some of the beliefs on which the decision-making process is based are unfounded. We will note in Chapter 6 that Hood and Shute in their research on Discretionary Conditional Release concluded that panels only released half of those who an actuarial risk predictor suggested were low-risk.[42] Padfield and Liebling questioned whether what Panels did during a hearing could accurately be called 'risk assessment'. The Panel formed a cumulative picture of the prisoner from the dossier and throughout the hearing. Panels arrived at hearings with concerns they wished to address. They looked for evidence of change, insight into the offence, evidence of offending behaviour work successfully undertaken and realistic release plans, with the prospect of effective supervision. *Level* of risk was rarely discussed. We noted in Chapter 4 how Parliament when creating the DLP had concentrated on procedural reform: the DLP had remarkably little substantive guidance. At a DLP the scales seem firmly in favour of protecting the public, and not in the direction of promoting the prisoner's right to liberty.

Perhaps this is inevitable, given the wording of section 28(6) of the Crime (Sentences) Act 1997. But this reinforces the view that inadequate attention was given by Parliament to the prisoner's special status once he has served the tariff part of his sentence. Although DLPs were created in response to the European Court of Human Right's recognition of this special status, it plays almost no part in the thinking of DLPs. In fact, some Panel members were clear that a long period of time spent in prison post-tariff could in itself indicate a high level of risk.

So, the first question here concerns the function of the Panel in assessing risk. It is as important to question the function of the Parole Board in relation to the functions of other criminal justice agencies. It was noted above that a prisoner must successfully negotiate a variety of Prison Service hurdles (categorisation, allocation, offending behaviour courses and so on) as a prerequisite to release. We will return to this in the final two chapters of the book.

The role of the Panel Secretary

We have already noted the ambiguous role of the Panel Secretary. Peay, in her review of Mental Health Review Tribunals,[43] suggests that the role of the tribunal clerk should be enhanced: 'their role is presently ill-defined, but in practice they act as a sort of Master of Ceremonies. They serve the coffee, usher in witnesses, pay their expenses, reassure

[42] See p. 111 below.
[43] See Chapter 6.

patients, sort out unexpected problems, phone the Home Office when so required'.[44] She suggests that legal training and an enhancement of their role might act as 'a deterrent effect on what might otherwise be errant decisions'. It is not obvious that in the context of the DLP that it would be the Panel Secretary who would function as the safeguard for prisoner's rights. Padfield and Liebling were concerned that some Panel secretaries became over-involved in the decision-making process, contributing their own views on the evidence during the deliberations. It would indeed be useful if they had more (legal) training on the precise contours of their role. However, whether the role should be enhanced is a very different question.

The role of the parties

At a typical DLP, the Secretary of State's representative introduces the case, but often plays only a minor role thereafter. The onus is on the prisoner and his representative to convince the Panel that they should direct release, or make some other recommendation. While the law is currently clear that the DLP can direct release only if it is satisfied that 'it is no longer necessary for the protection of the public that the prisoner should be confined' (section 34 of the Criminal Justice Act 1991, as amended), we will return in later chapters to explore whether the burden of proof should in fact be put firmly on the Home Office/Prison Service to justify detention.[45] Hearings also vary in the extent to which they are accusatorial: sometimes the questioning of witnesses is done entirely by the parties (or entirely by one party, the prisoner's legal representative), at other hearings, the questioning may come more strongly from the Panel itself, who would 'test' witnesses such as home probation officers, psychiatrists and psychologists in a probing way. In practice, because the DLP tends to be an adversarial/inquisitorial hybrid, the question of burden of proof is rarely raised as an issue. We will return in Chapter 7 to question the burden of proof and the inquisitorial/adversarial procedural balance at DLPs, suggesting that the Secretary of State's representative should take a more active role.

Delays

Padfield and Liebling (2000) found that although Panel members received dossiers about two or three weeks before a hearing, they were invariably supplemented with (often crucial) late reports at or shortly before the hearing. Late reports and papers were received either on the

[44] Peay (1989), at p. 220.

[45] We shall look in Chapter 6 at the recent changes in relation to Mental Health Review Tribunals.

day or shortly before the Panel date in many cases, which sometimes led to deferral of cases (for about six months), either before or sometimes at the hearing, wasting public money and risking considerable unfairness to the prisoner. An auditable standard on the timeliness of submitting reports has now been introduced.

More serious than late papers, were delays to the process itself. In Padfield and Liebling's sample of 69 cases, 13 were deferred before the hearing (19 per cent of the cases). Most of these deferrals were due to factors beyond the Panel's control, but some were related to disputed evidence (or evidence which might have been disputed): one case where a key probation witness failed to appear (the case was deferred more than four months); one case where the prisoner had a serious adjudication pending (the case was deferred for two months pending the adjudication); one case where the prisoner said he wanted legal representation but had failed to contact his solicitor. He complained that he had not been assisted (the case was relisted four months later). Prisoners themselves sometimes agree to defer hearings when they have been waiting for a place on a course or for an 'imminent transfer' to a lower category prison. It is obviously in their interests to move as far as they can through the system before a hearing so that the hearing may 'nudge' them further, but this raises the question of why they had not already moved. The most frequent reason for deferrals was the late arrival of reports: legal representatives applied shortly before the hearing for a deferral because the dossier was incomplete. This was both unfair on the prisoner and wasteful of resources.

Other hearings open, but are deferred part way into the hearing. This happened in three of Padfield and Liebling's hearings in open prisons: one because the home probation officer and psychologist were not present; one due to lack of up-to-date reports by the home probation officer, psychologist or psychiatrist; and the third because the prisoner was awaiting the outcome of an adjudication. At the subsequent deferred hearing, the Panel decided to release this prisoner. The cost (and anguish) of such last-minute delays are an important factor in suggesting that the pre-hearing review could be more effective.

Many cases are heard outside the agreed timetable: from the dossiers, this appeared to be the case in 20 of Padfield and Liebling's 52 cases. While this was no more than five months delay in 17 of these cases, the remaining three had been delayed nine months, 13 months and 21 months respectively. One of these concerned a man who had been released in 1983 but had been recalled in 1990. At a DLP in 1992, the Panel had recommended his transfer to Category C with a 12-month review after the date of transfer, which had taken place in April 1993. Since then, the case was regularly deferred while he underwent behaviour modification therapy. A Panel met in January 1999 but was again deferred following the late submission of a psychologist's report. It was again deferred in May 1999 for the reports to be rewritten, ready for hearing in July 1999, at which it was recommended that he should move to open conditions. The timetable of the DLP process seemed to have fitted uncomfortably with the Prison Service's own timetable of treatment for this and other prisoners.

Delays also appeared to happen because of the bureaucratic constraints of the DLP process. The Parole Board fixed a provisional timetable for hearings some eight or nine months in advance, on the assumption that the prisoner would remain in the same prison. There was evidence that a prisoner might not be moved on to another prison during that time, since he was waiting for a DLP. There were dangers that the prisoner's progress would freeze pending the next hearing. Thus while the DLP might well help to 'nudge' some prisoners through the lifer system, it seemed also inadvertently to slow others down.

Recall hearings

The differences between first oral recall hearings and ordinary DLPs are stark. An 'ordinary' DLP is held regularly as a discretionary lifer moves, albeit sometimes imperceptibly, towards open conditions and release. A recalled lifer on the other hand finds himself suddenly returned to a local prison and, of course, is unlikely to have been given advance notification of his recall. Few have committed further serious offences before they are recalled.[46] Within a few weeks, the case is considered by a 'Friday morning' Panel of the Parole Board. These Panels, which normally meet to consider mandatory life sentence cases, meet in the Parole Board headquarters.[47] The prisoner is not represented and may not even know that his case is being considered.

The first full DLP for recalled lifers may not happen for several months. The focus of the discussion and of the evidence at a recall DLP is on 'what went wrong' in the community rather than on any release plan. Panels are asked both to confirm the recall decision and to consider whether it is still necessary for the protection of the public that the prisoner should be confined.[48] However, since the Probation Service will not have prepared a release plan (it will usually have been as a result of Probation Service concerns that the prisoner was recalled), questions of release are usually glossed over, or at least easily decided.

[46] Weeks, Wilson and Gunnell were all recalled lifers. The facts of their cases were spelt out in Chapter 3 and reveal the factors which lead to the recall of those who had previously been deemed 'safe' to release.

[47] See Chapter 6 below, at p. 113.

[48] See *R* v. *Parole Board, ex parte Watson* [1996] 2 All ER 641, where the Court confirmed that both functions are necessary.

In Padfield and Liebling's research there were five cases where the Panel was considering representations against recall at the first oral hearing since the prisoner's return to prison. In each case, the recall was confirmed. The Panels' failure adequately to distinguish the confirmation of the recall from the fresh assessment on the necessity of detention and whether this should be in open conditions gave rise to concerns. The reality of power in recall cases seems to lie with the Probation Service, who having made the decision that they can no longer safely supervise the prisoner in the community, were unlikely to be swift to prepare a new release plan.[49] Tuddenham, in a critique of risk assessment in probation practice, states that 'current practice remains defensive; it over-estimates dangers, errs too far on the side of caution and, despite the rhetoric, lacks an evidence base . . . One of the main reasons for this is the impact of wider social and political imperatives on both the probation organisation and its staff, something which much must be recognised and responded to if risk assessment is to develop'.[50] Whether or not this defensive approach is due to a shortage of staff and other resources, or a desire to avoid the 'blame culture', the human rights implications for prisoners are too easily ignored.

Women and the DLP process

Redressing the imbalance of the past, there is now a considerable literature on the problems faced by women in the prison system[51] and, even more importantly, an increasing literature which seeks to understand female criminality.[52] But there is still little written on women lifers.[53] The fact that so few women commit crimes which result in life sentences means that research into why they committed the crime that resulted in the life sentence is particularly difficult. Many women lifers have suffered violence and sexual abuse. Women prisoners have often had particularly chaotic lifestyles prior to their imprisonment, and many have mental and physical health, drug, alcohol and substance abuse problems.[54] High rates of self-harm amongt women prisoners and their childcare and family responsibilities are other factors which may distinguish women prisoners from their male equivalents.

[49] See *R* v. *Secretary of State for the Home Department, ex parte Cummings* [2001] EWCA Civ 45, 22 January 2001, for a depressing account of the powerlessness of a recalled mandatory lifer.

[50] Tuddenham (2000), at p. 173. He calls for a more dynamic and 'reflexive' approach to risk assessment.

[51] See, for example, Prison Reform Trust (2000), HM Chief Inspector of Prisons for England and Wales (1997) and (2001).

[52] For a review of the literature, see Hedderman (1997).

[53] But see Genders and Player (1987b).

[54] See Maden (1996).

On 30 June 2000, there were 153 women serving a life sentence (including seven young offenders).[55] Only one woman's case fell within Padfield and Liebling's sample. Her DLP was held in the closed prison where she was held, and the prisoner was recommended for a 'progressive move' or hospital. There remains a shortage of programmes for female lifers,[56] and this is particularly serious in view of the finding that progress towards release often turns on completed accredited offending behaviour work. The Chief Inspector of Prison noted that short tariff female lifers are particularly disadvantaged.[57] The other obvious disadvantage faced by women lifers is the lack of pre-release hostels in urban centres. The Chief Inspector's follow-up report in 2001 called for 'transitional prisons in urban centres' to be developed to serve the needs of women prisoners. It is to be hoped that the government's strategy for women offenders[58] may release more resources to support work with this group of offenders.

Ethnicity and release

There has long been concern at the overrepresentation of black people within the prison system, but little work had been done until recently on ethnicity and release decisions. The Public Accounts Committee's 10th Report of 2000–1, on Parole[59] concluded that:

> A lack of information means that the Prison Service and Parole Board are not able to demonstrate fully that parole applications are dealt with in a consistent and equitable manner, for example according to the type of offender, educational attainment and region of origin. Figures from the Parole Board suggest that parole rates vary considerably between ethnic groups. While recent research[60] conducted for the Home Office concluded that most of the variation could be explained by the type of offences committed and other relevant factors, the Parole Board and Prison Service should monitor the relative success rates of different prisoner groups on a regular basis to ensure parole applications are being handled consistently and fairly.

Padfield and Liebling wondered whether the Parole Board sometimes subconsciously sought to counter the bias which they felt prisoners might have suffered in prison. An obvious example was where a prisoner's poor English seemed to have made him particularly difficult

55 Prison Statistics 2000, table 5.1.
56 See HM Chief Inspector of Prisons for England and Wales (2001), para. 2.141.
57 HM Chief Inspector of Prisons for England and Wales (2001), para. 2.142.
58 A strategy document was produced by a joint Home Office/Prison Service working group in October 2000.
59 Published on 29 March 2001.
60 This is a reference to Hood and Shute (2000).

to assess in prison, and had slowed down his progress from Category B. The Panel was keen to try and get him 'moved along'. Another concern is the problem of foreign nationals awaiting deportation.[61] Prison Service policy is that such prisoners are not held in open conditions. They may therefore be particularly disadvantaged in the release process. If a prisoner subject to a deportation order is not held in open conditions, and the Parole Board is very unlikely to release anyone not in open conditions, such a prisoner finds himself in an invidious position. There was just such a prisoner in Padfield and Liebling's sample.

Low intellectual ability and release

Another area which has been unexplored is the impact of intellectual ability on release decisions. It is well known that the average prisoner has a low IQ, though it is of course also known that social class and socio-economic disadvantage themselves affect IQ scores.[62] The important role played by the prisoner him or herself in the DLP process suggests that being articulate may well help a prisoner obtain release. Padfield and Liebling (2000) observed that the successful completion of offending behaviour courses was often a requirement before a prisoner would be considered for a progressive move through the prison system. This echoes the finding of Price (2000) that the completion, or otherwise, of offending behaviour programmes is a vital factor in persuading the Category A Committee to downgrade a prisoner from Category A status, which clearly has major consequences for the overall length of sentence in lifer cases. Yet a low level of learning ability may make a prisoner ineligible for a course. It seems clear that some lifers, perhaps particularly arsonists, may find that their low IQ limits their ability to progress towards release. The less literate as well as the less intelligent may find anger management and other similar courses a struggle. We should perhaps view with some concern the government's suggestions in *Skills for Life: a National Strategy for Improving Adult Literacy*[63] (at paragraph 38):

> We are also creating a literacy and numeracy skills pathfinder project to develop and then disseminate best practice. Prisoners in pathfinder area prisons will, from September 2001, have access to tutors trained in the new literacy and numeracy standards, core curriculum and National Tests. We are also exploring whether the Prison Service can require all prisoners eligible for early release who have literacy and numeracy skills needs to attend literacy and numeracy classes as a condition of licence. We are determined to make a significant impact on the numbers of people in prison or supervised in the

[61] Also highlighted in the House of Commons Public Accounts Committee (2001) report.
[62] See for example, Mackintosh (1998).
[63] Department for Education and Skills (2000).

community with literacy and numeracy needs. Evidence from our prison pathfinder will help us determine how we can best tackle this need. We expect our strategy to enable at least 40,000 people in prison and those supervised in the community to have improved their literacy and numeracy skills by 2004.

Whatever the merits of improved literacy, they can never justify prolonging imprisonment!

Duration of licences and licence conditions

Lifers are released on licence, and this licence continues in force until his or her death. This is an important point, completely misunderstood by many of those who complain that lifers are released too early. In practice supervision as a condition of licence may be lifted at any time by the Secretary of State (although in practice not sooner than four years after release). However, the government resisted attempts in the Criminal Justice Bill 1990 to give the Parole Board the right to give a prisoner unconditional release. There has been no published research on licence conditions. When the police were given the power to grant conditional bail, there was significant concern that this would not result in more people being granted bail who would previously have been remanded in custody, but that it would simply result in people finding greater restrictions imposed on their liberty.[64] Similar concerns arise if people are granted conditional liberty who could or should be granted unconditional release.

The standard life licence contains six conditions:

1. He/she shall place him/herself under the supervision of whichever probation officer is nominated for this purpose from time to time.
2. He/she shall on release report to the probation officer so nominated, and shall keep in touch with that officer in accordance with that officer's instructions.
3. He/she shall, if his/her probation officer so requires, receive visits from that officer where the licence holder is living.
4. He/she shall reside only where approved by his/her probation officer.
5. He/she shall work only where approved by his/her probation officer and shall inform his/her probation officer at once if he/she loses his/her job.
6. He/she shall not travel outside Great Britain without the prior permission of his/her probation officer.

[64] See, for example, Bucke and Brown (1997).

In most cases Panels simply impose the standard licence conditions, but they may add others such as a residence or treatment requirement, or a requirement that the licensee avoid a certain geographical area. Not only are such conditions sometimes difficult to enforce, they clearly infringe the prisoner's liberty. The Parole Board has no power to grant an unconditional licence. It will be remembered that the Sheerman proposals in the House of Commons would have given the Parole Board the duty to review licence conditions every five years. There has been no subsequent debate as to whether a formal review of parole licence conditions would be appropriate. As Hood and Shute suggest, 'whether or not it is realistic to expect so many conditions to be fulfilled by the prisoner and provided and enforced by the probation service are issues worthy of research'.[65] It would certainly be worth investigating further whether the stringent conditions imposed on lifers are 'necessary' restrictions on their liberty. The Parole Board could discuss in their letter making the decision to release whether less onerous conditions might be appropriate.

Summary

In this chapter we have seen how DLPs work in practice. Dossiers prepared by the Prison Service are studied by Panels in advance. Panels meet in the prison where the prisoner is held, and hear evidence from witnesses in a fairly consistent yet informal manner. The Secretary of State's representative, presenting the case against the prisoner, takes a minor role. Clearly witnesses can play a vital role, but the rules governing their appearance at hearings can appear haphazard. Even more important is the role of the prisoner, whose chances of success can be increased by good, realistic legal representation. While the procedural 'rules' at a DLP are relatively clear if flexible, the same cannot be said of either the evidential hurdles faced by the prisoner or the substantive risk principles to be applied.

Perhaps the most striking conclusion of Padfield and Liebling's research was that although the 'process' worked well, it had little impact in practice. Only prisoners held in an open prison are likely to be released. All recalls in the study were confirmed. All nine prisoners who were released were in open conditions and had the support of their probation officers. Future research might be able to explore whether those prisoners who were released were released earlier or later than they might otherwise have been if there had not been a DLP process. But before we move on to evaluate the DLP process further, we will divert to look at other release procedures.

[65] Hood and Shute (2000), at p. 32.

6

Release procedures compared

It is of course not only discretionary lifers who are detained against their wishes. The same is true of all prisoners, and in this chapter we will seek to describe the procedures which are followed before other long-term prisoners are released, as well as the procedures which are followed before those sentenced to a mandatory life sentence for murder, and those who have been detained against their will in mental hospitals, are released. Until the introduction of the DLP in 1992, all life sentence prisoners had been dealt with in a similar fashion. Since then the Home Secretary has retained the right to decide on the release of mandatory lifers. Until 1983 the Home Secretary also had the power to release, or to refuse to release, mentally abnormal offenders, but after an adverse decision of the European Court of Human Rights, this power was transferred to a new tribunal, the Mental Health Review Tribunal, by the Mental Health Act 1983. These Tribunals were in some sense, as we have seen,[1] the model for the DLP. Both systems will be described and compared. But let us start with a short description of the process which underlies the release of those facing long determinate sentences.

Determinate sentences

In Chapter 1 we saw how indeterminate 'life' sentences of imprisonment fitted into the general sentencing framework. The length of determinate (fixed length) sentences should be, as we saw, either commensurate with the seriousness of the offence, or where the offence is a violent or sexual offence, for such longer term as in the opinion of the court is necessary to protect the public from serious harm from the offender'.[2] Until recently determinate sentence prisoners had been treated similarly when it came to release and recall whether or not they had been sentenced to a commensurate or longer than commensurate sentence. However, this is no longer true.

[1] See p. 82 above.

[2] See sections 79 and 80 of the Powers of Criminal Courts (Sentencing) Act 2000.

A new early release scheme was introduced in the Criminal Justice Act 1991, following the recommendations of the Carlisle Committee. Here we will only explore the discretionary release system applicable to those sentenced to four years or over. At the halfway point in their sentence, they are eligible for Discretionary Conditional Release (DCR). If early release is not granted, they are released automatically at the two-thirds point in the sentence. They remain under licence, i.e. under the supervision of the probation service, until they reach the three-quarter point in their sentence (and some sex offenders for considerably longer[3]). Until recently, the Parole Board had not taken into account the different justifications for which the sentence might have been imposed. The point was considered by the European Commission on Human Rights in *Mansell* v. *United Kingdom*,[4] in 1997, who were unanimous that Article 5(4) had no application to sentences of this kind:

> The sentence imposed on the applicant was a fixed term sentence of five years. There is no question of the sentence being imposed because of the presence of factors which 'were susceptible to change with the passage of time, namely mental instability and dangerousness' (*Thynne, Wilson and Gunnell*, para. 73). Rather, there was an element of 'simple' punishment as well as an element of deterrence. It is true that the latter part of the sentence was imposed pursuant to Section 2 of the Criminal Justice Act 1991, which provides for sentences in the case of violent or sexual offences to be longer than 'normal' in order to protect the public from serious harm. Such an 'increased' sentence is, however, no more than the usual exercise by the sentencing court of its ordinary sentencing powers, even if the 'increase' has a statutory basis. In particular, nothing in the sentencing procedure indicates that the fixed term sentence of five years' imprisonment was anything other than a sentence which was imposed as punishment for the offences committed.

However, the question was explored once again in 2001 in an application for judicial review. In *R (Giles)* v. *Parole Board and the Secretary of State for the Home Department*[5] Elias J had to rule on the legality of the procedures and principles applied by the Parole Board when considering applications for parole from prisoners sentenced under section 80(2)(b) (previously section 2(2)(b) of the Criminal Justice Act 1991). Giles had been sentenced to seven years' imprisonment for two offences: the trial judge made it clear that he was passing the sentences under section 2(2)(b) of the Criminal Justice Act 1991 because of the danger that Giles posed to the public. His appeal had been refused. Although he had been released

[3] See section 44 of the Criminal Justice Act 1991, and section 20 of the Crime (Sentences) Act 1997, now sections 85 and 86 of the Powers of Criminal Courts (Sentencing) Act 2000.

[4] Application No. 32072/96, decided 2 July 1997.

[5] [2001] EWHC Admin 834.

on 17 May 2001, Elias J agreed that the application for judicial review should be heard because the argument was quite independent of any particular factual context. He found that Article 5(4) applied to the continuing detention of persons detained pursuant to section 80(2)(b) in circumstances where they would have been released but for the application of that subsection: in his view, there was no distinction if a person is subject, for example, to a sentence of two years as punishment and ten years as preventative, as opposed to a discretionary life sentence.

The implications of this decision were obviously huge. However the decision in *Giles* was reversed on appeal by the Court of Appeal (Civil Division) on 4 July 2002 (see *Times*, 23 July). The Parole Board would have had to be staffed and resourced to deal with a large number of extra oral hearings. Already, it has been accepted that prisoners serving extended sentences[6] who are recalled may make representations to an oral hearing of the Parole Board, organised on similar lines to a DLP, and this has already happened in a very small number of cases.

Release decisions

The power to release is given to the Home Secretary, acting on the recommendation of the Parole Board, but in practice the Home Secretary has delegated to the Parole Board the final decision in relation to prisoners sentenced to less than 15 years.[7] As we have seen, the Criminal Justice Act 1991 gave the Home Secretary the power to issue rules with respect to the proceedings of the Board and directions as to matters to be taken into account by the Board when discharging its functions. In giving such directions, he shall in particular have regard to

(a) the need to protect the public from serious harm from offenders; and
(b) the desirability of preventing the commission by them of further offences and of securing their rehabilitation.[8]

Whereas no directions have been issued to the Board concerning discretionary lifers, the Home Secretary has issued directions for the release and recall of determinate sentence prisoners. The first, issued in 1992, were replaced in 1996. The Report of the Carlisle Committee[9] on

[6] See Parole Board Annual Report 2000–1, at p. 29.
[7] Until December 1998, the Parole Board made only recommendations in the case of those sentenced to seven years or more.
[8] Section 32(6) of the Criminal Justice Act 1991: see Appendix 2.
[9] Carlisle, Lord (1988) *The Parole System in England and Wales. Report of the Review Committee*, Cm 532 (London: HMSO).

which the 1991 changes were based had made it quite clear that the Committee hoped that a higher proportion of prisoners would be released at the halfway point. The Report stated that the risk to be assessed, which was whether a further serious offence might be committed, had to be balanced against the benefit to the prisoner and to the public of his release under supervision 'which might assist his rehabilitation and thereby lessen the risk of his re-offending'. However, the Home Secretary's directions have put the priority firmly on the protection of the public. The 1996 directions explicitly state that the Parole Board 'shall take into account that safeguarding the public may often outweigh the benefits to the offender of early release'.

The Parole Board decides between 5,000 and 6,000 cases every year, sitting in Panels in London. Dossiers are prepared by parole clerks in the prisoner's prison (unlike lifer dossiers, which as we have seen, are prepared in the Lifer Unit at Prison Service headquarters). The prisoner will have been interviewed by a member of the Board in his prison, but this member will not be part of the final Panel. The results have been, not surprisingly, very cautious. In 1996–7, for example, only 36.4 per cent of those eligible were awarded release. This figure has been creeping upwards and by 2000–1 46.3 per cent of eligible prisoners were awarded parole. But this remains lower than the percentage released under the pre-1991 system, and a far cry from the aspirations of the Carlisle Committee. Why is this? The most detailed analysis of decision-making by the Parole Board in DCR cases has been carried out by Roger Hood and Stephen Shute. They have published three major reports: the first on parole before the implementation of the Criminal Justice Act 1991, the second looking at parole 'in transition' and the third assessing the impact of the changes over a decade.[10] They have 'no doubt' that the Home Secretary's Directions (and the training guidance) have created a 'generally cautious approach'. They also found that Parole Board members believed that the chance of a prisoner reoffending was substantially higher than that indicated by an actuarially based risk of reconviction score. It is hardly surprising that they comment: 'in a system which gives priority to risk, it is essential that risk should be re-assessed as accurately as possible, both to protect the public and to ensure that the liberty of prisoners who do not pose a high risk to the public is not unnecessarily restricted'.[11]

The Parole Board when deciding on Discretionary Conditional Release is deciding on the early release of prisoners. Discretionary Lifer Panels are deciding on 'late release': post-tariff release. We will return to the implications of this important distinction in Chapter 8.

[10] Hood and Shute (1994), (1995) and (2000).
[11] Hood and Shute (2000), at p. 78.

The release of mandatory lifers

As we saw in Chapter 1, although mandatory life sentence prisoners are treated in a similar fashion to discretionary life sentence prisoners within the prison setting, the procedure governing their release remains very different. After some time (often longer than a year[12]) the prisoner will discover what the judge and the Lord Chief Justice suggested as their tariff, and they are permitted to make representations to the Home Secretary, who then fixes the tariff. It will be remembered that in the House of Lords in 1990, during the debates on the introduction of DLPs, a number of peers were convinced that soon the European Court of Human Rights would impose a similar system on mandatory lifers as on discretionary lifers. This has not happened. In *Wynne* v. *UK*, as we saw in Chapter 3,[13] the European Court of Human Rights accepted the 'essential distinction' between mandatory and discretionary life sentences, and so the changes introduced for discretionary lifers are not applicable to mandatory lifers.[14]

The procedural improvements introduced by the House of Lords in *Doody* v. *Secretary of State for the Home Department*[15] were mentioned in Chapter 1. There the House of Lords granted a declaration that:

> (1) The Secretary of State is required to afford to a prisoner serving a mandatory life sentence the opportunity to submit in writing representations as to the period he should serve for the purpose of retribution and deterrence before the Secretary of State sets the date of the first review of the prisoner's sentence.
> (2) Before giving the prisoner the opportunity to make such representations, the Secretary of State is required to inform him of the period recommended by the judiciary as the period he should serve for the purpose of retribution and deterrence, and of any other opinion expressed by the judiciary which is relevant to the Secretary of State's decision as to the appropriate period to be served for these purposes.
> (3) The Secretary of State is obliged to give reasons for departing from the period recommended by the judiciary as the period which he should serve for the purpose of retribution and deterrence.[16]

Yet Lord Mustill, giving the main speech in *Doody*, was at pains to repeat emphatically that 'Parliament has left the discretion to release with the

[12] Sparks (1998) found that even those convicted after the decision in *Doody* (see below) had made tariff disclosure automatic were waiting as long as three years for information on their proposed tariffs.

[13] See p. 51.

[14] But note the decision of the European Court of Human Rights in the case of *Stafford* v. *UK* (see Preface).

[15] [1994] 1 AC 531.

[16] At p. 567.

Home Secretary, and that he has done nothing to yield up'.[17] Thus it is important to note that the procedural improvements introduced by *Doody* apply only to the first stage of the mandatory life sentence, the tariff setting stage.

Release decisions

Within the prison system, a convicted murderer will follow the same 'career' as does the discretionary lifer;[18] however, when he comes to be considered for release, it is the Home Secretary not the Parole Board who makes the final decision. Section 29 of the Crime (Sentences) Act 1997 provides that:

> (1) If recommended to do so by the Parole Board, the Secretary of State may, after consultation with the Lord Chief Justice together with the trial judge if available, release on licence a life prisoner who is not one to whom section 28 above applies.
> (2) The Parole Board shall not make a recommendation under subsection (1) above unless the Secretary of State has referred the particular case, or the class of case to which that case belongs, to the Board for its advice.

Thus it is clear that in these cases the Parole Board makes recommendations only. The dossier is compiled by the Prison Service, and the case is referred to the Parole Board by the Home Secretary, but as the Parole Board's Policy and Procedures Manual explains:

> The Secretary of State is not obliged by law to refer a mandatory lifer's case to the Board at any particular time, even after expiry of the tariff, though in practice and as a matter of administrative policy, the timing of reviews is very much in line with the practice in the discretionary lifer cases.[19]

Cases are considered by a panel of the Parole Board, but in the Parole Board headquarters in London (housed within the Prison Service). The prisoner is not present. Mandatory life sentence cases have been heard for many years on a Friday morning. Most cases will be heard for the first time three years before the tariff expiry date. The prisoner does not have the right to appear before the Panel but will have had the opportunity to present his case, both in writing and by way of an interview with a member of the Parole Board.[20] Written representations may well be prepared by a solicitor. The Parole Board member will make

[17] At p. 556.
[18] See p. 21 above.
[19] Para. 3.37.
[20] Prior to 1992, the reports in the dossiers were not disclosed to prisoners, which made something of a mockery of their 'right' to make representations.

a detailed report on the interview with the prisoner, but will not be a member of the Panel who consider the recommendation for the Home Secretary.[21] The Panel will have studied the dossiers in advance, and the three members will take in turns to lead the discussion of individual cases, several of which will be considered in one morning. The prisoner is not informed of the precise date of the hearing, nor of the result until the Home Secretary has decided whether or not to accept the Board's recommendation. To repeat, the Home Secretary does not have to accept the recommendation of the Board.

Between 460 and 630 cases are heard every year, with somewhere between 18–25 per cent recommended for release.[22] The Parole Board does not publish whether the recommendations are accepted by the Home Secretary.[23] In 1999–2000, 39 mandatory lifers were recalled to prison, and 26 were recalled in 2000–1. There has been little published research on the release of mandatory lifers. Hood and Shute observed during 1992–4 a number of panels but this research has not been published.[24] They analysed 122 mandatory life sentence cases, and found that 86 per cent (54 out of 63) of the mandatory lifers in their sample who were being reviewed before their tariff expired received a recommendation from the Board which, if all went well and the Minister did not object, meant that they could hope to be released at or very near their tariff. Fourteen per cent (9) could not realistically have hoped to be released within a year of their tariff expiring. Thus Hood and Shute concluded that, if their sample of cases was representative, a majority of mandatory lifers can expect to be released at or near tariff. However, 22 prisoners in their sample were already three years or longer post-tariff. The majority of these prisoners remained in closed conditions and their prospects for release seemed bleak. Even where the Parole Board recommended a move to open conditions, the Home Secretary exercised his veto in a number of cases. It does not seem surprising that many murderers are released on tariff: their recidivism rate is lower than that of discretionary lifers, and many are unlikely to be considered 'dangerous'. However, the minority who are considered 'dangerous' are understandably aggrieved that they do not benefit from the DLP procedure.

The Sentencing Advisory Panel's (2001) consultation paper on tariffs in murder cases also provides an insight. It states that the average tariff

21 Before 1992, the interview would have been conducted by a member of the local Review Committee, and in practice were significantly briefer than current reports.
22 See Parole Board Annual Report 2000–1 (House of Commons, 2001).
23 Unfortunately, they stopped doing so after 1996/7. It would be useful if the Board reintroduced the practice of publishing these figures, and indeed an analysis of the veto figures over the years might be revealing.
24 They submitted a memorandum to the Chief Inspectors of Prisons and of Probation which is cited in the Chief Inspectors' Thematic Review of Lifers (HMIPP, 1999).

of the 119 mandatory lifers released in 2000 was 12.6 years, and that the average time served after sentence was 14.3 years. If one takes into account the time likely to have been spent on remand (which counts towards time served), mandatory lifers continue to serve on average a couple of years or more post-tariff. This figure is difficult to analyse. An average can disguise wide fluctuations. It may be that some murderers are perceived to pose a significant risk to the public. However, process delays and vetoes by the Home Secretary of Parole Board recommendations are also likely to be part of the explanation. The Chief Inspectors state that the Hood and Shute research indicated that for the years 1992, 1993 and 1994, the recommendations for release were vetoed in 14.5, 9 and 19 per cent of cases respectively.[25] These figures are astonishingly high. Why does the Minister veto release? Perhaps it is because of political concerns about the 'public acceptability' of the release of murderers. Perhaps it is because the Minister is yet more cautious than the Parole Board about taking risks. It would be interesting to know if Labour Ministers follow similar practices. We return to the question of ministerial veto in the next section.

Why the difference?

The system applicable to mandatory lifers is in essence the same system that was applied to all lifers before 1992 (though it is now somewhat more open). It is difficult to assess whether it is necessarily a 'worse' system. What is undoubtedly true is that prisoners perceive the system to be less fair than the DLP system. Mandatory lifers envy the discretionary lifer their 'hearing', their 'day in court'. The issues are undoubtedly explored in greater depth at a DLP, where a hearing may well last half a day: the Parole Board deals with many mandatory cases in a morning. But it has to be remembered that the two types of case are often very different. Many murderers represent significantly less risk than do discretionary lifers: they are less 'dangerous'. If murderers were routinely released on tariff, subject to a brief check for 'risk', it might be appropriate to argue that the detailed review process should be reserved for the truly dangerous. But as we have seen, this does not appear to be the case. Of Hood and Shute's sample, half had already served the tariff when the Parole Board considered their case.

The explanation for the different treatment of mandatory and discretionary life sentence prisoners would appear to be purely political. As we saw in Chapter 4, the government was forced to introduce changes to the release process for discretionary lifers only reluctantly. They

[25] Her Majesty's Inspectorates of Prison and Probation (1999) *Lifers: A Joint Thematic Review* (London: Home Office), para. 3.21.

adopted a minimalist approach. Both the Sheerman proposals and the Nathan proposals introduced during the passage of the Criminal Justice Bill 1990 would have applied to all life sentence prisoners. However, the government insisted that the new procedures should only apply to discretionary lifers (the only group to whom the *Thynne* judgment applied). It is disappointing for those who would have welcomed wider reform that the Labour government elected in 1997 seems to have moved so far away from the position they held when in opposition in 1991.

This is not the place to rehearse in detail the arguments against the mandatory life sentence, but there have been many calls for its abolition, to add to those of the Nathan Committee, discussed in Chapter 4. For example, in an important review of the concept of dangerousness and the tariff, Maguire *et al.* (1984) commented that it would have been more satisfactory to allow judges to pass determinate sentences for murder in open court. The Lane Committee on the Penalty for Homicide (1993), a Committee set up under the auspices of the Prison Reform Trust, concluded that

1. The mandatory life sentence for murder is founded on the assumption that murder is a crime of such unique heinousness that the offender forfeits for the rest of his existence his right to be set free.
2. That assumption is a fallacy. It arises from the divergence between the legal definition of murder and that which the lay public believes to be murder.
3. The common-law definition of murder embraces a wide range of offences, some of which are truly heinous, some of which are not.
4. The majority of murder cases, though not those which receive most publicity, fall into the latter category.
5. It is logically and jurisprudentially wrong to require judges to sentence all categories of murder in the same way, regardless of the particular circumstances of the case before them.
6. It is logically and constitutionally wrong to require the distinction between the various types of murder to be decided (and decided behind the scenes) by the executive as is, generally speaking, the case at present.

However, there seems to be no more political will at this time to abolish the mandatory life sentence than there was in 1984. The Home Affairs Committee of the House of Commons held an inquiry in 1994–5 into the mandatory life sentence for murder. Their proposed solution was to maintain the mandatory sentence but to remove the Home Secretary from the process and in 1995–6 they heard further evidence on this proposal. In their memorandum to the Select Committee, the Parole Board was cautiously encouraging:

> The Committee recommended in paragraph 98 of its Report that the Parole Board procedures for assessing the risk of releasing mandatory life sentence prisoners should follow the DLP model. The Parole Board does not dissent from that conclusion: indeed we said in our evidence to the Committee that we felt it would make sense to extend the DLP system to all future lifer prisoners. Nevertheless we did also point out the considerably high cost of such a system and the need for the Board to have much greater resources if it were to undertake the responsibility.[26]

The Select Committee's 1996 supplementary report concluded that the mandatory life sentence should be retained and the political mood has not softened since then. However, it is worth noting that the Select Committee did recommend that the responsibility for setting the tariff and for taking decisions on release should be removed from the Home Secretary. They suggested that the tariff should be set by the trial judge, with a right of appeal to the Court of Appeal. On decisions to release, the Supplementary Report concluded that:

> We see no reason why Parole Board Lifer Panels should not have the power to direct the release of prisoners convicted of murder and sentenced to life imprisonment (para. 16)
>
> We recommend that Lifer Panels formed to consider the possible release of mandatory life sentence prisoners should consist of four members to include a judge, a psychiatrist and a senior probation officer (para. 17)
>
> We favour the suggestion that victims' relatives might have the right to nominate a legal representative to attend the panel hearing as an observer on their behalf (para. 19)
>
> We believe that, if questions of releasing prisoners convicted of murder are to be determined by Parole Board Lifer Panels, steps should be taken to ensure that the concerns of the Home Secretary are fully represented during the hearing; consideration should also be given to the provision of a right of appeal on behalf of the Home Secretary against decisions taken by Lifer Panels (para. 20).

These recommendations have not been heeded: the European Court of Human Rights has continued to accept the fundamental distinction

[26] See Appendix F, Annual Report of Parole Board for 1995 and 1995–6.

between mandatory and discretionary life sentences; the DLP procedure still applies only to discretionary lifers.[27]

Mental Health Review Tribunals[28]

It will be remembered from Chapter 4 that Discretionary Lifer Panels of the Parole Board were modelled in certain respects on MHRTs. These were strengthened as a result of the decision of the European Court of Human Rights in *X* v. *United Kingdom*[29] that Article 5(4) required the 'court' reviewing the lawfulness of the detention of a patient to have the power to order his or her discharge where the detention was unlawful.

The legal structure for compulsory detention in hospital is now governed by the Mental Health Act 1983 (as amended). A hospital order may be imposed as a criminal sentence, and a patient so detained may be released by the hospital or a Mental Health Review Tribunal. A restriction order may also be imposed by a Crown Court in cases where mentally disordered offenders are believed to be likely to inflict serious harm on others (see sections 37–41 of the Mental Health Act 1983). The effect of a 'restriction order' was, until 1983, that a patient detained in hospital under such an order could not be discharged without the consent of the Home Secretary. The Mental Health Act 1959 created Mental Health Review Tribunals, on the advice of the Royal Commission on the law relating to mental illness and mental deficiency (the Percy Commission[30]), but originally a patient under a restriction order had no right to apply to a tribunal for his discharge, nor was the Secretary of State required to accept the advice of a Tribunal. However, as a result of *X* v. *United Kingdom*, the law was amended to provide that a restricted patient may apply to a Mental Health Review Tribunal in the period between the expiration of six months and the expiration of 12 months beginning with the date of the relevant hospital order, hospital direction or transfer direction, and in any subsequent period of 12 months (see section 70). Section 71 gives the Secretary of State the power to refer the case of a restricted patient to a Mental Health Review Tribunal, and imposes on him the duty to do so every three years. The powers of the MHRT, to be found in sections 72 and 73, are to be found in full at Appendix 5. The Tribunal may order that the patient is discharged

[27] And, of course, 'automatic' life sentence prisoners, and children convicted of murder since the decision in *Hussein and Singh*: see p. 55 above. But now see *Stafford* v. *UK* (in Preface).

[28] For detailed analysis of MHRTs, see Peay (1989), Richardson (1993), Eastman and Peay (1999), Holloway and Grounds (forthcoming).

[29] (1982) 4 EHRR 188.

[30] Percy Report (1957) *Royal Commission on the Law relating to Mental Illness and Mental Deficiency 1954–7*, Cmnd 169 (London: HMSO).

'absolutely', in which case the restriction order ceases to have effect, or he may be discharged conditionally, in which case the Secretary of State has the power to recall him.

A Mental Health Review Tribunal is comprised of three members: a legal member (a circuit judge or recorder), a psychiatrist and a lay member, who may well be a social worker or psychologist. Under sections 70–72, restricted patients are entitled to a review of their case every 12 months, all cases must be reviewed every three years; and the Home Secretary may refer a case at any time 'he thinks fit'. The procedure is governed by the Mental Health Review Tribunals Rules 1983,[31] made by the Lord Chancellor under powers granted by section 78 of the 1983 Act. He has a duty to consult with the Council on Tribunals before making amendments to the Rules (see section 8 of the Tribunals and Inquiries Act 1992).

Once an application has been lodged with the MHRT Secretariat, reports are gathered from a wide variety of sources. They must include an up-to-date medical report from the patient's responsible medical officer (RMO), and a statement from the Home Secretary. A copy of every document relevant to the application must be sent to the patient, the responsible authority and the Home Secretary.

The role of the psychiatrist

A key difference with the DLP is that the medical member of the Tribunal is required to interview the patient and to make an assessment of his or her mental condition. Holloway (2000), in a review of MHRT cases heard between 1990 and 1999, found that the oral reports that the psychiatrist gave to his/her colleagues at the pre-hearing discussion were particularly influential (indeed her questionnaires revealed that Tribunal members found this oral report of greater assistance than the RMO's oral report). Given that this oral report was heard in private and was not open to challenge, it surely contravenes the principle of an oral hearing. It is not surprising that the recent White Paper[32] on reforming the Mental Health Act proposes to separate out the role of expert advisor from the role of Mental Health Tribunal decision-maker. When the government brings forward its Bill to change the MHRTs to Mental Health Tribunals,[33] a doctor from an 'independently appointed' expert panel will assess the patient and report to the Tribunal.

Holloway and Grounds (forthcoming), however, concluded that the greatest influence on Tribunals was the written opinion of the patient's RMO. The fact that the tribunal discharged patients against the RMO's

[31] SI 1983/942, as amended e.g. by SI 1996/314; SI 1998/1189; SI 2000/3712.

[32] Department of Health (2000), Cm 5016-I and II.

[33] See p. 123 below.

advice in only 4 per cent of cases led her to conclude that the Tribunal was apparently 'rubber-stamping' the RMO's views. It was the reputation of the individual RMO or his/her inability to communicate effectively in English which led the Tribunal to diverge from the RMO's opinion. This correlates closely with Padfield and Liebling's finding that DLPs were very unlikely to order release against the recommendation of key report writers.[34] Holloway singled out other factors associated with the decision (not) to discharge:

- the type of hospital in which the patient was detained – patients in maximum security hospitals were unsurprisingly less likely to be discharged than patients detained in medium or lower security;
- the long waiting lists for therapy and the lack of continuity of care;
- the absence of independent psychiatrists – the fact that an independent psychiatrist was confident enough to assume responsibility for the patient once released reassured Tribunals. This reflects the findings of Padfield and Liebling: the presence of a convincing home probation officer was important in convincing the DLP to direct release;
- the reputation of independent psychiatrists;
- marital status: single patients were less likely to be discharged.

It is hardly surprising that psychiatric evidence in these cases is crucial. What is interesting is that Holloway, like Padfield and Liebling, found that the decision-making of the MHRT is seriously constrained by factors far outside its sphere of control.

The burden of proof

Until 26 November 2001, sections 72 and 73 compelled a patient to prove that he or she was no longer a risk. Thus, section 72(1) provided that:

> (1) Where application is made to a Mental Health Review Tribunal by or in respect of a patient who is liable to be detained under this Act, the tribunal may in any case direct that the patient be discharged, and –
> (a) the tribunal shall direct the discharge of a patient liable to be detained under section 2 above if they are satisfied –
> (i) that he is not then suffering from mental disorder or from mental disorder of a nature or degree which warrants his detention in a hospital for assessment (or for assessment followed by medical treatment) for at least a limited period; or
> (ii) that his detention as aforesaid is not justified in the interests of his own health or safety or with a view to the protection of other persons;

34 See pp. 92, 96 above.

(b) the tribunal shall direct the discharge of a patient liable to be detained otherwise than under section 2 above if they are satisfied –
  (i) that he is not then suffering from mental illness, psychopathic disorder, severe mental impairment or mental impairment or from any of those forms of disorder of a nature or degree which makes it appropriate for him to be liable to be detained in a hospital for medical treatment; or
  (ii) that it is not necessary for the health or safety of the patient or for the protection of other persons that he should receive such treatment; or
  (iii) in the case of an application by virtue of paragraph (g) of section 66(1) above, that the patient, if released, would not be likely to act in a manner dangerous to other persons or to himself.

This negative definition had long been criticised. Thus Eastman and Peay (1999) commented that proving a negative is a 'sufficiently problematic if not impossible' task to achieve.[35] However, it was the decision of the Court of Appeal in *R (ex p. H)* v. *Mental Health Review Tribunal, North and East London Region and the Secretary of State for Health (intervenor)*[36] which forced a change. H was convicted of manslaughter in 1988, and ordered to be detained under sections 37 and 41 of the Mental Health Act 1983. In 1999 he applied to an MHRT for a discharge, but the Tribunal decided on 29 March 2000 to reject the application. This he challenged by way of judicial review, specifically challenging the negative formulation used in section 72(1)(b). The Court of Appeal was persuaded to issue a declaration of incompatibility under the Human Rights Act 1998. As the Master of the Rolls explained:

> In the course of argument it was suggested that, in the context of review of a patient's detention, the phrase burden of proof was not appropriate. The phrase suggests an adversarial process, whereas proceedings of a Mental Health Review Tribunal are inquisitorial in nature. Furthermore, a reference under section 71 may not be made by the patient. There is some force in this. The essential question is the nature of the test to be applied when determining the entitlement of a patient to release. Does the tribunal have to order discharge of the patient if it is not satisfied that each of the criteria is made out, or is the patient only entitled to release if the tribunal is satisfied that at least one of the criteria is not made out. If the latter is the position, however, it is not inappropriate, where a patient makes an application under section 73, to say that the burden of proof is on the patient. To speak of reversing the burden of proof is a useful shorthand to describe the effect of the section (para. 24).
>
> . . . It is of course the duty of the court to strive to interpret statutes in a manner compatible with the convention and we are aware of instances where

[35] At p. 10. See also Richardson and Thorold (1999), at p. 117.
[36] [2001] 3 WLR 512.

> this has involved straining the meaning of statutory language. We do not consider however that such an approach enables us to interpret a requirement that a tribunal must act if satisfied that a state of affairs does not exist as meaning that it must act if not satisfied that a state of affairs does exist. The two are patently not the same. If the requirements of the Convention can only be satisfied if the tribunal is required to order the discharge of a patient unless satisfied that the three criteria justifying admission are made out, section 72 and 73 are incompatible with the Convention (para. 27).

Thus the Master of the Rolls held that although the courts are under a duty to interpret statutes in a way which is compatible with the European Convention of Human Rights where possible, it was not possible to do so here. The burden of proof should be clearly on the state, not the patient. Meanwhile, the White Paper on reforming the Mental Health Act,[37] published in December 2000, had already suggested a new Mental Health Tribunal. Part I explains the new legal framework. Although the issue of the burden of proof is not confronted directly it would appear that the government had accepted that the tribunal would not have a 'reversed onus of proof'. Thus, at para. 3.42:

> The Tribunal hearing will take place within 7 days of receipt of the application for review. If the Tribunal decides that the conditions for continued use of compulsory powers are not met, the patient will be discharged from compulsory care and treatment straight away . . .

The government accepted the need to remove the incompatibility without waiting for the new Bill. The Secretary of State at the Department of Health therefore issued a remedial order on 18 November 2001, which took effect on 26 November 2001. This amended, by way of statutory instrument, sections 72(1) and 73(1) and (2).[38] It is the amended versions which appear in Appendix 5.

The role of the Council on Tribunals

It was noted in Chapter 4 that there was a concern in the House of Lords during the passage of the Criminal Justice Bill 1990 that the Parole Board should be supervised by the Council on Tribunals. For example, Lord Harris had pointed out that the Council had usefully drawn attention to the substantial delays which occur in hearings before MHRTs. It is worth

[37] Cmnd 5016-I.

[38] The constitutional significance of SI No. 3712 seems to have passed without remark: one would have expected the first example of a government minister using his powers under the Human Rights Act 1998 to amend primary legislation by delegated legislation to have had much greater publicity.

noting that these criticisms have not abated during the 1990s. In its Annual Report of 1998/99, the Council on Tribunals stated that:

> Over many years we have expressed serious concerns about the working of MHRTs. We have drawn attention to unacceptable delays in listing and hearing cases, to pressures on administrative staff arising from lack of resources, to the need for training for tribunal members, and to the lack of central judicial direction which a presidential system can provide. We have also had concerns about the confusion caused by the separate system of manager's hearings, about the late submission of hospital reports, about the increasing incidence of unclerked hearings, about a shortage of medical members, about the inadequacy of tribunal accommodation, and about the capacity of the system to handle an increasing workload.[39]

In 2000 the Council produced a Special Report on MHRTs which sought to examine the operation of MHRTs within the framework of the proper conditions for independence and integrity of tribunals set out in other Council on Tribunals documents. This recommended, among other changes, that:

- a consistent policy should be in place to ensure that every tribunal hearing is properly supported by a tribunal clerk;[40]
- there was a need for good quality Community Legal Service funded representation at tribunal hearings to be made more available to mental health patients;
- there should be a review of MHRT accommodation with a view to securing greater consistency and an improvement in standards.

The success or otherwise of the Council on Tribunals in achieving improvements remains a moot point. Many of the Council's recommendations appear not to have been adopted by the government in the White Paper. However, the involvement of the Council in the supervision of these tribunals is some recognition of the importance of the MHRT as an 'independent' tribunal.

The future for those with severe personality disorders

The law in this area is soon to change. A Bill will be published shortly (later in 2002?) which will propose new criteria for compulsory treatment under the Mental Health Act. The Criminal Justice and Court Services Act 2000 has already imposed a duty on the police and probation

[39] At para. 2.112.

[40] We noted at pp. 99–100 above Peay's concerns that Tribunal clerks needed greater training and an 'enhanced' role.

services to assess and manage relevant sexual or violent offenders (as well as publish annual reports on the arrangements established to discharge this duty).[41] Under the proposed new legislation, the relevant statutory agencies will be able to refer the individual for an initial assessment and, if the initial criteria are satisfied, apply for a 28-day period of compulsory care and treatment to allow for more detailed assessment. Beyond 28 days, compulsory care will have to be authorised by a new body, the Mental Health Tribunal. The White Paper confirms that all those detained under compulsory powers will also have the right to:

- free legal representation;
- access to independent specialist advocacy services; and,
- provisions to cover the use of certain specified treatments for mental disorder and all long-term treatment without consent.

The White Paper also promises new arrangements for the 'oversight of the new legislation' and for the provision of annual reports through the creation of a new Commission for Mental Health.

Conclusions

In this chapter we have looked at the procedures which govern the release of several 'categories' of people who are detained against their wishes. Our division fell into three categories:

- those subject to long determinate sentences;
- those sentenced to a mandatory life sentence;
- those detained under the Mental Health Act 1983.

Law (and practice) applies differently to each category. For example, the MHRT scheme may well be more 'court' like in many ways than is the DLP, and it is more obviously 'independent'. But what is particularly striking about this categorisation is the impact of the categorisation itself: once a person is labelled a restricted patient, he or she has different procedural rights than does the 'dangerous' person detained in prison. Yet people with similar characteristics may find themselves in one, rather than another, category. And, conversely, the people within the different categories do not necessarily share the same characteristics. Thus, for example, the courts are beginning to recognise that the Discretionary Conditional Release scheme includes within it many

[41] See section 67.

people detained not only because their crime 'deserved' a sentence of a certain length, but also those who are detained beyond this time because of the risk that they present. It is time to use the descriptions of these alternative release schemes described in this chapter to assess the DLP, the main focus of this book.

7

The spirit of *Weeks/Thynne* and the reality

In the last two chapters we looked first at how Discretionary Lifer Panels of the Parole Board have developed in practice, and then at other processes followed in England and Wales for deciding the question of whether those compulsorily detained should be released. Now the time has come to return to the reasoning of the European Court of Human Rights in order to consider whether the practice developed in DLPs lives up to that reasoning. Were the expectations generated in the minds of discretionary life sentence prisoners and their advisers exaggerated? The first point which must be stressed is that the Court's role is to set a minimum standard of fairness and it leaves to domestic courts the duty of developing the detail. The principles established in Convention case law have to accommodate hugely different legal systems

> ... as diverse as those of the former soviet legal systems of Central and Eastern Europe, continental legal systems and common law systems, with an emphasis on jury trial. It is inevitable that any constitutional standards which are applicable to so many different legal traditions will be insufficiently detailed to afford a comprehensive guide to the application of the Convention in the United Kingdom criminal law.[1]

In this chapter we explore in more depth what it was the European Court seemed to be seeking to achieve.

The judicial function

The European Court of Human Rights in *Weeks*[2] made it clear that the judicial function is limited:

> Article 5(4) does not guarantee a right to judicial control of such scope as to empower the 'court', on all aspects of the case, including questions of

[1] Emmerson and Ashworth (2001), at p. 255.
[2] (1988) 10 EHRR 666.

> expediency, to substitute its own discretion for that of the decision-making authority. The review should, however, be wide enough to bear on those conditions which, according to the Convention, are essential for the lawful detention of a person subject to the special kind of deprivation of liberty ordered against Mr. Weeks.[3]

Thus the European Court of Human Rights does not require the 'court' to substitute its own discretion, but simply to review the conditions which justify detention. The first question we will ask is why judicial review is inadequate. Judicial review is the classic English remedy whereby anyone sufficiently affected by a decision can ask the High Court to review the legality, the lawfulness, of the exercise of executive power. It has never been easy to define this role precisely: the role of the court is to review the legality of the decision-making process, but not the merits of a particular decision. The distinction is a fine one. The classic summary of the modern grounds for judicial review is the statement of Lord Diplock in *Council of Civil Service Unions* v. *Minister for the Civil Service*:[4]

> One can conveniently classify under three heads the grounds upon which administrative action is subject to control by judicial review. The first ground I would call 'illegality', the second 'irrationality' and the third 'procedural irregularity'.[5]

Having described these three grounds in more detail, Lord Diplock readily recognised that there could in future be additions to the three heads which he had identified. Constitutional lawyers have been particularly interested by the principle of 'proportionality', which is recognised in the administrative law of many other EU countries as well as in the jurisprudence of the European Court of Justice and European Court of Human Rights.[6] However, English courts have been reluctant to adopt the doctrine since it is argued that to do so is to blur the important distinction between appeal and review: the courts in an application for judicial review are reviewing the legality and not the merits of a decision. Why did the European Court in Human Rights decide in *Weeks*, and the other cases, that judicial review was an inadequate remedy?

> As the Commission pointed out, the scope of the control afforded is thus not wide enough to bear on the conditions essential for the 'lawfulness', in the

3 At para. 59 (see Appendix 1).
4 [1985] AC 374; [1984] 3 All ER 935.
5 [1984] 3 All ER 935, at p. 950.
6 See Emmerson and Ashworth (2001) pp. 92–8.

> sense of Article 5(4) of the Convention, of Mr. Weeks' detention, that is to say, whether it was consistent with and therefore justified by the objectives of the indeterminate sentence imposed on him. In the Court's view, having regard to the nature of the control it allows, the remedy of judicial review can neither itself provide the proceedings required by Article 5(4) nor serve to remedy the inadequacy, for the purposes of that provision, of the procedure before the Parole Board.[7]

The Court does not explore this issue further. It is to be noted that the three dissenting judges were impressed by judicial review as a speedy remedy for those who wished to challenge the legality of Parole Board decision-making. But for the majority, it lacked something essential.

Reviewing an executive process

In requiring a process of judicial control, the European Court of Human Rights could be meaning one of two different processes. Whichever route is taken, the review has to be wide enough to bear on those conditions which are essential for someone to be lawfully detained. The first possible process of judicial control would leave to experts on risk the task of making decisions about risk. This decision would then be subject to review by a court. On this scenario, where the executive (perhaps the Home Office or one of its 'offshoots') decided that a prisoner should not be released, the prisoner would be able to challenge this decision before a judicial tribunal.

The advantage of such a process is that 'experts' on risk assessment make the primary decision. Assessing risk, especially risk of dangerousness, is no easy task, and, it can be argued, should be left to experts. We saw in Chapter 5 how, with this population of prisoners, assessing risk is a complex and unpredictable business, requiring a clinical not only an actuarial approach. Under this 'reviewing an executive process' model, the judicial tribunal would simply assess or review an earlier process, undertaken by experts. The reviewing court to satisfy the European Court of Human Rights has to have the power to review the conditions which justify detention. The conditions which justify the post-tariff detention of discretionary lifers is their 'dangerousness'. Thus the reviewing court has to review the factors which make the prisoner a danger to the public. If this option were to be followed, the 'review' powers of the High Court would have to be more extensive. We will explore later in this chapter recent developments in judicial review which may make this a more realistic option. But the government in 1991 chose the second option, which we will now describe.

[7] At para. 69 (see Appendix 1).

Making the primary decision

The second route to satisfactory judicial supervision is a process whereby a judicial tribunal makes the primary decision and decides the lawfulness of the detention, including the question whether the conditions which justified the original detention (in this case, the 'risk' posed by the prisoner) continue to exist. The tribunal takes in effect two decisions: the decision on the lawfulness of the detention rests inevitably on a prior decision on risk, also to be taken by the 'court'. This involves 'judges' having to assess 'dangerousness' and making decisions on risk.

The involvement of the judiciary in decisions on risk is not necessarily problematic, as long as the process in which they are involved provides them with relevant expert evidence. Judges may not be in a position to predict dangerousness, but they should be able to weigh up expert opinion, and to explain to a prisoner why they have chosen to accept one 'expert' opinion rather than another.[8] Indeed, John Allison, in his *A Continental Distinction in the Common Law*,[9] goes further, pointing out that in administrative disputes, judges are frequently involved in policy issues, and a judge is an expert in much more than just due process. He argues that the judge must be not only independent but also an expert. This administrative expertise combined with that of other experts, in this context a psychiatrist, is invaluable. The Nathan proposals, it will be remembered, had proposed that the third member of the Tribunal should also be an 'expert': a chief probation officer. Without such expertise, Allison argues that the judge becomes the 'enemy' of the administration. Thus he praises the French *conseil d'état*: with this administrative expertise, French judges have been able to develop principles ('les principes généraux de droit et le principe de proportionalité', for example) which have worked to the benefit of victims. A contrast can be drawn by looking at the position within the Prison Service/Home Office where the judge is often perceived as a threatening presence, 'the judge on your shoulder'.[10]

The government chose the judicial model. Indeed a model whereby the decision-making body would be a judicial body was also the preferred option of both the other proposals considered in Parliament. But it is important to remember that, traditionally, English judges have been wary of involving themselves in such decision-making. In traditional legal theory, judges should not step into the political or policy arena: their proper constitutional role is to apply fundamental rules of natural justice and fairness to the treatment of prisoners, for example, but not to

[8] See the discussion on adversarial/inquisitorial procedures below.

[9] Allison (2000).

[10] This is the name of a booklet prepared for civil servants on the judicial review process.

second-guess executive decision-makers. In practice, of course, things are not so straightforward. But before we explore further the appropriate administrative procedure, we should return to *Weeks*.

What is a court?

In *Weeks*, the European Court of Human Rights explained that the 'court' referred to in Article 5(4) did not necessarily have to be a classic 'court of law':

> The 'court' referred to in Article 5(4) does not necessarily have to be a court of law of the classic kind integrated within the standard judicial machinery of the country.[11] The term 'court' serves to denote 'bodies which exhibit not only common fundamental features, of which the most important is independence of the executive and of the parties to the case . . . but also the guarantees . . . appropriate to the kind of deprivation of liberty in question . . . of [a] judicial procedure', the forms of which may vary from one domain to another.[12] In addition, as the text of Article 5(4) makes clear, the body in question must not have merely advisory functions but must have the competence to 'decide' the 'lawfulness' of the detention and to order release if the detention is unlawful.[13]

This paragraph builds on what was said in *De Wilde, Ooms and Versyp* v. *Belgium*[14], the case of the Belgian vagrants, where the Court explored the meaning of the Convention by comparing the official texts in both English and French. This led them to conclude that, although at first sight the wording of Article 5(4) might make one think that it guarantees the right of the detainee always to have supervised by a 'court' the lawfulness of a previous decision to deprive him of his liberty, this was not necessarily the case. The Court pointed out the English text spoke of 'proceedings' and not of 'appeal', 'recourse' or 'remedy' and that in Article 5(4) the word 'court' ('tribunal') is used in the singular and not in the plural. This led them to conclude (at para. 76) that:

> Where the decision depriving a person of his liberty is one taken by an administrative body, there is no doubt that Article 5(4) obliges the Contracting States to make available to the person detained a right of recourse to a court; but there is nothing to indicate that the same applies when the decision is made by a court at the close of judicial proceedings. In the latter case, the supervision required by Article 5(4) is incorporated in the decision; this is so,

[11] See *X* v. *United Kingdom* (1982) 4 EHRR 373, para. 53.
[12] See *De Wilde, Ooms and Versyp* (1979) 1 EHRR 373, paras 56 and 58.
[13] At para. 61.
[14] See note 12 above.

for example, where a sentence of imprisonment is pronounced after 'conviction by a competent court' (Article 5(1) (a) of the Convention). It may therefore be concluded that Article 5(4) is observed if the arrest or detention of a vagrant, provided for in paragraph (1)(e), is ordered by a 'court' within the meaning of paragraph (4).

It results, however, from the purpose and object of Article 5, as well as from the very terms of paragraph (4) ('proceedings', 'recours'), that in order to constitute such a 'court' an authority must provide the fundamental guarantees of procedure applied in matters of deprivation of liberty. If the procedure of the competent authority does not provide them, the State could not be dispensed from making available to the person concerned a second authority which does provide all the guarantees of judicial procedure.

In sum, the Court considers that the intervention of one organ satisfies Article 5(4), but on condition that the procedure followed has a judicial character and gives to the individual concerned guarantees appropriate to the kind of deprivation of liberty in question.

The Court went on to explain that the Convention uses the word 'court' (French: 'tribunal') in Articles 2, 5 and 6 in order to mark out 'one of the constitutive elements of the guarantee afforded to the individual' by the provision in question. Thus:

In all these different cases, it [the word 'court' or 'tribunal'] denotes bodies which exhibit not only common fundamental features, of which the most important is independence of the executive and of the parties to the case,[15] but also the guarantees of judicial procedure. The forms of the procedure required by the Convention need not, however, necessarily be identical in each of the cases where the intervention of a court is required. In order to determine whether a proceeding provides adequate guarantees, regard must be had to the particular nature of the circumstances in which such proceedings takes place. Thus, in the *Neumeister* case, the Court considered that the competent courts remained 'courts' in spite of the lack of 'equality of arms' between the prosecution and an individual who requested provisional release, nevertheless, the same might not be true in a different context and, for example, in another situation which is also governed by Article 5(4).[16]

Later, in *X* v. *United Kingdom*,[17] the decision which led to the creation of the Mental Health Review Tribunals, the European Court explained more briefly that:

53. It is not within the province of the Court to enquire into what would be the best or most appropriate system of judicial review in this sphere, for the Contracting States are free to choose different methods of performing their

[15] See *Neumeister* v. *Austria (No. 1)* (1968), 1 EHRR 91, 132, para. 24.

[16] At para. 78.

[17] (1982) 4 EHRR 188.

> obligations. Thus, in Article 5(4) the word 'court' is not necessarily to be understood as signifying a court of law of the classic kind, integrated within the standard judicial machinery of the country. This term, as employed in several Articles of the Convention (including Art. 5(4)), serves to denote –
>
> bodies which exhibit not only common fundamental features, of which the most important is independence of the executive and of the parties to the case, but also the guarantees ('appropriate to the kind of deprivation of liberty in question') of [a] judicial procedure, the forms of which may vary from one domain to another.[18]

Thus the European Court enforces the minimum standard of human rights, leaving individual states to choose the appropriate route to achieving those standards. The essential elements of a court seem to be its independence and the appropriateness of its procedures. Both key values are difficult to interpret. The Court in *Weeks* also stressed the importance of the court's 'competence to decide'. Does the DLP live up to the standard set?

The independence of the Parole Board

The Parole Board was set up by Parliament in 1967 simply to 'advise' the Home Secretary. All cases were subject to ministerial veto. Section 59 of the Criminal Justice Act 1967 set out the constitution and functions of the Parole Board (and of local review committees, which were abolished in 1991). Subsection (1) provides that the Parole Board should consist of a chairman and not less than four other members to be appointed by the Secretary of State. According to subsection (4), the Board

> (a) shall deal with the case on consideration of any documents given to it by the Secretary of State and of any reports it has called for and any information whether oral or in writing that it has obtained; and
> (b) if in any particular case the Board thinks it is necessary to interview the person to whom the case relates before reaching a decision, the Board may request one of its members to interview him and shall take into account the report of that interview by that member . . .

Subsection (6) gave the Home Secretary the power to make rules for the establishment and constitution of local review committees and for the interviewing of prisoners by a member of a local review committee.

Schedule 2 to the 1967 Act provided more details:

[18] See *De Wilde, Ooms and Versyp* v. *Belgium (No. 1)* (1979), 1 EHRR 373, 407, 408, paras. 76, 78.

1. The Parole Board shall include among its members – (a) a person who holds or has held judicial office; (b) a registered medical practitioner who is a psychiatrist; (c) a person appearing to the Secretary of State to have knowledge and experience of the supervision or aftercare of discharged prisoners; and (d) a person appearing to the Secretary of State to have made a study of the causes of delinquency or the treatment of offenders.

When constituting the Board in the autumn of 1967, the Home Secretary made 16 appointments for an initial period of 18 months.[19] The Report of the Parole Board for 1969 noted that 'there is a need for adequate continuity of membership to preserve consistency and development of policy, and there is also a need to maintain, within the membership, the categories of members required by the Act, Schedule 2. In order to meet these needs the Home Secretary has informed the Board that it is his intention to appoint members for a three-year term, one-third of the membership retiring each year'.[20] The numbers have increased steadily, most dramatically from 62 to 86 in 1992, mainly to deal with the extra work arising from the abolition of local review committees and the creation of DLPs.

In practice, the Board has always sat in small panels when deciding determinate as well as lifer cases. Only in the case of life sentence prisoners must the panel include a judge and a psychiatrist. The Parole Board has always had a High Court judge as Vice-Chairman, and a number of other High Court and circuit judges have sat on the Board. Then as now, the Home Secretary appointed the judges on the Board after consultation with the Lord Chief Justice.

Since 1 July 1996 the Parole Board has been an Executive Non-Departmental Public Body, an executive agency of the Home Office, sponsored by the Prison Service. What does this mean? According to the Report of the Parole Board for 1995 and 1995–6, the Board was established as an Executive NDPB 'because of' their new executive responsibility in regard to the release of discretionary lifers and 'because of' the need for greater accountability.[21] But agency status does not in itself create independence from the Home Office: agency status was created to put greater emphasis on the financial and managerial responsibility of the individual agency. The Parole Board remains an executive agency of the Home Office. It is housed within the Prison Service headquarters in London. The Prison Service is regarded as a 'related party', providing grant-in-aid, seconded staff, accommodation, facilities management, personnel, postage, IT, telecommunications, etc.

[19] House of Commons (1969).
[20] House of Commons (1970), para. 3.
[21] House of Commons (1996), para. 3.

all at nil cost to the Parole Board.[22] That the staff of the Parole Board secretariat have often worked for the Prison Service, and may indeed be on secondment from the Prison Service, is surprising for an 'independent' body. These close links between the Prison Service and the Parole Board obviously smooth the wheels of the administration. The Chairman of the Parole Board was keen to highlight these links in the latest Parole Board annual report: he noted that the excellent results of the Parole Board are 'a testament to the close links the Board has with staff in the Prison Service'.[23] While the effectiveness and efficiency of the Board may well be fostered by close links, they may also undermine its independence.

It is of course the members of the Parole Board and not the staff who make the decisions at a DLP. But questions can also be asked about their independence. The Home Secretary appoints them for periods of six years. In *Weeks*, the Court concluded that

> the Court is satisfied that the judge member and the other members of the Board remain wholly independent of the executive and impartial in the performance of their duties.

It is not clear on what grounds the Court found this to be proved. They cited in support of their conclusion the case of *Campbell and Fell* v. *United Kingdom*,[24] where the Court disagreed with the Commission, who had concluded that a prison's Board of Visitors was not an independent tribunal. Boards of Visitors are statutory bodies[25] with the duty to 'satisfy themselves as to the state of prison premises, the administration of the prison and the treatment of the prisoners'.[26] Until 1991, they also had the duty of adjudicating on disciplinary offences in prisons. The Court in *Campbell and Fell* were asked to rule on the 'independence' of Boards. But here too the Court does not explain the factual basis, the evidence on which they relied, for the finding of independence.

The Home Secretary's control over the Parole Board extends to the making of rules and directions.[27] (We have already noted how, in relation to discretionary lifers, rules but not directions have been issued.) Most tribunals come under the umbrella of the Lord Chancellor's Department, and the Lord Chancellor therefore draws up the rules for most 'independent' tribunals. A comparison can be made with the

[22] See the Annual Report and Accounts of the Parole Board (House of Commons, 2001), p. 47.

[23] Ibid., at p. 2.

[24] (1985) 7 EHRR 165.

[25] See section 6 of the Prison Act 1952, as amended.

[26] Rule 77, Prison Rules 1999 (SI 1999 No. 728).

[27] Section 32(5) and (6) of the Criminal Justice Act 1991.

recently drafted regulations for the new Care Standards Tribunal which was the subject of a consultation document at the end of 2001.[28] The 50-page detailed document (to be the subject matter of a statutory instrument) stands in contrast to the lack of detail in the Parole Board Rules. Not only are these Rules drafted by the Home Secretary, they are not even delegated legislation. They thus avoid Parliamentary scrutiny. The objections to this by both the Opposition in the House of Commons and by significant numbers of peers in the House of Lords during the passage of the Criminal Justice Bill 1990 were noted in Chapter 4.

Another example of the Home Secretary's continuing control over the Parole Board has been his refusal to allow the DLP to be supervised by the Council on Tribunals. In the last chapter, the Council's long-standing critiques of the Mental Health Review Tribunal were noted. It was not only peers in the House of Lords who tried to bring the DLP under the same umbrella, but also the Council on Tribunals itself. In its 1994–5 Annual Report, the Council reports that the government rejected their claim to supervision of DLPs. The reasons given by the government seem to undermine the very purpose of the Council: it was argued that formal jurisdiction would enable the Council to do no more on a formal basis than they already did by way of informal visits and consultations. Unsurprisingly the Council on Tribunals was disappointed by this response:

> While we value the opportunity to comment on procedural rules and to attend hearings, we do not consider that the present arrangements afford a real opportunity for adequate or in-depth study of the working of discretionary lifer panels, such as we are able to undertake in respect of tribunals under our supervision. We feel that our experience of tribunal systems such as the Mental Health Review Tribunals (where the presence of senior judicial members has not been thought to detract from the desirability of our supervision) would enable us to make a helpful contribution to the working of the panels, if we were given a formal role.[29]

Given that their claim to oversight was rejected and that the Council on Tribunals has to focus on their allotted responsibilities, it is perhaps not surprising that they do not appear to have maintained their interest in DLPs. The Home Office's response revealed here is perhaps symptomatic of their attitude to DLPs generally: this is a quasi-court or tribunal in the most limited sense of the term.[30] Again, the new Care Standards Tribunal provides an interesting contrast since it will be clearly under the umbrella of the Council on Tribunals. Bradley, commenting in 1991 on

28 www.doh.gov.uk/rht/carestandardtribunal/htm.

29 Para. 2.98–102.

30 Another explanation for the exclusion of the Council might be the ongoing 'power struggle' between the Lord Chancellor's Department and the Home Office.

the numerous bodies outside the supervision of the Council on Tribunals, stated that 'presumably these procedures are not admitted to the benefits of supervision by the Council on Tribunals because in terms of fairness, openness and impartiality, they are not thought to make it to the starting gate'.[31] It would be depressing to conclude that the government thought that the DLP did not make it through the starting gate of fairness, openness and impartiality. It would be a 'vote of confidence' in the DLP to admit it to supervision by the Council.

It is also worth remembering that the European Court of Human Rights recognised that whatever their analysis of the 'objective' independence of Parole Board members, independence also includes the requirement of 'an appearance of independence', notably to the prisoners involved. Prisoners are well aware of the close connection between the Parole Board, the Prison Service and the Home Office.

The power to decide

The 'court' in question must have not merely advisory functions but also the competence to 'decide' the 'lawfulness' of the detention and to order release if the detention is unlawful. The European Court of Human Rights in *Weeks* held that the 'right to judicial control' meant that the tribunal must have the power to give a binding decision on the matter before it.[32] The British government took a narrow interpretation of the decision in question. The DLP has the power to decide only questions of release. Yet the 'matter before' the DLP is frequently not release. It is well understood by prisoners and their legal representatives that the Parole Board is very unlikely to order the release of a prisoner who has not spent a period of time in open conditions, in a Category D prison. He or she will also be expected to have done the appropriate accredited courses in prison. In Padfield and Liebling (2000), only 23 per cent of DLPs were held in open prisons.[33] For virtually all the other prisoners the important 'decision' that they wanted from the DLP was a recommendation, probably that they should be moved on to a lower category prison or given priority for suitable courses. As we saw in Chapter 5, such recommendations are much more common than a direction for release. Yet such recommendations can be (and frequently are) vetoed by the Home Secretary, and this final decision is not subject to appeal or challenge.[34] It would be useful to research further why this is: the culture of the relevant parts of the Home Office and Prison Service headquarters, or the tension between prison establishments and headquarters, may

31 Bradley (1991), at p. 9.
32 At para. 64.
33 Padfield and Liebling (2000), at p. 5.
34 See *ex parte Burgess*, discussed below at p. 149.

lead to a certain 'institutional inertia'. It may also be a question of limited resources. This is in line with the findings of Peay (1989) whose study of MHRTs concluded similarly that sufficient resources and a suitable compassionate attitude in staff are also necessary for the law adequately to protect the individual prisoner (or patient, in her study). A court-like body alone is inadequate to the task.

We have already noted that the primary decision required of the court or tribunal concerns 'dangerousness'. But it seems also to be accepted that prisoners should be required to show that they are 'safe' to be released by spending time in an open prison. The decision of the DLP in reality hangs on a chain of earlier decisions taken primarily by the Prison Service (but also, of course, the sentencing judge).[35] The role of the DLP as monitor of speedy progress towards possible release on tariff, or as soon as possible afterwards, is also important. It was for this reason that Padfield and Liebling (2000) recommended that Parole Board recommendations should, unless rejected by the Home Secretary within a fixed time frame and with written reasons, create a substantive 'legitimate expectation' for prisoners that the recommendations will be acted on.[36] An alternative would, of course, be a more powerful tribunal with authority to decide these matters.

Proper participation of the prisoner

The European Court of Human Rights in *Weeks* appeared somewhat ambivalent about the role that the prisoner should play before the court or tribunal. Commenting on the rights of the prisoner in the 1980s to make representations to the Parole Board, the court mildly comments that 'there remains a certain procedural weakness in the case of a recalled prisoner'.[37] But all three proposals considered in Parliament, including that of the government itself, readily accepted the need for the prisoner to be present.

In fact, it is difficult to assess whether an oral hearing results in a 'better' decision than a paper review.[38] It is clear that most participants

35 See Padfield and Liebling (forthcoming).

36 For a discussion of this concept, see p. 98 above.

37 At para. 66.

38 It is interesting to note that Coker and Martin (1985), in criticising changes taking place at the time they were writing felt able to say that their research showed 'the life sentence policy and procedures evolved by the Home Office to be one of the unsung achievements of that much maligned department . . . in many of its acts it was trying to practise its traditional paternalism in ways that do not satisfy the legalistic temper of the age . . . we have examined the handling of over 200 licences, and our abiding impression is that of the care, impartiality and integrity shown in their cases. Within the limits of the politically possible the Home Office evolved an effective procedure' (pp. 246 and 248). Open procedures do not necessarily lead to better decision-making.

in the DLP process considered an oral hearing important. Most obviously prisoners appreciated being present in order that they could assess whether the process was 'fair and open'. Perhaps this point should not be exaggerated: prisoners are also well aware that real decisions were made elsewhere in the Prison Service. But mandatory life sentence prisoners are keenly aware of the extra level of personal involvement by discretionary lifers, and of the opportunity that they have to be legally represented by an advocate. They sense too that the mandatory sentence process is more 'secret'[39] and universally seem to press for an oral hearing. Risk decisions in these cases are 'human judgements' and there was clear evidence that just seeing the prisoner could inform the decision (rightly or wrongly). In Padfield and Liebling (2000), one independent member was quoted as saying that 'by seeing him, it's taken away my concerns', and another commented repeatedly that the particular prisoner gave her the creeps.[40] Clearly the impact of the oral hearing on decision-making in practice is an area for further research.

As important as the presence of the prisoner is the requirement for legal representation. In Chapter 5 we saw the impact that the legal representative could have on a DLP hearing. Many legal studies of courts and court processes put the emphasis entirely on the judicial role: the role played by other participants is equally important.[41] In this context, the availability of good quality Community Legal Service funded representation is of huge significance. Research into the interpretation of funding rules would be useful.

In Chapter 5 we also saw how at a DLP, the Prison Service will have prepared the dossier, the paperwork which the DLP receives in advance of the hearing. These reports tend to be subjective and judgmental. Another problem with dossiers was the time-lag between the preparation of the reports and the hearing itself. In Chapter 6 we saw how, in contrast, the Mental Health Review Tribunal procedure requires the tribunal secretariat to prepare the paperwork, not the hospital itself. This does not seem to have resulted in a more timely procedure, but it may create less 'one-sided' dossiers. Given the enormous importance of a prisoner's dossier, it is curious that they have not been subject to greater critical analysis. Thus it would be useful if a contents analysis and a process analysis of the construction of the DLP dossier were to be carried out which focused on the quality and usefulness of the various items in the dossier. Comparative work with the preparation of files for other

[39] The reality is, of course, that the deliberation stage is equally secret for both mandatory and discretionary lifers.

[40] At p. 60 and p. 51.

[41] For a challenging call for socio-legal analysis of all players in court processes, and not just judges, see Schlanger (1999).

decision-making bodies would also be useful. For example, the analysis by McConville, Saunders and Leng (1991) of the way in which Crown Prosecution Service files are 'constructed' by the police could be usefully applied to the construction of DLP dossiers.

A 'speedy' decision

The European Court of Human Rights has acknowledged on many occasions that the requirement in article 5(4) that a court should decide 'speedily' on the lawfulness of a prisoner's detention also implies that an automatic review must follow at reasonable intervals.[42] Recently, in *Oldham* v. *UK*,[43] the European Court of Human Rights has found that a two-year delay between reviews was not reasonable. Oldham was a recalled discretionary lifer who had completed a number of relevant courses in eight months and the Court held that requiring him to wait another 16 months for another review was not sufficiently speedy. In an attitude reminiscent of their response to the decision in *Weeks* in the case of *Thynne, Wilson and Gunnell*, the UK government tried to limit the implications of *Oldham* in the later case of *Hirst* v. *UK*.[44] They argued (unsuccessfully) that mental disorder in the context of mental illness is more susceptible to change over time than mental instability posing risks of dangerousness, and that therefore a two-year review was sufficient for a post-tariff discretionary lifer. The European Court of Human Rights disagreed: on the facts of the case, periods of 21 months and two years were not justified by considerations of rehabilitation and monitoring. The DLP process is therefore having to become less rigid in terms of the normal biennial review. However, the Court of Appeal made it very clear in *MacNeil* v. *Discretionary Lifer Panel*[45] that the decision of the European Court of Human Rights in *Oldham* v. *UK* gave rise to no general proposition about the maximum permissible period between reviews. On the facts of this case (a recalled murderer with a tariff of ten years who has now served nearly twenty years), a two-year review was reasonable.

It is not only the length of time between reviews which is problematic but also the frequent delays found at many stages in the process. As we saw in Chapter 5, Padfield and Liebling (2000) found that late reports and papers were received either on the day or shortly before the hearing date in many cases, which sometimes led to deferral of cases (for about six months), either before, or sometimes at the hearing, wasting public money and risking considerable unfairness to the prisoner. The most

42 *AT* v. *UK* (commission report 29 November 1995); *Herczegfalvy* v. *Austria* (1992) 15 EHRR 437.

43 (2000) 31 EHRR 813; [2000] Crim LR 1011.

44 [2001] Crim LR 919.

45 [2001] EWCA 448, 21 March 2001.

frequent reason for deferrals was the late arrival of reports which was both unfair on the prisoner and wasteful of resources.

A 'speedy decision' might not happen because of the bureaucratic constraints of the DLP process. As we saw in Chapter 5, the Parole Board fixes a provisional timetable for hearings some eight or nine months in advance, on the assumption that the prisoner would remain in the same prison. A prisoner might not be moved on to another prison during that time, since he is waiting for a DLP. There is a danger that a prisoner's progress freezes pending the next hearing. Thus while the DLP process may well help to 'nudge' some prisoners through the lifer system, it may also slow others down. This listing procedure has been held to be lawful, even when it means that some lifers may not have a review until a couple of months after their tariff expires.[46] The court held that piecemeal referrals would be less efficient and would result in longer delays for some prisoners. But it is certainly worth considering whether the low 'status' of the DLP as a quasi-court may explain the significant problem of delays. If the Nathan proposals had been adopted, and a new tribunal well outside the umbrella of the Home Office had been created, would the executive have done more to meet deadlines? We return to this in the final chapter.

The 'court' must follow appropriate procedures

Initiation of proceedings

The language of Article 5(4) makes it clear that the prisoner should 'be entitled to take proceedings', i.e. initiate proceedings. We have already noted that the Court in *Weeks* was somewhat ambivalent about the proper participation of the prisoner.[47] The Court was content, perhaps surprisingly, to decide that since the Home Secretary is obliged to refer certain cases to the Parole Board, this gives sufficient access. The fallacy in this argument is the assumption that that the Home Secretary refers cases efficiently. As we have seen, not all discretionary lifers find their cases referred on time to the Parole Board: it can therefore be argued that a greater emphasis should be put on the prisoner's 'right' to initiate proceedings.

Adversarial or inquisitorial?

The European Court of Human Rights in *Hussain and Singh* put particular emphasis on the need for an 'adversarial procedure' involving

[46] *R (on behalf of Noorkoiv)* v. *Secretary of State for the Home Department*, 2 July 2001, *Criminal Law Week* 01/26/70.

[47] See p. 137 above.

legal representation and the calling and questioning of witnesses.[48] The term 'adversarial' is usually taken to describe a system in which the judge takes the role of umpire, leaving the presentation of the case to the parties on each side. The parties separately prepare their case and call, examine and cross-examine their witnesses. The term 'inquisitorial' describes systems where judges may supervise the pre-trial preparation of the evidence and play a major part in the presentation of the trial.[49] Used in this way, the procedure at a DLP is in some sense a hybrid, lying some way between the two models. The Panel may enter the arena by asking questions and indeed by choosing which witnesses they wish to call. They need this power to investigate the case properly.[50]

It would appear that, when the DLP was created, an inquisitorial model was preferred in order to facilitate the Panel's search for the 'right' answer. But as the years have gone by the process has moved in a more accusatorial direction. This is not simply because the judges who chair proceedings are used to the more accusatorial format of the traditional English court hearing. The adversarial model has advantages: it forces the parties to clarify the key issues and to argue their case. Giving the parties the key role legitimates the process. Why is it that prisoners unanimously welcome the oral hearing? Why is it that mandatory lifers are jealous of the discretionary lifers 'day in court'? It is, it is argued, because the prisoner becomes part of the process. In a certain sense, he or she is made party to the decision whether or not he should be released. He is, in a certain sense, empowered. Trevor Allan, is his recent *Constitutional Justice: A Liberal Theory of the Rule of Law*, goes further and argues that it is the essentially collaborative nature of adversarial adjudication that explains its special moral force as an impartial means of dispute settlement:

> The adversarial hearing embodies that element of respect for persons that consists, not merely in treating them correctly, according to formally adopted rules, but with proper dignity, in a manner that responds directly to their own perceptions of their due as equal citizens ... The greater the litigant's participation – the stronger his control over the nature of the proceedings – the greater the moral authority of the outcome.[51]

Allan robustly defends adversarial procedures, primarily because they oblige government agencies to account for their decisions in terms that the ordinary person can understand: 'if the legitimate needs of the

[48] See p. 57 above.
[49] See Report of the Royal Commission on Criminal Justice (1993), p. 3.
[50] Richardson's important *Law, Process and Custody: Prisoners and Patients* (1993) argues strongly for an 'actively inquisitorial model'.
[51] Allan (2001), at p. 87.

administration cannot be satisfactorily explained to a non-expert court, they cannot be justified to the citizen whose interests are directly affected'.[52] But this argument implies that in an adversarial procedure both adversaries take part. At present, the DLP can appear remarkably one-sided: the Prison Service/Home Office present a dossier of reports and then leave the prisoner (or his representative) to try and prove why he should be released. It could be described as adversarial, but with a sleeping adversary.

Of course the adversarial and inquisitorial models are simply models. There is no reason why the body charged with deciding the legality of a prisoner's detention should not be a hybrid. But this discussion serves to underline the need for clarity. At present the DLP might be seen as adopting the worst of both worlds: because the Secretary of State's representative takes a minor role at the hearing, it is left to the Panel to enter the arena, but not on the side of the prisoner who is at that stage well represented. In its search for 'truth', there is a danger that the Panel appears on the side of the Prison Service. The 'independence' of the Panel would be enhanced if the Secretary of State's representative took a greater role at the hearing, intervening more actively to establish the need for continued detention, leaving the Panel to judge.

But even then the DLP as an adversarial process can only reach a fair outcome if both sides can put their case with equal effectiveness. At a DLP, the Home Office has constructed the dossier and has greater access to experts. It is important that an actively inquisitorial Panel can search for the genuine justifications for the continued detention of the prisoner. Applying Allison's analysis[53] to the DLP, it is clear that Allison would call for the greater involvement of the tribunal itself:

> When procedures are adversarial rather than inquisitorial courts are judicially informed only by the representatives of two parties to the administrative dispute – usually the administration and the complainant – and are unable properly to investigate the complex repercussions of judicial intervention. Improperly informed, the courts are unable to intervene confidently. And informed as if the administrative dispute only involves two parties, they struggle to develop acceptable principles sufficiently different from those designed for the bipolar disputes of private law.[54]

Padfield and Liebling (2000) concluded that Panels could be consciously proactive in two senses: testing for risk/safety and testing whether the Prison and Probation Services are respecting the prisoner's human rights. This raises the difficult question of who has to prove what.

52 Ibid., at p. 10.
53 See note 9 above.
54 Allison (2000), at p. 39.

The burden of proof

If the DLP was truly inquisitorial, then it might be argued that any discussion of burdens of proof in this context was misleading. The law states simply that the Parole Board cannot release unless they are satisfied that 'it is no longer necessary for the protection of the public that the prisoner should be confined'.[55] In practice it is not surprising that Panels appear to feel that the prisoner has a 'persuasive' burden of proof. Richardson (1990) commented before the DLPs had been created that it would be essential that the burden of proof be clearly located: 'there must either be a duty on the detaining authority to prove the existence of a real risk that the behaviour will recur after release, or the tribunal must be required to satisfy itself of the existence of such a risk'.[56] Padfield and Liebling concluded that the DLP should operate with two legal presumptions:

- a safety presumption: they cannot release unless they are satisfied that 'it is no longer necessary ... that the prisoner should be confined'; and
- a human rights presumption: post-tariff discretionary lifers must be released as soon as possible, and should be given every opportunity to be 'tested for safety'.

It is this second presumption which needs to be reinforced and which led the Court of Appeal in *R (ex p. H)* v. *Mental Health Review Tribunal, North and East London Region and the Secretary of State for Health (intervenor)*,[57] discussed in Chapter 6, to issue a declaration of incompatibility. As we saw, the Master of the Rolls held the burden of proof should not be on the patient.[58]

We saw in Chapter 6 how the government has now amended the Mental Health Act to make clear that the burden lies on the hospital authorities to prove the mental disorder. In order to satisfy the requirements of the European Court of Human Rights, a similar burden should surely be applied at the DLP. A prisoner should be entitled to release unless the DLP is satisfied that it is not safe to release him or her. These developments suggest that, in the context of the DLP, it should be made clear that the post-tariff lifer shall be released unless the 'court' is satisfied (on a balance of probabilities) that it is not safe to do so. The burden should be clearly on the Home Office to show why it remains necessary to detain the prisoner.

[55] Section 34(4) of the Criminal Justice Act 1991, now section 28(6) of the Crime (Sentences) Act 1997: see Appendices 1 and 2.
[56] Richardson (1990), at p. 39.
[57] [2001] 3 WLR 512.
[58] At para. 24.

We have seen that many discretionary lifers spend many years in prison post-tariff. One interpretation of this is that they are particularly dangerous. The longer a prisoner has been in prison the less likely he is to be 'releasable'. But taking a human rights agenda, the opposite can also be true: the longer a prisoner has spent in prison after the tariff part of his sentence has been completed, the more certain the court should be that it is necessary to detain him. This was the approach taken by Stuart-Smith LJ in *Bradley*.[59] Explaining the Parole Board's test of dangerousness, that they had to be convinced that the level of risk which the prisoner presented was 'a substantial risk of further offences dangerous to life or limb, including serious sexual offences', he added:

> The Parole Board have to carry out a balancing exercise between the legitimate conflicting interests of both prisoner and public. They must clearly recognise the price which the prisoner personally is paying in order to give proper effect to the interests of public safety. They should recognise too that it is a progressively higher price. Accordingly, the longer the prisoner serves beyond the tariff period, the clearer should be the Parole Board's perception of public risk to justify the continued deprivation of liberty involved.[60]

While this does not reflect the current position, it is an important argument in support of greater recognition of the rights of post-tariff life sentence prisoners.

Recent developments in judicial review

So far we have seen that decisions of the European Court of Human Rights are ambiguous, and indeed have not explored the appropriate procedures to be followed in any depth. But it is doubtful whether the DLP lives up to the requirements of the Court. It is doubtful whether the Parole Board is truly 'independent'. It has very limited powers. Its procedures are not obviously always appropriate. Before reaching conclusions on why this might be, we should consider recent developments in domestic law. Have domestic courts had an impact in achieving fair procedures and fair outcomes? Indeed, have they gone further than the European Court sought to go?

As we saw at the beginning of this chapter, the standard of judicial review is not rigid. There is no doubt that the standards of judicial review are being refashioned, partly as a result of the incorporation of the European Convention of Human Rights into domestic law by the

59 See p. 27 above.
60 At p. 146.

Human Rights Act 1998. As Craig and Schonberg put it, the courts are increasingly willing to recognise the totality of the tools available to them.[61] A leading case now is *R (Daly)* v. *Secretary of State for the Home Department*[62] where the House of Lords had the opportunity to explore whether the contours of judicial review had changed as a result of the Human Rights Act 1998. The case concerned a prisoner's challenge to the policy which required prisoners to leave their cells even when their legally privileged correspondence was being examined (but not read!) during cell searches. Lord Bingham, the Lord Chief Justice, delivered the main speech. Having decided that such cell searches infringed the prisoner's right to legal professional privilege, he had to consider whether the policy could be justified as a necessary and proper response. To do this, he explored the policy in detail, as well as looking at the policy as applied in Scotland, and at a report of the Prisons Ombudsman. He concluded that the policy provided for a greater degree of intrusion than was justified. He agreed with the additional observations of Lord Steyn on the differences in approach between the traditional grounds of judicial review and the proportionality approach, which must be applied in cases involving Convention rights. In a Convention case, the court must be able to decide, if there was a prima facie justified interference with a person's right, whether the interference was really proportionate to the legitimate aim being pursued. The important difference, their Lordships stress, between the 'traditional' heads of judicial review and proportionality is the question of balance. With proportionality, as Lord Steyn made clear, the reviewing court may have to assess the balance that the decision-maker has struck in weighing the relative weight to be accorded to different interests and considerations. Having admitted that the different approaches could sometimes lead to different results,[63] Lord Slynn ended rather enigmatically by saying that the respective role of judges and administrators will remain fundamentally distinct and that the intensity of the review will depend on the subject matter in hand: 'In law context is everything'.[64] Lord Cooke hinted more boldly that that the standard of review must be robust: 'it may well be that the law can never be satisfied in any administrative field merely by a finding that the decision under review is not capricious or absurd'.[65]

[61] Craig and Schonberg (2001), at p. 701.

[62] [2001] 2 AC 532.

[63] A clear example is the decision of the Court of Appeal in *R* v. *Ministry of Defence, ex parte Smith* [1996] QB 317 and the decision of the European Court of Human Rights in *Smith and Grady* v. *United Kingdom* (1999) 29 EHRR 493. The European Court applying a test of proportionality struck down the policy ban on homosexuals serving in the armed forces whereas the domestic courts had not done so.

[64] At para. 28.

[65] At para. 32.

We need to investigate whether there is any evidence that the intensity of judicial review in this area is in fact increasing. Certainly there has been a striking increase in the number of applications for judicial review of Parole Board decisions since the Human Rights Act 1998 came into force: during 2000–1, 71 applications were lodged against the Parole Board, more than double the figure for 1999–2000.[66] The Parole Board suggests that this increase arises from greater awareness on the part of prisoners of the process. However, the likelihood of success remains very small. Only five prisoners were successful in 1999–2000, and three in 2000–1. However, even the rare successes may have a large impact: after the Court of Appeal in *R* v. *Parole Board, ex parte Oyston*[67] held that the Parole Board had given undue weight to Oyston's continued denial of his offences, there was a marked increase in applications from prisoners who felt that their case was comparable.[68]

There are other striking examples of cases where judges have struck down the decision of the Parole Board as either irrational or unlawful. In *R (on the application of Jordan)* v. *Parole Board*,[69] Henriques J quashed a decision of the Parole Board as irrational where the decision letter referred to further work being required on 'impulse control and perspective taking' when three reports were forcefully in Jordan's favour, with none of them identifying any necessary further work and where the decision letter made no reference to these reports. This followed another dramatic example of the potential role of judicial review in the context of the life sentence prisoner (though here a mandatory lifer): in *R* v. *Parole Board, ex parte Hart*,[70] Turner J held that not only were the reasons given to Hart deficient, but also that the decision of the Parole Board not to recommend a transfer to open conditions was itself irrational. Hart had been convicted of murder in 1975 aged 23 and at the time of the decision under review had already served 23 years, ten years post-tariff. Having quoted extensively from the many reports before the Board, Turner J concluded:

> There were . . . many positive factors in favour of the risk, which undeniably exists, being capable of being contained and monitored if the applicant were to be transferred into open conditions ... It was as though the letter was concerned and concerned only with risk.

Turner J emphasised that the Board should make it clear that they had considered the positive efforts that the prisoner had made and the benefit

[66] Parole Board (2001), p. 31.
[67] (2000) 1 March, unreported.
[68] Parole Board (2001), p. 21.
[69] (2000) EWHC Admin, 26 October; [2001] ACD 261, *Criminal Law Week* 01/13/9.
[70] (2000) 70 24 May, unreported.

that he would derive from being able to address areas of concern about his behaviour in an open prison.

Another mandatory lifer to benefit from a similar decision was Ross Gordon. He had been convicted of murder in 1977, and had already served more than ten years beyond his tariff of 13 years. He had appeared to have been on the cusp of release in 1992 when he was withdrawn from a Pre-Release Employment Scheme because of incidents involving drink: he had returned to Category C conditions. In 2000 the Parole Board continued to refuse to recommend that he should be returned to Category D (open) conditions. In *R* v. *Parole Board, ex parte Gordon*,[71] Smith J ordered that the Board should reconsider their decision promptly. She was concerned that the basis on which the risk was said to be unacceptable was fallacious: past failures on PRES were the only reasons given for why he could not now be transferred to conditions in which he had not previously failed and which were in any event more closely supervised than PRES. She said that she was not sure that she would have quashed the decision if the only ground had been that of irrationality, but she had no doubt that the decision was unlawful as there had been no real balancing of risk and benefit. Smith J also made it clear that she was shocked that Gordon had been left in something of a limbo. Nothing had happened in Gordon's treatment since the Parole Board decision of ten months earlier.

These cases may reflect a more interventionist High Court bench. But they were mandatory cases, in which judges were able to rely on the directions issued by the Home Secretary in mandatory life sentence cases. As we saw in Chapter 4, the Home Secretary has not issued directions in discretionary life sentence cases.[72] Discretionary lifers may be disadvantaged by the absence of substantive criteria against which to measure the DLP's decision-making.

There seems to be a growing trend in judicial review cases for the courts to look beyond the narrow impact of the Parole Board's decision-making and to acknowledge the role of the Prison Service in release decisions. Thus, in *R* v. *Secretary of State for the Home Department, ex parte Hirst*.[73] A post-tariff prisoner had been recategorised from Category C to Category B. The Divisional Court had held that it should be very slow to impose procedural standards upon the internal workings of the prison system in so sensitive a context. However, the Lord Chief Justice, in the Court of Appeal, recognising that the recategorisation of a prisoner significantly affects the prospects of his being released on licence, concluded:

[71] (2000) 7 November, unreported.
[72] See p. 78 above.
[73] [2001] EWCA 378 , 3 March 2001.

> . . . the rules of fairness and natural justice are flexible and not static; they are capable of developing not only in relation to the expectations of contemporary society, but also to meet proper operational requirements. The ability of the Prison Service to meet both their operational needs and the needs for prisoners to be treated fairly can usually be achieved within the panoply of the requirements of fairness.

The Court of Appeal therefore made a declaration that a post-tariff discretionary lifer is 'entitled to be told prior to his category being changed retrogressively, the reasons for the proposed change and given a reasonable opportunity to make representations as to the change'. (They added that the fact that a decision to change the category of a prisoner has not been made does not prevent a prisoner being moved for operational reasons.) This case was followed in *R (on the application of Blagden)* v. *Secretary of State for the Home Department*.[74] The Home Secretary acknowledged that although the Prison Service was entitled to move Blagden, an arsonist serving a discretionary life sentence, back to closed conditions, it had failed formally to reclassify him. He undertook to return Blagden to open conditions within ten days.

Very recently in *Williams* v. *Secretary of State for the Home Department*[75] the Court of Appeal has held that a prisoner may be entitled to an oral hearing before the Category A Committee. Williams had appealed against the dismissal of his application for judicial review of the decision of the Director of High Security Prisons that his classification as a category A prisoner should continue. Williams, serving five discretionary life sentences, and who had made two escape attempts, one of which had been successful, had been categorised as a 'high risk' prisoner. In rejecting his referral for parole on the ground that he continued to represent a risk to the public, the Discretionary Lifer Panel of the Parole board had recognised that he had made as much progress in addressing his offending behaviour as had been possible in Category A conditions. He therefore sought recategorisation, submitting that his continued classification as a Category A prisoner would prevent any future DLP concluding he was fit for release. A request for an oral hearing before the Category A review committee and for full disclosure of reports had been denied. The Court of Appeal, led by the Master of the Rolls, in allowing the appeal, held that there were exceptional cases where a prisoner who sought recategorisation was entitled to an oral hearing before the Category A review committee and to full disclosure of the reports on which his categorisation was based subject to the requirements of public interest immunity. Such cases would occur where the

[74] [2001] EWHC Admin 393, 11 April 2001.
[75] [2002] EWCA Civ 498,17 April 2002.

differing approach taken by the DLP and the review committee to public safety issues would, as in the instant case, result in the possibility of inconsistent decisions. This decision provides a welcome recognition of the vital importance of protecting the rights of post-tariff lifers.

But it is important to stress that judicial review should not be seen as a panacea for all ills. Many more challenges are unsuccessful than successful. The Parole Board may face an increasing number of challenges a year, but the vast majority are unsuccessful. For example, we have already seen how in *MacNeil* v. *Discretionary Lifer Panel*,[76] the Court of Appeal successfully resisted the argument that the European Court of Human Rights had forced a more flexible review timetable. In any case, the Parole Board, as we have seen, has limited powers, and judicial review is unlikely to curb the vast powers of the Home Secretary. Thus in *R (on the application of Burgess)* v. *Secretary of State for the Home Department*[77] the court held that Article 5 of the European Convention is concerned with the lawfulness of detention, and not with where prisoners are detained within the prison system. Article 5(4) was not engaged by the Home Secretary's decision not to accept the advice of a DLP to move Burgess to open conditions, even though such a refusal was accepted in practice to be likely to delay his eventual release. The decision was particularly disappointing to Burgess and his legal advisers since they had not been given a copy of the civil servant's advice on which the Home Secretary had based his decision. They were given no opportunity to make representations on new points which were raised at this late stage. But the court held that this was not a case of recategorisation, but simply a refusal of a recommendation with which the court would not interfere. In the context of MHRTs, Richardson and Mackin have recently shown that the influence of judicial review is at best patchy, even with regard to procedural fairness.[78] It is unlikely that its impact is any greater in this area.

A brief review of recent relevant judicial review cases shows that 'trends' are difficult to identify. On a positive footing, judicial review has been important in safeguarding the rights of individual prisoners. The careful review of the release process as applied to such prisoners as Jordan, Hart and Gordon has speeded them on their way towards release. The spectre of the 'judge on their shoulder' has doubtless created a culture of greater care, certainly in the preparation of the reasons for decisions, than might otherwise exist. Recent developments, notably in relation to the use of proportionality following the incorporation of the Human Rights Act 1998, may lead to further improvements. But at the

76 See p. 139 above.
77 (2000) EWHC, 3 November; *Daily Telegraph*, 5 December; *Criminal Law Week* 00/44/17.
78 See Richardson and Mackin (2000).

same time one should be aware that the proliferation of judicial review cases may not be so much proof of successful activism but, as Allison might suggest, a symptom of the enduring uncertainties which continue to hang over the DLP process, about the required procedure, the relevant substantive principles, and the likely judicial role.[79] Ashworth, for example, is wary of the courts' attraction to 'balancing' competing human rights: 'the notion of "balancing" is itself rather nebulous, unless a clear indication is given of the relative weight of the factors being balanced, and unless the notion of "public interest" is carefully unpacked'.[80]

In this chapter, we began by exploring in more detail the reasoning behind the judgments of the European Court of Human Rights which led to the creation of DLPs. The requirements of a 'judicial process' were analysed to see whether the DLP lives up to the necessary standard. The process of judicial control required might simply be a court making the primary decision (the DLP?), or a court reviewing an executive process (judicial review?). But it is important to remember that the European Convention on Human Rights lays down merely minimum standards: there is no reason why English law should not provide both safeguards and indeed higher standards than those required by the European Convention. It is time to draw some final conclusions together.

[79] Allison (2000), at p. 183.
[80] Ashworth (2001), at p. 871. See also p. 155 below.

8

Theory and practice

Summary

This book has traced the origins and developments of Discretionary Lifer Panels of the Parole Board from their roots in the key decisions of the European Court of Human Rights which caused Parliament to legislate for a more 'court-like' body to decide the question of the release of post-tariff life sentence prisoners. We then looked at the way Parliament created 'Discretionary Lifer Panels' of the Parole Board. The government was prepared to legislate for the minimum procedural safeguards required by the Court but without examining in detail whether the Parole Board was independent or, perhaps more importantly, without laying down the substantive criteria for release. Chapter 5 described the way DLPs work in practice, and Chapter 6 offered a description of other comparable release procedures in England and Wales. Chapter 7 returned to explore the ambiguities in the decisions of the European Court, raising also the ambiguities in recent decisions of the domestic courts in applications for judicial review. The main question for this final chapter is whether DLPs have achieved their purpose. That depends on what we understand their purpose to be.

Back to basics

Article 5(4) provides that:

> Everyone who is deprived of his liberty by arrest or detention shall be entitled to take proceedings by which the lawfulness of his detention shall be decided speedily by a court and his release ordered if the detention is not lawful.

There is nothing unusual, or unusually demanding, in this statement. It is a fundamental right in modern democratic states that people should not be detained without justification. The common law of England provides just such a safeguard. Let us go back to the facts of *Weeks*: a lad of 17 is sentenced to prison for life for a minor robbery. We should ask two questions. Why was an indeterminate sentence justified? What criteria should be applied to check whether this detention is still justified?

Indeterminate detention

Indeterminate or life sentences may be justified in English law for many reasons, and these justifications must provide a key to understanding release criteria. In *Weeks* v. *UK*. the justification was clear: the European Court of Human Rights held that he was detained because of the risk that he presented, or, in their words, for 'social protection and rehabilitation . . . grounds [which] are by their nature susceptible to change with the passage of time'.[1] The 'dangerous' may be detained in order to incapacitate them and to allow for their rehabilitation. Others (i.e. murderers) are detained because of the gravity of their initial offence. A life sentence may also be imposed as a deterrent (see, for example, automatic life sentences imposed under the Crime (Sentences) Act 1997). Indeterminate sentences on children have been justified both because of the seriousness of the offence and on the grounds of the welfare of the individual offender.

It is not a central ambition of this book to undermine the justifications for indeterminate 'life' sentences, though there is an increasing literature that seeks to refute all such justifications. Thus, for example, Van Zyl Smit (2001) reviews an important book by the German Hartmut-Michael Weber, which van Zyl Smit describes as a 'full throated call for the total repeal of the law providing for life imprisonment as a penal sanction'.[2] These arguments merit further discussion in English.[3] For example, there is no evidence that deterrence is likely to have an effect on those who commit the most serious crimes for which a life sentence is likely to be imposed. Nor can deterrence itself justify disproportionate penalties. As soon as one accepts that not all lifers are 'dangerous' one has admitted that the sentence is sometimes disproportionate. Nor can life imprisonment be easily justified as an incapacitation or as social protection: many people will be falsely included in the net of the incapacitated. 'Risk', as we have seen, is notoriously difficult to predict. Weber also stresses the

[1] See para. 58.

[2] At p. 301.

[3] See van Zyl Smit (1999), and his *Taking Life Imprisonment Seriously in National and International Law* (2002), which adds a welcome comparative analysis to the literature. For example, he states that 'the fear of indeterminacy as a source of uncontrolled executive power has been one of the factors that has persuaded some modern states to outlaw life imprisonment' (1999, p. 29), citing Portugal, Brazil and Columbia. He also points out that the Spanish constitution specifies that each offender must be given a realistic opportunity to return to society to exercise the basic freedoms that they may have learnt to use responsibly. Such a principle is not adequately evident in English law or practice at the moment.

undesirability of coerced rehabilitation, giving as it does wide discretionary powers to prison authorities. It is time for Parliament to lay down for the first time a clear statement of the purposes and function of imprisonment. At the moment, the government seems to be inclined towards 'greater use of life sentences'.[4] They should think long and hard about the justifications for so doing.

In England the inconsistencies and doubtful philosophical justifications for life sentences are exacerbated by the mandatory life sentence for murder. The European Court of Human Rights has now had the chance to review its own decisions on the distinction between mandatory and discretionary lifers in *Stafford* v. *UK*[5]. Once it is recognised, as it is, that the sentence of life imprisonment for murder authorises, but does not require, lifelong punitive detention, and is imposed regardless of the facts of a particular case and the circumstances of the individual offender, it is difficult to maintain the distinction. Such arguments led judges in both the Divisional Court and in the Court of Appeal in the recent case of *Anderson and Taylor*[6] to admit openly that they hoped that the European Court of Human Rights would reconsider their position. It may be that this book serves in some small way to underline the inconsistencies which underlie the many different (and inconsistent) justifications for life sentences. But this argument, welcome as it is, should not divert us from the main subject of this book which is the release procedures applicable to those who find themselves before a DLP.

A theoretical framework

We have already noted that predicting future 'dangerous' offending is an unreliable business, because of the infrequency of such events and the 'bluntness' of prediction tables.[7] With this in mind, we should be wary of justifying the detention of people on grounds of prevention alone. The threat for civil liberties has long been recognised: reporting in England in 1981, the influential Floud Report[8] argued that the wholly indeterminate life sentence of imprisonment should cease to be available for non-homicide offences and that any determinate protective sentence should be restricted to those who had proved to be 'likely to do further grave harm'. Strong procedural and evidential safeguards (including a 'quasi-judicial' review tribunal) should, they argued, limit the use of such protective sentences.

[4] Home Office (2002), at p. 18.
[5] See also the decision of the House of Lords in *R* v. *Secretary of State, ex parte Stafford* [1999] 2 AC 38, and the comments in the Preface, added when this book was at proof stage.
[6] [2001] EWCA Civ 1698.
[7] See p. 93 above.
[8] See Floud and Young (1981).

The renewed interest in protective sentences was at that time 'pushed' by a desire to reduce sentence lengths for non-dangerous offenders. This element of the equation seems to have disappeared from the current debate. The Floud Report also generated an interest in the theoretical justifications for protective (incapacitative) sentences. Walker (1983), adopting a utilitarian or protectionist approach, argued that the difficulties of defining dangerousness should not be exaggerated and that detention can be accepted as a last resort. However, arguments justifying the detention of people for social protection reasons need to be considered in the context of the language of rights. A starting point is Dworkin's famous *Taking Rights Seriously* (1977). Dworkin, as the title suggests, defends the case for individual rights. The courts have a duty to safeguard these rights of individuals against undue interference by other social institutions which may act in the pursuit of wider goals such as the general welfare of society. In his analysis, Dworkin holds that courts should decide hard cases on grounds of principles, not policy: principles, which can be seen as requirements of justice or fairness, define rights, and individual rights operate as 'political trumps held by individuals' (p. xi). Policies merely define the collective goals of the community as a whole. He is keen to marginalise the role of discretion in defending his liberal theory of law and does this by arguing that judicial decisions are based on arguments of principle. Thus he argued that a person should only be detained against his will for preventative reasons if the 'danger he presents is vivid',[9] not whenever we calculate that it would probably reduce crime if we did.

Bottoms and Brownsword (1983) argued that this concept of vivid danger needed more analysis than Dworkin gave it:

> We suggest that it [the concept of vivid danger] has three main components: *seriousness* (what type and degree of injury is in contemplation?); *temporality*, which breaks down into *frequency* (over a given period, how many injurious acts are expected?) and *immediacy* (how soon is the next injurious act?) and *certainty* (how sure are we that this person has acted as predicted?). The certainty element is pivotal. If there is a very low score on the certainty factor, then whatever the danger it is certainly not vivid. However, as the score increases on certainty, the risk becomes increasingly vivid and we then have to look very carefully at the kind of danger threatened.[10]

If individual rights are 'political trumps held by individuals', we should of course be wary of any potential 'over-trumps', or what Von Hirsch calls 'an override claim' based on consequentalist notions of future harm:

[9] Dworkin (1977), at p. 11.
[10] Bottoms and Brownsword (1983), at p. 17.

'No single intellectual currency exists into which these competing considerations can be translated and compared'.[11] The danger is that a narrow justification for departing from a person's right to liberty may be expanded in the name of protection of the public. In Padfield and Liebling (2000), the Parole Board concluded in 83 per cent of the cases that the prisoner was sufficiently dangerous that their detention was necessary to protect the public. Did all these prisoners present a 'vivid' danger? Such a test demands that the *level* of risk as well as its presence or absence should be considered, and that both the *seriousness* and the *certainty* of the risk must be assessed as rigorously as possible. That is, high certainty of a minor offence is insufficient, and very low certainty of a serious offence is insufficient, to constitute a substantial risk.

In Dworkin's terms, clear principles, based on justice or fairness, need to be developed to ensure that arguments of policy do not restrict individual rights. Walker proposes five 'rules' (which are 'an appeal to values'):[12]

1. Protective sentences should be used only to prevent serious and lasting hardship to other individuals.
2. There should have to be good reason to believe that such harm in the past was not an isolated, out-of-character episode.
3. If it can reasonably be argued that the offender is unlikely to repeat his behaviour, this argument should operate in his favour.
4. Less drastic measures than detention which have a reasonable prospect of protecting others should be used instead of detention.
5. Where detention is purely for public protection, its conditions should be no worse, apart from the deprivation of liberty, than those which a law-abiding wage-earner would enjoy outside.

Protectionist and libertarian alike agree that clear principles are essential.

Release criteria

Let us look first at the criteria applicable to 'classic' discretionary lifers such as Thynne, Wilson and Gunnell. They, like Weeks, were detained for 'social protection and rehabilitation' because of the risk that they presented. They are *not* being detained for punishment: post-tariff they

[11] Von Hirsch (1983), at p. 50. In von Hirsch's words, 'one is left largely with intuitions on these questions, because they involve apple and oranges comparisons'. See also Ashworth's concern about the 'nebulous' notion of balancing, mentioned at p. 150 above.

[12] See Walker (1983). Walker recognises that the fifth rule is an idealistic standard to set, but as a principle it is an important one, certainly not respected in the prison system today.

have served their proportionate sentence imposed as punishment. Such people have no chance of early release, but are only considered for release once they have served the total sentence which would be the 'tariff' for the offence itself, ignoring the element of risk. This book has sought to question not only the procedure but also the grounds which justify their continued detention after they have served the 'tariff'.

The following four principles are offered as an alterantive to Walker's five rules mentioned above. Someone who is detained post-tariff only because of the risk that they present to the public is entitled:

1. to know the level of risk that they are held to present, and the precise criteria which justify their detention;
2. to be detained in an environment which allows them as much liberty as the 'risk' allows;
3. to expect the state to help them 'speedily' reduce that risk;
4. to expect the state to have to prove the necessity for their detention, the evidence of risk: it should not be the prisoner who has to prove the absence of evidence of risk.

How does the current release procedure satisfy these four principles? As we have seen, the DLP itself has very limited powers. The management of prisons and prison regimes has been left clearly by Parliament in the hands of the Prison Service. One conclusion of this book is that it would be wrong to expect too much of the DLP in curing the inefficiency of the lifer system, which was well catalogued by the Chief Inspectors of Prisons and Probation Thematic Review of Lifers.[13] For both mandatory and discretionary lifers, the 'process of release' should start from the moment of sentence. The wheels of internal Prison Service processes need constant oiling to ensure that suitable lifers have progressed over the categorisation/transfer/offending behaviour courses hurdles to ensure that suitable prisoners are routinely released on tariff. As we have seen, the need for speedy progress has been accentuated with the introduction of 'automatic' life sentences, where judges frequently specify very short 'tariffs'. DLPs as currently constituted can have little impact on Principles 2 and 3 above.

It may be that the Parole Board could have done more itself to underline the importance of these principles. It could most certainly have been clearer in its interpretation of Principles 1 and 4. But it was argued in Chapter 4 that Parliament itself was remiss in failing to lay down clear criteria for release. We saw how when the Criminal Justice Act 1991

[13] HMIPP (1999).

created DLPs, Parliament delegated to the Home Secretary the power to give to the DLP directions as to the matters it should take into account when considering release. The Home Secretary has not done this, though directions do exist on the release of mandatory lifers and determinate sentence prisoners. This leaves a vacuum at the heart of the DLP process. While it may be constitutionally right that the Home Secretary has not sought to issue directions to an independent judicial tribunal, it is not surprising that, given the vacuum, the Parole Board appears to apply similar criteria when releasing discretionary lifers as it does when deciding whether to release other prisoners. Yet this ignores the fundamental difference between discretionary lifers and the other categories of offenders whose cases are considered by the Parole Board: determinate sentence prisoners are being considered for early release, for release before they have served their 'tariff'; murderers, the government insists and the courts have until now accepted, are serving a different sort of life sentence, one in which detention for life is justified by the heinousness of the offence. The position of a discretionary life sentence prisoner is different, closer perhaps to the position of those detained against their wishes in mental hospitals only because of the risk that they present to themselves or the public. Parliament has failed to lay down clear criteria on any of the four principles listed above.

Developments elsewhere in the United Kingdom

Scottish amendments

Before we reach our final conclusions it is worth noting the important changes which have been made recently elsewhere in the United Kingdom. The Convention Rights (Compliance) (Scotland) Act 2001 was enacted to ensure that certain elements of Scots law were Convention compatible. The Scottish Executive conducted a detailed ECHR 'audit' across all its departments and the main focus of the Act of the Scottish Parliament which resulted from it are prisoners and parole. A detailed Policy Memorandum was published with the Bill explaining the need for change.[14] The Act brings the arrangements for adult mandatory life sentence prisoners into line with the arrangements for other prisoners (known in Scotland as 'designated life prisoners', a term designed to embrace both discretionary lifers and those convicted of murder when under the age of 17). The Scottish Ministers considered

> that there is a risk of a domestic court taking the view that, in practice, the arrangements for the release of [adult mandatory lifers] are no different from

[14] See www.scotland.gov.uk.

> those applying to other prisoners sentenced to indeterminate terms of imprisonment. In those circumstances, a domestic court would find a breach of Article 5(4) (since after the expiry of the punishment period the question of risk must be considered by a court-like body) and a breach of Article 6 (since the punishment part would require to be set by a court) . . . The Executive believes that the system for sentencing life prisoners should be clear and transparent with no room for misunderstanding.[15]

This new system has now come into force, including transitional arrangements for the 500 or so existing murderers in Scottish prisons. The High Court is considering ten cases a week, at a special sitting, in order that the punishment part of their sentence is fixed in open court. All life sentence prisoners will now be entitled to a regular oral hearing before the Parole Board at a 'Designated Life Tribunal', once they have served the punishment part of their sentence. The Parole Board for Scotland is now able to direct the release of any post-tariff lifer.

The Act also strengthens the independence of the Parole Board by extending the period of initial appointment of Parole Board members from three to six years. The Policy Manual cites the case of *Findlay* v. *UK*,[16] a case which concerned the courts martial system, setting out the well-established ECHR test for independence and impartiality:

> In order to establish whether a tribunal can be considered 'independent' regard must be had inter alia to the manner of appointment of its members and their term of office, the existence of guarantees against outside pressures and the question of whether the body presents an appearance of independence.

Scotland has become well sensitised to the issue of 'independence'. The High Court of Justiciary in *Starrs* v. *Procurator Fiscal, Linlithgow*[17] famously held that the post of 'temporary sheriff' (junior judges, in the English vocabulary) did not satisfy the requirements of independence and impartiality since they did not have security of tenure. The Bail, Judicial Appointments etc. (Scotland) Act 2000 made new provisions for part-time sheriffs who are now appointed for a five-year term. Reappointment is mandatory unless one of a number of conditions applies. The Scottish Executive decided that the system whereby members of the Parole Board could be reappointed at the discretion of the Executive immediately after their initial term of three years, together with the possibility of removal by the Executive, could be seen as incompatible with the Convention. The Convention Rights (Compliance) Act 2001

[15] www.scotland.gov.uk, at para. 29 and 35.
[16] (1997) 24 EHRR 221.
[17] [2000] SC 208; [2000] HRLR 191.

therefore enhances the security of tenure of Parole Board members and seeks to ensure that their reappointment does not give rise to the appearance of either dependence upon or partiality towards the executive. Appointment is still made by the Scottish Ministers, but in accordance with published regulations. Parole Board members are now appointed for six years, and may be appointed for a further six years but only after a gap in service of six years.

Most recently, a Criminal Justice (Scotland) Bill, introduced in the Scottish Parliament on 26 March 2002, will amend the Criminal Procedure (Scotland) Act 1995 to introduce a new life sentence of an 'Order of Life-long Restriction' (OLR). This builds on the recommendation of the MacLean Committee, which was appointed in 1999 by the then Scottish Home Affairs Minister, Henry McLeish, to examine the law in relation to serious violent and sexual offenders. Chaired by a High Court Judge, Lord MacLean, the Committee included expert members of the judiciary and representatives of the legal profession, the prison service, the police, social work, forensic psychiatry, clinical psychology, psychotherapy and the voluntary sector and it reported on 26 June 2000. Under the new proposals, the OLR will involve 'life-long control' of any offender considered by the court to be high risk; Risk Management Plans for offenders sentenced to OLRs will be designed to 'ensure the offender's risk is properly managed and controlled'; and a new expert body, the Risk Management Authority (RMA), will be created to assist the agencies responsible for offenders in managing the Plans.

A key to the 'success' of these new orders will be the new risk assessment framework. Whether Risk Management Plans will ensure 'continuity of management and supervision of offenders from prison back into the community', as the Scottish executive suggests,[18] remains to be seen. What is important for the purpose of our review is to ask whether sufficient resources will be allocated to this initiative to ensure that offenders detained under these orders do not spend unnecessary time in unnecessarily restricted conditions. Will the relevant bodies operate under clearly articulated principles which recognise the human rights 'trumps' of the offender?

A new body in Northern Ireland

Meanwhile, as a result of both the Human Rights Act 1998 and the Criminal Justice Review which arose out of the Good Friday Agreement,[19] a new body was created in Northern Ireland in 2001, taking effect

[18] For details of the Bill and Explanatory Notes, see the Scottish Parliament's website.

[19] A 'questions and answers' news release is available on www.niprisonservice.gov.uk/news/lifesetenorder.htm.

from 8 October 2001. The Life Sentences (Northern Ireland) Order 2001[20] created the 'Life Sentence Review Commissioners' to replace the previous Life Sentence Review Board. The Commissioners are an advisory body, with the power to direct the release of any life sentence prisoner who has served the 'relevant part' of his sentence. The Secretary of State is then under a duty to release the prisoner. The new body considers the cases of all life sentence prisoners. The Commissioners, appointed by the Secretary of State, should include a judge or senior lawyer, a psychiatrist, a chartered psychologist, a person with knowledge and experience of the supervision or aftercare of discharged prisoners, and a person who has made a study of the causes of delinquency or the treatment of offenders.[21] The numbers of affected prisoners in Northern Ireland are very small: as of 8 October 2001, there were 82 prisoners to whom the new procedure applied. Seventeen 'transitional' Commissioners had been appointed until 15–20 permanent Commissioners 'can be appointed' later in 2002.[22]

An Adhoc Committee of the Northern Ireland Assembly was set up to consider the Order, and agreed that there should be a clear statement outlining that the Commissioners should be independent of the government and appointed by open competition. The Life Sentence Review Commissioners' Rules[23] came into operation on 8 October. While these are closely modelled on the Parole Board Rules 1997, there are significant differences. For example, the Rules do not specify that the legally qualified members should chair the panel; they specify that, subject to the provisions of the Rules, the Commissioners may regulate their own procedure in dealing with each case as they consider appropriate; the Rules include a provision for the appointment of a special advocate in cases involving confidential information.

It is too early to assess the new procedures in Scotland and Northern Ireland, and indeed it is beyond the remit of this book to do so. The developments are mentioned for the sake of completeness and to remind us that the procedures in place in England and Wales are in no sense 'fixed in stone'.

Does the DLP pass the test?

It is clearly arguable that the Parole Board is not the appropriate body to decide on 'late release' as opposed to 'early release'. We have already

[20] SI 2001 No. 2564 (NI 2).
[21] See Article 3 of the Order.
[22] See www.niprisonservice.gov.uk/news/lifesetenorder.htm.
[23] See Statutory Rules of Northern Ireland 2001 No. 317.

questioned its 'independence' and its caution. Hood and Shute (2000) point out, in the context of determinate sentenced prisoners, a 'dramatic decline'[24] in the use of parole in recent years. They have no doubt that this cautious approach to parole is created by the emphasis placed on risk by the directions and training given to Parole Board members. Using existing actuarial predictors, Hood and Shute suggest that many more prisoners could be released every year without any increase in the average reconviction rate of parolees as a whole. To repeat, the Parole Board has developed this culture of caution within a legal framework governing the release of determinate sentence prisoners which allows them to release people even before they have served their 'tariff'. It is not obvious that such caution should operate in a similar way on those who are already post-tariff, who have in effect served the determinate part of their indeterminate sentence. Yet there is no reason to believe that the Parole Board is less cautious in the case of DLPs.

In Chapter 4 we looked briefly at the proposals of the Nathan Committee for Life Sentence Review Tribunals. If Parliament had accepted these proposals, the Tribunal which would now exist to decide on the release of discretionary lifers would not be a Panel of the Parole Board. It would be more obviously independent. It is impossible to guess whether it would release more prisoners, or fewer, and whether it would be more efficient or effective. But it is difficult not to believe that it would have been forced to consider its basic criteria, both substantive and procedural, closely. The Council on Tribunals and other outside bodies might have had a greater influence on the new Tribunal.

Procedural safeguards are required not simply because procedural safeguards are good in themselves but because fair procedures are likely to lead to fairer outcomes. Are the outcomes of DLPs fair? It is of course difficult to say. While it has been suggested above that the DLP has serious limitations as an independent process, it is equally important to underline the advantages that it has over what went before. Prisoners are given an oral hearing at which they and their legal advisers have the opportunity to challenge the 'evidence' for continued detention. The Panel gives written reasons for their decisions, which give some guidance to prisoners as to what they have to do to move towards release. This decision-letter may also be of use in giving a message to the Prison Service on what they should be doing. Measured in terms of what it actually does, the process was perceived by Padfield and Liebling (2000) to be very fair.

Too much should not be expected of the Parole Board. It is arguable that the creation of the DLP has diverted attention away from those who have day-to-day responsibility for helping prisoners move towards

[24] At p. 81.

release and on those who have the duty to allocate the resources and policy guidance which should make this possible. Paradoxically this book, while focusing on the DLP, concludes that to concentrate on the DLP is to miss the central point. Padfield and Liebling's research concluded that an emphasis on the operation of the Discretionary Lifer Panel process was in danger of clouding the larger question of the fairness of the substantive outcome.[25] As we have seen, while the Parole Board may direct release, no prisoner, whose case was observed during that study, was released unless he was in open conditions. When the Parole Board recommended a transfer to open conditions (i.e. a necessary step on the journey towards release), the Secretary of State held the trump card and could veto (or delay) the transfer. Thus although for prisoners, and indeed for all those involved, the DLP process was hugely significant, it appeared that the key decisions were taken at the transfer stage and that the power to make these decisions rested firmly with the Prison Service and the Home Secretary. The power of the Parole Board to direct release was seriously constrained by powers and inertias lying elsewhere, to hold up progress. Similarly, this book has sought to show that the procedural improvements forced upon the British government by the European Court of Human Rights have been interpreted narrowly and have resulted in a process which does not survive detailed analysis in human rights terms.

If the Discretionary Lifer Panel of the Parole Board fails the test as an independent court, as has been suggested, there are various options to remedy this :

- The powers and independence of the Parole Board could be strengthened. Thus the Parole Board could be encouraged to develop clearer guidelines, to demand of the Secretary of State's representative a clear argument in favour of detention, with compelling evidence of serious risk of 'dangerousness', which should be clearly defined. A start was made in the decisions of the High Court in the 1980s which required an actual likelihood of dangerousness, a serious risk to life or limb.[26] Before a strengthened DLP, the Secretary of State's representative should have to present a clear case, bearing in mind the four principles mentioned above.
- The power to direct the release of post-tariff lifers, those detained simply for 'social protection and rehabilitation' could be given to a more obviously 'independent' body. The proto-type lies in the proposals of the Nathan Committee, cast aside by Parliament in 1991, which would have created a new tribunal under the umbrella of the

[25] Padfield and Liebling (2000), at pp. 141–3.
[26] See p. 28 above.

Lord Chancellor's Department and under the scrutiny of the Council on Tribunals.

Whichever option is accepted (indeed, especially if neither is accepted), the 'ordinary' courts should more clearly acknowledge their role in providing an appropriate review. The High Court should be more active in forcing the DLP to articulate more clearly the balancing act that they are forced to confront. Unless the Home Office can convince the DLP on a balance of probabilities that the risk that a person seriously reoffending is so high as to outweigh his fundamental right to liberty, then he should be released. The DLP should be forced to develop a more rigorous scrutiny of the prisoner's right to liberty. The Home Office should be forced to articulate more clearly the grounds on which they seek to continue to detain the prisoner. To suggest this is not to overestimate the capacity of judicial review to change administrative decision-making. It would simply be a step in the direction of a genuine recognition of the importance of the right to liberty to everyone in our society.

Lessons for the future

It is not surprising that there is a lack of clarity, and indeed a degree of instability, in the precise relationships between the different organs of the state, made worse perhaps by the absence of a written Constitution. In theory, there is an efficient system of checks and balances: Parliament makes laws, the executive carries them out and the judges check that they are acting lawfully.[27] Traditionally it has been accepted in this country that the balance between human rights and competing public policy claims is primarily for the executive: the courts only intervene if the executive's evaluation of the relative importance of the two factors is so untenable as to be absurd. This book has sought to show in some small way how the system in practice breaks down. Parliament does not lay down adequate laws; the executive is left with an inadequate framework; the judges, perhaps mindful of their unelected status, are wary of undue intervention. The rights of the individual are liable to be forgotten.

The discretionary life sentence is really a fixed-term sentence with a quite separate preventive detention order.[28] A legal system which allows indeterminate sentences, while acknowledging that only a fixed term within that sentence is imposed as punishment, must also require its courts to scrutinise the lawfulness of that detention. That is the meaning

[27] For a useful analysis, see Elliott (2001), at p. 306.
[28] See van Zyl Smit (2002).

of Article 5(4). There needs to be a formal acknowledgement of society's obligation to enhance the quality of a detainee's life in detention as much as is possible consistent with security.[29] The European Court of Human Rights has proved to be a useful backstop, a reminder of minimum standards of human rights, leaving to the UK government the choice of methods for implementing its human rights obligations. This book has painted a depressing picture of a government reluctant to do more than the minimum to secure compliance. But if Parliament (dominated of course by the government) remains reluctant to set its own clear standards, human rights will continue to be undermined. There may be signs that domestic courts are likely now to be more vigilant in balancing competing interests, that judicial review may become a more adequate remedy. Lord Steyn suggested in *Daly*[30] that the doctrine of proportionality might require the reviewing court to assess the balance which the decision-maker had struck, the balance between the protection of the public (the risk that a person represents) and his or her fundamental right to liberty. But it is not only the judges who must be vigilant. The 'culture' of human rights principles must affect the thinking and decision-making of all those who work within criminal justice agencies, prison, probation and elsewhere. The beneficiaries of a more principled approach would be those individuals who remain in prison simply and only because of the imprecise and undefined risk that they present to the public.

[29] This is Walker's argument in Walker (1997), at p. 620.

[30] See p. 145 above.

Appendix 1

Extracts from the majority and dissenting opinions in *Weeks*

41. It must therefore be determined whether the fresh deprivation of liberty suffered by Mr. Weeks consequent upon that decision complied with Article 5(1)(a).

42. It was not contested that Mr. Weeks' re-detention as from 30 June 1977 was in accordance with a procedure prescribed by English law and otherwise lawful under English law. That, however, is not necessarily decisive. The 'lawfulness' required by the Convention presupposes not only conformity with domestic law but also, as confirmed by Article 18, conformity with the purposes of the deprivation of liberty permitted by sub-paragraph (a) of Article 5(1). Furthermore, the word 'after' in sub-paragraph (a) does not simply mean that the detention must follow the 'conviction' in point of time: in addition, the 'detention' must result from, 'follow and depend upon' or occur 'by virtue of' the 'conviction'. In short, there must be a sufficient causal connection between the conviction and the deprivation of liberty at issue . . .

44. The objectives to be pursued by the Home Secretary in exercising his discretion to release and recall are not spelt out in the 1967 Act or in its predecessor, the Prison Act 1952. Nevertheless, the statements made by the trial judge and the judges in the Court of Appeal make it quite plain what purpose the life sentence and any subsequent release into the community were meant to serve in Mr. Weeks' case . . .

46. . . . it may be extremely difficult, if not impossible, to disentangle different elements underlying a particular sentence in a given case and to determine which of those elements was accorded more importance by the sentencing judge; in the present case, however, it was the trial court itself and the Court of Appeal that explained in detail the reasons why Mr. Weeks received a life sentence as opposed to a determinate sentence. The Court agrees with the Commission and the applicant that the clearly stated purpose for which Mr. Weeks' sentence was imposed, taken together with the particular facts pertaining to the offence for which he was convicted places the sentence in a special category . . . The intention was to make the applicant, who was qualified both by the trial judge and by the Court of Appeal as a 'dangerous young man', subject to a continuing security measure in the interests of public safety . . .

The grounds expressly relied on by the sentencing courts for ordering this form of deprivation of liberty against Mr. Weeks are by their very nature susceptible of change with the passage of time, whereas the measure will remain in force for the whole of his life. In this, his sentence differs from a life sentence imposed on a person because of the gravity of the offence.

47. In this sense, the measure ordered against Mr. Weeks is thus comparable to the Belgian measure at issue in the Van Droogenbroeck case,[1] that is the placing of a recidivist or habitual offender at the disposal of the government – although in the present case the placement was for a whole lifetime and not for a limited period. The legitimate aim (of social protection and the rehabilitation of offenders) pursued by the measure and its effect on the convicted person are substantially the same in both cases.

Having regard to Mr. Weeks' age at the time and to the particular facts of the offence he committed, if it had not been for the specific reasons advanced for the sentence imposed, one could have serious doubts as to its compatibility with Article 3 of the Convention, which prohibits, inter alia, inhuman punishment. The remarks of Salmon L.J. in the Court of Appeal are instructive in this connection: . . . The sentencing judges were hoping for, though could not predict, an early release back into the community.

48. The special character of Mr. Weeks' sentence is further borne out by the statistics: between 1 January 1969 and 31 December 1984, of the 54,580 persons convicted of robbery only 17 have been sentenced to life imprisonment.[2]

49. Applying the principles stated in the Van Droogenbroeck judgment, the formal legal connection between Mr. Weeks' conviction in 1966 and his recall to prison some ten years later is not on its own sufficient to justify the contested detention under Article 5(1)(a). The causal link required by sub-paragraph (a) might eventually be broken if a position were reached in which a decision not to release or to re-detain was based on grounds that were inconsistent with the objectives of the sentencing court. 'In those circumstances, a detention that was lawful at the outset would be transformed into a deprivation of liberty that was arbitrary and, hence, incompatible with Article 5'.

50. In the submission of the applicant, the objectives of the courts in 1966 and 1967 as regards the length of his loss of liberty were satisfied on his release in March 1976; the requisite link was broken at that stage, so that his full rights under Article 5 were restored to him and his re-detention fifteen months later was no longer justified under Article 5(1)(e).

The Court does not accept this contention. As a matter of English law, it was inherent in Mr. Weeks' life sentence that, whether he was inside or outside prison, his liberty was at the discretion of the executive for the rest of his life (subject to the controls subsequently introduced by the 1967 Act, notably the Parole Board). This the sentencing judges must be taken to have known and intended. It is not for the Court, within the context of Article 5, to review the appropriateness of the original sentence, a matter which moreover has not been disputed by the applicant in the present proceedings.

[1] 4 EHRR 433, para. 40.

[2] Hansard, House of Commons, vol. 90, no. 43, 24 January 1986, col. 325: written answer by the Home Secretary.

It remains to examine the sufficiency of the grounds on which his re-detention in June 1977 and thereafter was based. In this area, as in many others, the national authorities are to be recognised as having a certain discretion since they are better placed than the international judge to evaluate the evidence in a particular case.[3]

51. . . . In view of this unstable, disturbed and aggressive behaviour, there were grounds for the Home Secretary to have considered that the applicant's continued liberty would constitute a danger to the public and to himself. The Minister's decision to re-detain remained within the bounds of the margin of appreciation available to the responsible national authorities; it cannot be regarded as arbitrary or unreasonable in terms of the objectives of the sentence imposed on Mr. Weeks . . .

In the Court's view, therefore, a sufficient connection, for the purposes of sub-paragraph (a) of Article 5(1), existed between his conviction in 1966 and his recall to prison in 1977 . . .

53. Accordingly, the applicant's recall to prison in 1977 and the period of his subsequent detention as in issue in the present proceedings were not incompatible with Article 5(1).

III. Alleged breach of Article 5(4) . . .

A. Whether the requisite judicial control was incorporated in the original conviction

. . .

58. The Court has already held in the context of paragraph (1)(a) of Article 5 that the stated purpose of social protection and rehabilitation for which the 'indeterminate' sentence was passed on Mr. Weeks, taken together with the particular circumstances of the offence for which he was convicted, places the sentence in a special category: unlike the case of a person sentenced to life imprisonment because of the gravity of the offence committed, the grounds relied on by the sentencing judges for deciding that the length of the deprivation of Mr. Weeks' liberty should be subject to the discretion of the executive for the rest of his life are by their nature susceptible of change with the passage of time. The Court inferred from this that if the decisions not to release or to re-detain were based on grounds inconsistent with the objectives of the sentencing court, Mr. Weeks' detention would no longer be 'lawful' for the purposes of sub-paragraph (a) of paragraph (1) of Article 5.

It follows that, by virtue of paragraph (4) of Article 5, Mr. Weeks was entitled to apply to a 'court' having jurisdiction to decide 'speedily' whether or not his deprivation of liberty had become 'unlawful' in this sense; this entitlement should have been exercisable by him at the moment of any return to custody after being at liberty and also at reasonable intervals during the course of his imprisonment[4]

[3] See, *inter alia*, *X* v. *United Kingdom* 4 EHRR 188, para. 43 and *Luberti* v. *Italy* (1984) 6 EHRR 440, para. 27.

[4] See, *mutatis mutandis*, *Van Droogenbroeck*, para. 48 in fine.

59. Article 5(4) does not guarantee a right to judicial control of such scope as to empower the 'court', on all aspects of the case, including questions of expediency, to substitute its own discretion for that of the decision-making authority. The review should, however, be wide enough to bear on those conditions which, according to the Convention, are essential for the lawful detention of a person subject to the special kind of deprivation of liberty ordered against Mr. Weeks.

B. Whether the proceedings available subsequent to conviction satisfied the requirements of Article 5(4)

60. The government submitted in the alternative that the requirements of Article 5(4) were sufficiently met by the Parole Board's jurisdiction, supplemented as it was by the availability of judicial review before the High Court. Both the applicant and the Commission disagreed with this analysis.

1. General principles

61. The 'court' referred to in Article 5(4) does not necessarily have to be a court of law of the classic kind integrated within the standard judicial machinery of the country.[5] The term 'court' serves to denote 'bodies which exhibit not only common fundamental features, of which the most important is independence of the executive and of the parties to the case . . . but also the guarantees . . . appropriate to the kind of deprivation of liberty in question . . . of [a] judicial procedure', the forms of which may vary from one domain to another.[6] In addition, as the text of Article 5(4) makes clear, the body in question must not have merely advisory functions but must have the competence to 'decide' the 'lawfulness' of the detention and to order release if the detention is unlawful.

There is thus nothing to preclude a specialised body such as the Parole Board being considered as a 'court' within the meaning of Article 5(4) provided it fulfils the foregoing conditions.[7]

2. Parole Board

(a) Independence and impartiality

62. The applicant maintained that the Parole Board is not independent of the Home Secretary, primarily because he appoints the members of the Board, provides its staff and makes the rules under which it conducts its procedures.

The Parole Board sits in small panels, each of which in the case of life prisoners includes a High Court judge and a psychiatrist. The manner of appointment of the Board's members does not, in the Court's opinion, establish a lack of independence on the part of the members.[8] Furthermore, the Court is satisfied that the judge member and the other members of the Board remain wholly independent of the executive and impartial in the performance of their duties.

[5] See *X* v. *United Kingdom*, para. 53.
[6] See *De Wilde, Ooms and Versyp* judgment paras 56 and 58.
[7] See *X* v. *United Kingdom*, para. 61.
[8] See, *mutatis mutandis, Cambell and Fell* v. *United Kingdom* (1985) 7 EHRR 165, para. 79.

There remains the question whether the Board presents an appearance of independence, notably to persons whose liberty it considers. On this point, as the government stated, the functions of the Board do not bring it into contact with officials of the prisons or of the Home Office in such a way as to identify it with the administration of the prison or of the Home Office.

The Court therefore sees no reason to conclude that the Parole Board and its members are not independent and impartial.

(b) Powers and procedural guarantees

63. The Commission, together with the applicant, took the view that the Board lacked the necessary powers and procedural guarantees for the purposes of Article 5(4). The applicant further contended that the Board's proceedings were not 'speedy'. He pointed out that, whereas his licence was revoked in June 1977, the Board did not give its decision until December 1977.

(i) Powers

64. According to the wording of the 1967 Act, the duty of the Parole Board is to 'advise' the Home Secretary on the exercise of his powers to release prisoners on licence and to revoke such licences, and its decisions take the form of 'recommendations' to the Home Secretary.

The Board's functions are without doubt purely advisory, both in law and in substance, as regards the periodic review that it carries out in relation to the question of the possible release on licence of a detained person serving a sentence of life imprisonment. The Home Secretary may not, it is true, release on licence a life prisoner unless recommended to do so by the Parole Board. However, where the Board does recommend release of such prisoners, the Home Secretary must also consult the Lord Chief Justice, together with the trial judge if available and, as demonstrated by the facts of Mr. Weeks' own case, the Home Secretary is free, in the light of all the material before him, not to accept the Board's recommendation. Quite apart from any consideration of procedural guarantees, the Board therefore lacks the power of decision required by Article 5(4) when dealing with this category of case.

On the other hand, the Board's recommendation to release is binding on the Home Secretary when the Board has to consider, as it did in December 1977 in relation to Mr. Weeks' recall to prison after release on licence. The procedure applicable in the event of recall must therefore be examined.

(ii) Procedural guarantees

65. The language of Article 5(4) speaks of the detained individual being entitled to initiate proceedings. Under the British system of parole of life prisoners, although only the Home Secretary may refer a case to the Board, referral is obligatory in recall cases except where a person recalled after a recommendation to that effect by the Board has chosen not to make written representations. In these circumstances, the recalled person can be considered as having sufficient access to the Parole Board for the purposes of Article 5(4).[9]

[9] See *X* v. *United Kingdom*, para. 52.

66. The Board deals with individual cases on consideration of the documents supplied to it by the Home Secretary and of any reports, information or interviews with the individual concerned it has itself called for. The prisoner is entitled to make representations with respect to his recall, not only in writing to the Board but also orally to a member of the Local Review Committee. The individual is free to take legal advice in preparing such representations. Furthermore, he must be sufficiently informed of the reasons for his recall in order to enable him to make sensible representations.

Whilst these safeguards are not negligible, there remains a certain procedural weakness in the case of a recalled prisoner. Thus, the Court of Appeal established in the Gunnell case that the duty on the Board to act fairly, as required under English law by the principles of natural justice, does not entail an entitlement to full disclosure of the adverse material which the Board has in its possession. The procedure followed does not therefore allow proper participation of the individual adversely affected by the contested decision, this being one of the principal guarantees of a judicial procedure for the purposes of the Convention, and cannot therefore be regarded as judicial in character.[10]

67. In view of this finding, the Court does not consider it necessary to rule on the remaining points raised by the applicant and the Commission, that is: firstly, whether, in relation to the special category of deprivation of liberty ordered against Mr. Weeks, this requirement of a proper procedure calls for the holding of an oral hearing in addition to the existing possibility of making written submissions;[11] and, secondly, whether the proceedings before the Board were 'speedy'.

(c) Conclusion

68. Consequently, neither in relation to consideration of Mr. Weeks' recall to prison in 1977 nor in relation to periodic examination of his detention with a view to release on licence can the Parole Board be regarded as satisfying the requirements of Article 5(4).

3. Judicial review

69. The Court has in previous cases recognised the need to take a comprehensive view of the system in issue before it, as apparent shortcomings in one procedure may be remedied by safeguards available in other procedures.[12] In this connection, an application for judicial review undoubtedly represents a useful supplement to the procedure before the Parole Board: it enables the individual concerned to obtain a control by the ordinary courts of both the Parole Board's decisions and the Home Secretary's decisions . . .

As the Commission pointed out, the scope of the control afforded is thus not wide enough to bear on the conditions essential for the 'lawfulness', in the sense of Article 5(4) of the Convention, of Mr. Weeks' detention, that is to say, whether it was consistent with and therefore justified by the objectives of the

[10] See, *mutatis mutandis*, *Sanchez-Reisse* v. *Switzerland* (1987) 9 EHRR 71, para. 51.
[11] See, *mutatis mutandis*, ibid.
[12] See, for example, *X* v. *United Kingdom*, para. 60.

indeterminate sentence imposed on him. In the Court's view, having regard to the nature of the control it allows, the remedy of judicial review can neither itself provide the proceedings required by Article 5(4) nor serve to remedy the inadequacy, for the purposes of that provision, of the procedure before the Parole Board.

70. In conclusion, there has been a violation of Article 5(4).

Dissenting opinions

There was two dissenting opinions. First, the partly concurring and partly dissenting opinion of Judges Thór Vilhjálmsson, Lagergren, Sir Vincent Evans and Gersing, who held that there had been no violation of Weeks' rights:

We share the view of our colleagues that the imposition of a penalty of such severity as life imprisonment in the circumstances of this case (as they appear in the material before the Court) can be comprehended only in the light of the explanation given by Thesiger J. and Salmon L.J. that, although seemingly 'terrible', it was passed with merciful intent. It is true that in this connection the judges emphasised that the sentence was 'indeterminate', in that it did not predetermine the period for which Mr. Weeks should remain in custody but left this to the discretion of the Secretary of State. Nevertheless, there can be no doubt whatever that both the sentencing judge and the Court of Appeal were fully aware and must be understood to have intended that, in the absence of the exercise of the Royal Prerogative to pardon Mr. Weeks or to remit or reduce his sentence, he would remain subject thereto with its consequences for the restriction of his liberty for the rest of his life. As a matter of English law therefore and for all practical purposes, the life sentence imposed on Mr. Weeks is indistinguishable from any other sentence of life imprisonment imposed by the English courts. Consequently, we are unable to agree with the majority of the Court that it was in a special category distinguishing it from other life sentences and was comparable, for the purposes of Article 5(1)(a) and (4) of the Convention, to the Belgian measure at issue in the Van Droogenbroeck case, that is the placing of a recidivist or habitual offender at the disposal of the government.

In the Van Droogenbroeck case, as the Court pointed out, the sentence imposed on the applicant under Belgian law had two components – he was sentenced to two years' imprisonment as a penalty for the offences of theft and attempted theft of which he was convicted and, as a recidivist, he was also placed by the court at the government's disposal for an additional period of ten years pursuant to the 'Social Protection' Act of 1964, a measure the execution of which could take different forms ranging from remaining at liberty under supervision to detention.[13] In that case, the Court agreed with

[13] See 4 EHRR 433, paras 9 and 39.

the Commission that the Belgian system for the treatment of recidivists which was at issue was 'fundamentally different from that ... of the conditional release of prisoners sentenced by a court to a period of imprisonment imposed by the court as being appropriate to the case'.[14] In our opinion, the measures to which Mr. Weeks was subject fall squarely within the latter category. And it has to be borne in mind that the alternative sentence considered by the British judges was a lengthy determinate sentence.

While, therefore, we agree with the conclusion of the majority of the Court that the applicant's recall to prison in 1977 and his subsequent detention were compatible with sub-paragraph (a) of Article 5(1), we do so for the rather different reasons and we do not agree with the conclusion of the majority that there has been a violation of Article 5(4). On both aspects of the case, our views are the same as those of the minority in the Commission.

Article 5(1)(a)

The question at issue is whether the detention of Mr. Weeks following his recall to prison in 1977 was 'the lawful detention of a person after conviction by a competent court'. We accept that the word 'after' in sub-paragraph (a) does not simply mean that the detention must follow the conviction in point of time but 'must result from, follow and depend upon or occur by virtue of the conviction'. It is not disputed that, though severe, the life sentence imposed on Mr. Weeks was one which the British judges could properly give under English law, and in fact gave, for a crime of which he had been convicted after a proper trial. Nor is it contested that his recall to prison in 1977 and subsequent detention were in accordance with domestic law. In the terms of section 62(9) of the Criminal Justice Act 1967, he was re-detained 'in pursuance of' his original life sentence. This meant that he continued to serve his sentence, the sentence imposed by the trial court. In our opinion, these elements were enough to satisfy the requirements of Article 5(1)(a).

Article 5(4)

It is well established in the Court's case law that when the decision depriving a person of his liberty is made by a court at the close of judicial proceedings the supervision required by Article 5(4) is incorporated in that decision.[15] Inasmuch therefore as Mr. Weeks continued to serve the sentence imposed by the trial court, no further provision is required by Article 5(4) to enable him to take proceedings to test the lawfulness of his detention.

We accept, of course, that what has just been said relates only to the initial decision (in this case the sentence of imprisonment) depriving a person of his liberty and that the ruling referred to in the De Wilde, Ooms and Versyp judgment does not go beyond this. Further issues of lawfulness could arise concerning decisions taken by the authorities in exercise of their power of release and recall in regard to the execution of the sentence. However, Mr. Weeks did not dispute the lawfulness of his recall or detention in terms of

14 Ibid., para 47.

15 See, *inter alia, De Wilde, Ooms and Versyp* v. *Belgium* 1 EHRR 438, para. 76.

English law. If he had wished to challenge the decisions of the authorities relevant to his recall or re-detention on grounds of 'illegality', 'irrationality' or 'procedural impropriety', he would have had available to him a remedy before the ordinary courts by way of an application for judicial review, which could be granted speedily.

We conclude, therefore, that there was no violation of Article 5(4) in the present case.

Finally, there was the partly dissenting opinion of Judge De Meyer who believed, at the other end of the scale, that there was a breach of both relevant paragraphs of Article 5:

My reasons for that conclusion are as follows.

1. The sentence imposed upon the applicant, though formally a life sentence, was in fact an indeterminate sentence. It was explicitly so qualified, both at the Hampshire Assizes and at the Court of Appeal, by the judges who dealt with his case. They simply meant to enable him to be 'released much sooner than if a long term of imprisonment had been imposed'. They wanted to act 'in mercy to the boy'. It cannot be assumed that their real intention was to put him on a life-time's leash to be drawn back at any moment.

2. Life imprisonment in its ordinary sense would indeed have been a punishment too 'terrible' for a somewhat aggressive young man of seventeen, guilty of robbing – after menacing his victim with a starting pistol loaded with blank cartridges – a sum of 35 old pence, which he did not even take away. It would have exceeded any reasonable relationship of proportionality with what actually happened. It would have been what the Eighth Amendment to the Constitution of the United States of America calls 'cruel and unusual punishment', and what Article 3 of the European Convention on Human Rights terms 'inhuman punishment'.

3. The sentence was also unique. In their answer to one of the questions put by the Court subsequent to the hearing held on 17 March 1986, the respondent government stated that it was 'not aware of any other cases where young people were given life sentences for non-homicide where the circumstances of the offence were comparable to those in the Weeks case'; it further admitted, referring to recent case law, that 'it is obviously open to question whether, if the criteria now followed by the Court of Appeal had been strictly applied' in the applicant's case, 'a life sentence would have been passed and upheld'.

4. In executing the sentence, special care and caution were therefore required. In the circumstances of the case, the sentence of life imprisonment, as explained by Thesiger J., and by Salmon L.J., entitled the Home Secretary to keep the applicant in prison only for such a period of time as was really necessary.

5. When the applicant was first released on licence (31 March 1976), more than nine years had elapsed since he was sentenced at the Hampshire Assizes (6 December 1966). Except for his mental breakdown in 1969 and his

subsequent stay at Grendon Underwood in 1970, the pleadings, arguments and documents submitted to the Court reveal nothing either about his behaviour while detained, until his escape from Swansea Prison at the end of 1974, or about any consideration which might have been given to his situation by the authorities responsible for the execution of the sentence, before the Parole Board's recommendation that same year. Neither has anything been submitted to justify why so much precious time was wasted. In 1974, the applicant's detention had already lasted long enough to have lost any reasonable connection, not only with the offence he was sentenced for, but also with the necessity of protecting the public and promoting his rehabilitation. It was still technically legal under the terms of the judicial decision on which it was founded and which it was supposed to execute. It had, however, ceased to be lawful, since it had gone far beyond the real object and purpose of that decision. It could therefore no longer be considered as 'the lawful detention of a person after conviction by a competent court'. Neither could it be further justified on any other ground.

6. The applicant has been involved in a certain number of incidents since 1974. These incidents cannot justify the length of his detention until 1974.

7. Accordingly, the applicant's detention had ceased to be compatible with Article 5(1) of the Convention.

Appendix 2

Sections 32 and 34 of the Criminal Justice Act 1991

32. [The Parole Board] –

(1) There shall continue to be a body to be known as the Parole Board ('the Board') which shall discharge the functions conferred on it by this Part.

(2) It shall be the duty of the Board to advise the Secretary of State with respect to any matter referred to it by him which is connected with the early release or recall of prisoners.

(3) The Board shall deal with cases as respects which it makes recommendations under this Part on consideration of –

(a) any documents given to it by the Secretary of State; and

(b) any other oral or written information obtained by it,

and if in any particular case the Board thinks it necessary to interview the person to whom the case relates before reaching a decision, the Board may authorise one of its members to interview him and shall consider the report of the interview made by that member.

(4) The Board shall deal with cases as respects which it gives directions under this Part on consideration of all such evidence as may be adduced before it.

(5) Without prejudice to subsections (3) and (4) above, the Secretary of State may make rules with respect to the proceedings of the Board, including provision authorising cases to be dealt with by a prescribed number of its members or requiring cases to be dealt with at prescribed times.

(6) The Secretary of State may also give to the Board directions as to the matters to be taken into account by it in discharging any functions under this Part; and in giving any such directions the Secretary of State shall in particular have regard to –

(a) the need to protect the public from serious harm from offenders; and

(b) the desirability of preventing the commission by them of further offences and of securing their rehabilitation.

(7) Schedule 5 to this Act shall have effect with respect to the Board.

34. [Duty to release discretionary life sentence prisoners] –

(1) A life prisoner is a discretionary life prisoner for the purposes of this Part if –

(a) his sentence was imposed for a violent or sexual offence the sentence for which is not fixed by law; and

(b) the court by which he was sentenced for that offence ordered that this section should apply to him as soon as he had served a part of his sentence specified in the order.

(2) A part of a sentence so specified shall be such part as the court considers appropriate taking into account –
  (a) the seriousness of the offence, or the combination of the offence and other offences associated with it; and
  (b) the provisions of this section as compared with those of section 33(2) above and section 35(1) below.

(3) As soon as, in the case of a discretionary life prisoner –
  (a) he has served the part of his sentence specified in the order ('the relevant part');
  and
  (b) the Board has directed his release under this section, it shall be the duty of the Secretary of State to release him on licence.

(4) The Board shall not give a direction under subsection (3) above with respect to a discretionary life prisoner unless –
  (a) the Secretary of State has referred the prisoner's case to the Board; and
  (b) the Board is satisfied that it is no longer necessary for the protection of the public that the prisoner should be confined.

(5) A discretionary life prisoner may require the Secretary of State to refer his case to the Board at any time –
  (a) after he has served the relevant part of his sentence; and
  (b) where there has been a previous reference of his case to the Board, after the end of the period of two years beginning with the disposal of that reference; and
  (c) where he is also serving a sentence of imprisonment for a term, after he has served one-half of that sentence;
  and in this subsection 'previous reference' means a reference under subsection (4) above or section 39(4) below made after the prisoner had served the relevant part of his sentence.

(6) In determining for the purpose of subsection (3) or (5) above whether a discretionary life prisoner has served the relevant part of his sentence, no account shall be taken of any time during which he was unlawfully at large within the meaning of section 49 of the [15 & 16 Geo. 6 & 1 Eliz. 2 c. 52.] Prison Act 1952 ('the 1952 Act').

(7) In this Part 'life prisoner' means a person serving one or more sentences of life imprisonment; but –
  (a) a person serving two or more such sentences shall not be treated as a discretionary life prisoner for the purposes of this Part unless the requirements of subsection (1) above are satisfied as respects each of those sentences; and
  (b) subsections (3) and (5) above shall not apply in relation to such a person until after he has served the relevant part of each of those sentences.

Appendix 3

Sections 28–32 of the Crime (Sentences) Act 1997 (as amended) Section 82A of the Powers of Criminal Courts (Sentencing) Act 2000

Sections 28–32 of the Crime (Sentences) Act 1997 (as amended)

28. (1) A life prisoner is one to whom this section applies if –
(a) the conditions mentioned in subsection (2) below are fulfilled; or
(b) he was under 18 at the time when he committed the offence for which his sentence was imposed.

(2) The conditions referred to in subsection (1)(a) above are –
(a) that the prisoner's sentence was imposed for an offence the sentence for which is not fixed by law; and
(b) that the court by which he was sentenced for that offence ordered that this section should apply to him as soon as he had served a part of his sentence specified in the order.

(3) A part of a sentence specified in an order under subsection (2)(b) above shall be such part as the court considers appropriate taking into account –
(a) the seriousness of the offence, or the combination of the offence and other offences associated with it; and
(b) the effect of any direction which it would have given under section 9 above if it had sentenced him to a term of imprisonment.

(4) Where in the case of a life prisoner to whom this section applies the conditions mentioned in subsection (2) above are not fulfilled, the Secretary of State shall direct that this section shall apply to him as soon as he has served a part of his sentence specified in the direction.

(5) As soon as, in the case of a life prisoner to whom this section applies –
(a) he has served the part of his sentence specified in the order or direction ('the relevant part'); and
(b) the Parole Board has directed his release under this section it shall be the duty of the Secretary of State to release him on licence.

(6) The Parole Board shall not give a direction under subsection (5) above with respect to a life prisoner to whom this section applies unless –
(a) the Secretary of State has referred the prisoner's case to the Board; and
(b) the Board is satisfied that it is no longer necessary for the protection of the public that the prisoner should be confined.

(7) A life prisoner to whom this section applies may require the Secretary of State to refer his case to the Parole Board at any time –
(a) after he has served the relevant part of his sentence; and
(b) where there has been a previous reference of his case to the Board, after the end of the period of two years beginning with the disposal of that reference; and
(c) where he is also serving a sentence of imprisonment or detention for a term, after the time when, but for his life sentence, he would be entitled to be released; and in this subsection 'previous reference' means a reference under subsection (6) above or section 32(4) below.

(8) In determining for the purpose of subsection (5) or (7) above whether a life prisoner to whom this section applies has served the relevant part of his sentence, no account shall be taken of any time during which he was unlawfully at large within the meaning of section 49 of the Prison Act 1952.

(9) An offence is associated with another for the purposes of this section if it is so associated for the purposes of Part I of the 1991 Act.

29. (1) If recommended to do so by the Parole Board, the Secretary of State may, after consultation with the Lord Chief Justice together with the trial judge if available, release on licence a life prisoner who is not one to whom section 28 above applies.

(2) The Parole Board shall not make a recommendation under subsection (1) above unless the Secretary of State has referred the particular case, or the class of case to which that case belongs, to the Board for its advice.

30. (1) The Secretary of State may at any time release a life prisoner on licence if he is satisfied that exceptional circumstances exist which justify the prisoner's release on compassionate grounds.

(2) Before releasing a life prisoner under subsection (1) above, the Secretary of State shall consult the Parole Board, unless the circumstances are such as to render such consultation impracticable.

31. (1) Where a life prisoner is released on licence, the licence shall, unless previously revoked under section 32(1) or (2) below, remain in force until his death.

(2) A life prisoner subject to a licence shall comply with such conditions (which shall include on his release conditions as to his supervision by a probation officer) as may for the time being be specified in the licence; and the Secretary of State may make rules for regulating the supervision of any description of such persons.

(3) The Secretary of State shall not include on release, or subsequently insert, a condition in the licence of a life prisoner, or vary or cancel any such condition, except –

(a) in the case of the inclusion of a condition in the licence of a life prisoner to whom section 28 above applies, in accordance with recommendations of the Parole Board; and

(b) in any other case, after consultation with the Board.

(4) For the purposes of subsection (3) above, the Secretary of State shall be treated as having consulted the Parole Board about a proposal to include, insert, vary or cancel a condition in any case if he has consulted the Board about the implementation of proposals of that description generally or in that class of case.

(5) The power to make rules under this section shall be exercisable by statutory instrument which shall be subject to annulment in pursuance of a resolution of either House of Parliament.

(6) In relation to a life prisoner who is liable to removal from the United Kingdom (within the meaning given by section 24(2) above), subsection (2) above shall have effect as if the words in parentheses were omitted.

32. (1) If recommended to do so by the Parole Board in the case of a life prisoner who has been released on licence under this chapter, the Secretary of State may revoke his licence and recall him to prison.

(2) The Secretary of State may revoke the licence of any life prisoner and recall him to prison without a recommendation by the Parole Board, where it appears to him that it is expedient in the public interest to recall that person before such a recommendation is practicable.

(3) A life prisoner recalled to prison under subsection (1) or (2) above –

(a) may make representations in writing with respect to his recall; and

(b) on his return to prison, shall be informed of the reasons for his recall and of his right to make representations.

(4) The Secretary of State shall refer to the Parole Board –

(a) the case of a life prisoner recalled under subsection (1) above who makes representations under subsection (3) above; and

(b) the case of a life prisoner recalled under subsection (2) above.

(5) Where on a reference under subsection (4) above the Parole Board –

(a) directs in the case of a life prisoner to whom section 28 above applies; or

(b) recommends in the case of any other life prisoner, his immediate release on licence under this section, the Secretary of State shall give effect to the direction or recommendation.

(6) On the revocation of the licence of any life prisoner under this section, he shall be liable to be detained in pursuance of his sentence and, if at large, shall be deemed to be unlawfully at large.

Section 82A of the Powers of Criminal Courts (Sentencing) Act 2000

82A Determination of tariffs.

(1) This section applies if a court passes a life sentence in circumstances where –
  (a) the sentence is not fixed by law; or
  (b) the offender was aged under 18 when he committed the offence.

(2) The court shall, unless it makes an order under subsection (4) below, order that the provisions of section 28(5) to (8) of the Crime (Sentences) Act 1997 (referred to in this section as the 'early release provisions') shall apply to the offender as soon as he has served the part of his sentence which is specified in the order.

(3) The part of his sentence shall be such as the court considers appropriate taking into account –
  (a) the seriousness of the offence, or the combination of the offence and one or more offences associated with it;
  (b) the effect [which section 67 of the Criminal Justice Act 1967 would have had][16] if it had sentenced him to a term of imprisonment; and
  (c) the early release provisons as compared with sections 33(2) and 35(1) of the Criminal Justice Act 1991.

(4) If the court is of the opinion that, because of the seriousness of the offence or of the combination of the offence and one or more offences associated with it, no order should be made under subsection (2) above, the court shall order that, subject to subsection (5) below, the early release provisions shall not apply to the offender.

(5) If, in a case where an order under subsection (4) above is in force, the offender was aged under 18 when he committed the offence, the Secretary of State shall at the appropriate stage direct that the early release provisons shall apply to the offender as soon as he has served the part of his sentence which is specified in the direction.

(6) The appropriate stage, for the purposes of subsection (5) above, is when the Secretary of State has formed the opinion, having regard to any factors determined by him to be relevant for the purpose, that it is appropriate for him to give the direction.

(7) In this section –
  'court' includes a court-martial;
  'life sentence' has the same meaning as in Chapter II of Part II of the Crime (Sentences) Act 1997.

(8) So far as this section related to sentences passed by a court-martial, section 167(1) below does not apply.

Appendix 4

The Parole Board Rules 1997

Made	6 October 1997
Coming into force	6 October 1997

Part I Introductory

Part II General

Part III The hearing

Part IV Miscellaneous

Schedules

Part I Introductory

Title and commencement and revocation

1. (1) These Rules may be cited as the Parole Board Rules 1997 and shall come into force on 6th October 1997.
   (2) The Parole Board Rules 1992 are hereby revoked.

Application and interpretation

2. (1) Subject to rule 19, these Rules apply where a prisoner's case is referred to the Board by the Secretary of State under section 28(6)(a), section 28(7) or section 32(4) of the Act.
   (2) In these Rules, unless a contrary intention appears –
   'Board' means the Parole Board, continued by section 32(1) of the Criminal Justice Act 1991,
   'Chairmen' means the chairman of the Board appointed under paragraph 2 of Schedule 5 to the Criminal Justice Act, 1991,
   'governor' includes a director of a contracted out prison,
   'panel' means those members of the Board constituted in accordance with rule 3,
   'parties' means the prisoner and the Secretary of State,
   'prisoner' means a person to whom section 28 of the Act applies,
   'the Act' means the Crime (Sentences) Act 1997.

Part II General

Appointment of panel

3. (1) The Chairman shall appoint three members of the Board to form a panel for the purpose of conducting proceedings in relation to a prisoner's case.

(2) The members of the panel appointed under paragraph (1) shall include a person who holds or who has held judicial office and who shall act as chairman of the panel.

Listing the case for hearing

4. The Board shall list the case for hearing and, as soon as practicable thereafter, notify the parties of the date when the case was so listed.

Information and reports by the Secretary of State

5. (1) Within eight weeks of the case being listed, the Secretary of State shall serve on the Board and, subject to paragraph (2), the prisoner or his representative –
(a) the information specified in Part A of Schedule 1 to these Rules,
(b) the reports specified in Part B of that Schedule, and
(c) such further information that the Secretary of State considers to be relevant to the case.
(2) Any part of the information or reports referred to in paragraph (1) which, in the opinion of the Secretary of State, should be withheld from the prisoner on the ground that its disclosure would adversely affect the health or welfare of the prisoner or others, shall be recorded in a separate document and served only on the Board together with the reasons for believing that its disclosure would have that effect.
(3) Where a document is withheld from the prisoner in accordance with paragraph (2), it shall nevertheless be served as soon as practicable on the prisoner's representative if he is –
(a) a barrister or solicitor,
(b) a registered medical practitioner, or
(c) a person whom the chairman of the panel directs is suitable by virtue of his experience or professional qualification;
provided that no information disclosed in accordance with this paragraph shall be disclosed either directly or indirectly to the prisoner or to any other person without the authority of the chairman of the panel.

Representation, etc.

6. (1) Subject to paragraph (2), a party may be represented by any person who he has authorised for that purpose.
(2) The following are ineligible to act as a representative before the Board –
(a) any person liable to be detained under the Mental Health Act 1983,

(b) any person serving a sentence of imprisonment;
(c) any person who is on licence having been released under Part III of the Criminal Justice Act 1967 or under Part II of the Criminal Justice Act 1991 or under Part II of the Act,
(d) any person with a previous conviction for an imprisonable offence which remains unspent under the Rehabilitation of Offenders Act 1974.

(3) Within three weeks of the case being listed, a party shall notify the Board and the other party of the name, address and occupation of any person authorised in accordance with paragraph (1).

(4) Where a prisoner does not authorise a person to act as his representative, the Board may, with his agreement, appoint someone to act on his behalf.

(5) A party may apply, in accordance with the procedure set out in rule 7 (1) and (2), to be accompanied at the hearing by such other person or persons as he wishes, in addition to any representative he may have authorised; but before granting any such application the Board shall obtain the agreement of –
(a) in the case where the hearing is to be held at a prison, the governor, and
(b) in any other case, the person in whom is vested the authority to agree.

Witnesses

7. (1) Where a party wishes to call witnesses at the hearing, he shall make a written application to the Board, a copy of which he shall serve on the other party, within 12 weeks of the case being listed, giving the name, address and occupation of the witness he wishes to call and the substance of the evidence he proposes to adduce.

(2) The chairman of the panel may grant or refuse an application under paragraph (1) and shall communicate his decision to both parties, giving reasons in writing, in the case of a refusal, for his decision.

Evidence of the prisoner

8. (1) Where the prisoner wishes to make representations about his case, he shall serve them on the Board and the Secretary of State within 15 weeks of the case being listed.

(2) Any other documentary evidence that the prisoner wishes to adduce shall be served on the Board and the Secretary of State at least 14 days before the date of the hearing.

Directions

9. (1) Subject to paragraph (3), the chairman of the panel may give, vary or revoke directions for the conduct of the case, including directions in respect of –
   (a) the timetable for the proceedings,
   (b) the varying of the time within which or by which an act is required, by these Rules, to be done,
   (c) the service of documents,
   (d) as regards any documents which have been received by the Board but which have been withheld from the prisoner in accordance with rule 5(2), whether the disclosure of such documents would adversely affect the health or welfare of the prisoner or others, and
   (e) the submission of evidence;

   and following his appointment under rule 3, the chairman of the panel shall consider whether such directions need to be given at any time.

   (2) Within 14 days of being notified of a direction under paragraph (1)(d), either party may appeal against it to the Chairman, who shall notify the other party of the appeal; the other party may make representations on the appeal to the Chairman whose decision shall be final.

   (3) Directions under paragraph (1) may be given, varied or revoked either
   (a) of the chairman of the panel's own motion, or
   (b) on the written application of a party to the Board which has been served on the other party and which specifies the direction which is sought;

   but in either case, both parties shall be given an opportunity to make written representations or, where the chairman of the panel thinks it necessary, and subject to paragraph (6)(b), to make oral submissions at a preliminary hearing fixed in accordance with paragraph (4).

   (4) Where the chairman of the panel decides to hold a preliminary hearing, he shall give the parties at least 14 days' notice of the date, time and place which has been fixed in respect thereof.

   (5) A preliminary hearing shall be held in private and information about the proceedings and the names of any persons concerned in the proceedings shall not be made public.

   (6) Except in so far as the chairman of the panel otherwise directs, at a preliminary hearing –
   (a) the chairman of the panel shall sit alone, and
   (b) the prisoner shall not attend save where he is unrepresented.

(7) The chairman of the panel shall take a note of the giving, variation or revocation of a direction under this rule and serve a copy on the parties as soon as practicable thereafter.

Part III The hearing

Oral hearing

10. (1) Except in so far as both parties and the chairman of the panel agree otherwise, there shall be an oral hearing of the prisoner's case.
(2) The prisoner shall, within five weeks of the case being listed, notify the Board and the Secretary of State whether he wishes to attend the hearing.

Notice of hearing

11. (1) When fixing the date of the hearing the Board shall consult the parties.
(2) The Board shall give the parties at least three weeks' notice of the date, time and place scheduled for the hearing or such shorter notice to which the parties may consent.

Location, privacy of proceedings

12. (1) The hearing shall be held at the prison or other institution where the prisoner is detained.
(2) The hearing shall be held in private and, except in so far as the chairman of the panel otherwise directs, information about the proceedings and the names of any persons concerned in the proceedings shall not be made public.
(3) The chairman of the panel may admit to the hearing such persons on such terms and conditions as he considers appropriate.

Hearing procedure

13. (1) At the beginning of the hearing the chairman of the panel shall explain the order of proceeding which the panel proposes to adopt.
(2) Subject to this rule, the panel shall conduct the hearing in such manner as it considers most suitable to the clarification of the issues before it and generally to the just handling of the proceedings; it shall so far as appears to it appropriate, seek to avoid formality in the proceedings.

(3) The parties shall be entitled to appear and be heard at the hearing and take such part in the proceedings as the panel thinks proper; and the parties may hear each others' evidence, put questions to each other, call any witnesses who the Board has authorised to give evidence in accordance with rule 7, and put questions to any witness or other person appearing before the panel.

(4) The chairman of the panel may require any person present at the hearing who is, in his opinion, behaving in a disruptive manner to leave and may permit him to return, if at all, only on such conditions as he may specify.

(5) The panel may receive in evidence any document or information notwithstanding that such document or information would be inadmissible in a court of law but no person shall be compelled to give any evidence or produce any document which he could not be compelled to give or produce on the trial of an action.

(6) The chairman of the panel may require the prisoner, or any witness appearing for the prisoner, to leave the hearing where evidence is being examined which the chairman of the panel, in accordance with rule 9(1)(d) (subject to any successful appeal under rule 9(2)), previously directed should be withheld from the prisoner as being injurious to the health or welfare of the prisoner or another person.

(7) After all the evidence has been given, the prisoner shall be given a further opportunity to address the panel.

Adjournment

14. (1) The panel may at any time adjourn a hearing for the purpose of obtaining further information or for such other purposes as it may think appropriate.

(2) Before adjourning any hearing, the panel may give such directions as it thinks fit for ensuring the prompt consideration of the application at a resumed hearing.

(3) Before the panel resumes any hearing which was adjourned without a further hearing date being fixed it shall give the parties not less than 14 days' notice, or such shorter notice to which all parties may consent, of the date, time and place of the resumed hearing.

The decision

15. (1) Any decision of the majority of the members of the panel shall be the decision of the panel.

(2) The decision by which the panel determines a case shall be recorded in writing with reasons, signed by the chairman of the

panel, and communicated in writing to the parties not more than seven days after the end of the hearing.

Part IV Miscellaneous

Time

16. Where the time prescribed by or under these Rules for doing any act expires on a Saturday, Sunday or public holiday, the act shall be in time if done on the next working day.

Transmission of documents etc.

17. Any document required or authorised by these Rules to be served or otherwise transmitted to any person may be sent by pre-paid post or delivered,
    (a) in the case of a document directed to the Board or the chairman of the panel, to the office of the Board;
    (b) in any other case, to the last known address of the person to whom the document is directed.

Irregularities

18. Any irregularity resulting from failure to comply with these Rules before the panel has determined a case shall not of itself render the proceedings void, but the panel may, and shall, if it considers that the person may have been prejudiced, take such steps as it thinks fit, before determining the case, to cure the irregularity, whether by the amendment of any document, the giving of any notice, the taking of any step or otherwise.

References to the Board following recall

19. Where the Secretary of State refers a prisoner's case to the Board under section 32(4) of the Act, and the prisoner has made representations under section 32(3) of the Act, these Rules shall apply subject to the following modifications –
    (a) rules 5(1), 6(3), 7(1), 8(1) and (2), 9(2) and (4), 10(2), 11(2), 14(3) and 15(2) shall apply as if for references to the periods of time specified therein there were substituted a reference to such period of time as the chairman of the panel shall in each case determine, taking account of both the desirability of the Board reaching an early decision in the prisoners' case and the need to ensure fairness to the prisoner;
    (b) rule 5 shall apply as if for the references in paragraph (l)(a) and (b) of that rule to the information and reports specified in

Schedule 1 there were substituted a reference to the information and reports specified in Schedule 2.

Rule 5 (1)

Schedule 1 Information and reports for submission to the Board by the Secretary of State on a reference to the Board under section 28(6)(a) or 28(7) of the Act

Part A Information relating to the prisoner

1. The full name of the prisoner.
2. The age of the prisoner.
3. The prison in which the prisoner is detained and details of other prisons in which the prisoner has been detained, the date and reasons for any transfer.
4. The date the prisoner was sentenced and the details of the offence.
5. The previous convictions and parole history, if any, of the prisoner.
6. The comments, if available, of the trial judge in passing sentence.
7. Where applicable, the conclusions of the Court of Appeal in respect of any appeal by the prisoner against conviction or sentence.
8. The details of any life sentence plan prepared for the prisoner which have previously been disclosed to him.

Part B Reports relating to the prisoner

1. Any pre-trial and pre-sentence reports examined by the sentencing court and any post-trial police report on the circumstances of the offence(s).
2. Any report on a prisoner while he was subject to a transfer direction under section 47 of the Mental Health Act 1983.
3. Any current reports on the prisoner's performance and behaviour in prison and, where relevant, on his health including any opinions on his suitability for release on licence (reports previously examined by the Board need only be summarised) as well as his compliance with any sentence plan.
4. An up-to-date home circumstances report prepared for the Board by a Probation Officer, including reports on the following:
   (a) details of the home address, family circumstances, and family attitudes towards the prisoner;
   (b) alternative options if the offender cannot return home;
   (c) the opportunity for employment on release;
   (d) the local community's attitude towards the prisoner (if known), including the attitudes and concerns of the victim(s) of the offence(s);

(e) the prisoner's response to previous periods of supervision;
(f) the prisoner's behaviour during any temporary leave during the current sentence;
(g) the prisoner's response to discussions of the objectives of supervision where applicable;
(h) an assessment of the risk of re-offending;
(i) a programme of supervision;
(j) a recommendation for release; and
(k) recommendations regarding any special licence conditions.

Rule 5(1) and 19(b)

Schedule 2 Information and reports for submission to the Board by the Secretary of State on a reference to the Board under section 32(4) of the act

Part A Information relating to the prisoner

1. The full name of the prisoner.
2. The age of the prisoner.
3. The prison in which the prisoner is detained and details of other prisons in which the prisoner has been detained, the date and reasons for any transfer.
4. The date the prisoner was sentenced and the details of the offence.
5. The previous convictions and parole history, if any, of the prisoner.
6. The details of any life sentence plan prepared for the prisoner which have previously been disclosed to him.
7. The details of any previous recalls of the prisoner including the reasons for such recalls and subsequent re-release on licence.
8. The statement of reasons for the most recent recall which was given to the prisoner under section 32(3)(b) of the Act.
9. The details of any memorandum which the Board considered prior to making its recommendation for recall under section 39(1) of the Act or confirming the Secretary of State's decision to recall under section 32(2) of the Act, including the reasons why the Secretary of State considered it expedient in the public interest to recall that person before it was practicable to obtain a recommendation from the Board.

Part B Reports relating to the prisoner

1. The reports considered by the Board prior to making its recommendation for recall under section 32(1) of the Act or its confirmation of the Secretary of State's decision to recall under section 32(2) of the Act.
2. Any other relevant reports.

Appendix 5

Sections 72 and 73 of the Mental Health Act 1983, as amended by the Mental Health Act 1983 (Remedial) Order 2001 (SI 2001 No. 3712)

72 Powers of Tribunals

(1) Where application is made to a Mental Health Review Tribunal by or in respect of a patient who is liable to be detained under this Act, the tribunal may in any case direct that the patient be discharged, and –

(a) the tribunal shall direct the discharge of a patient liable to be detained under section 2 above if they are satisfied –

(i) that he is not then suffering from mental disorder or from mental disorder of a nature or degree which warrants his detention in a hospital for assessment (or for assessment followed by medical treatment) for at least a limited period; or

(ii) that his detention as aforesaid is not justified in the interests of his own health or safety or with a view to the protection of other persons;

(b) the tribunal shall direct the discharge of a patient liable to be detained otherwise than under section 2 above if they are satisfied –

(i) that he is not then suffering from mental illness, psychopathic disorder, severe mental impairment or mental impairment or from any of those forms of disorder of a nature or degree which makes it appropriate for him to be liable to be detained in a hospital for medical treatment; or

(ii) that it is not necessary for the health or safety of the patient or for the protection of other persons that he should receive such treatment; or

(iii) in the case of an application by virtue of paragraph (g) of section 66(1) above, that the patient, if released, would not be likely to act in a manner dangerous to other persons or to himself.

(2) In determining whether to direct the discharge of a patient detained otherwise than under section 2 above in a case not falling within paragraph (b) of subsection (1) above, the tribunal shall have regard –

(a) to the likelihood of medical treatment alleviating or preventing a deterioration of the patient's condition; and

(b) in the case of a patient suffering from mental illness or severe mental impairment, to the likelihood of the patient, if discharged, being able to care for himself, to obtain the care he needs or to guard himself against serious exploitation.

(3) A tribunal may under subsection (1) above direct the discharge of a patient on a future date specified in the direction; and where a tribunal do not direct the discharge of a patient under that subsection the tribunal may –

(a) with a view to facilitating his discharge on a future date, recommend that he be granted leave of absence or transferred to another hospital or into guardianship; and

(b) further consider his case in the event of any such recommendation not being complied with.

(3A) Where, in the case of an application to a tribunal by or in respect of a patient who is liable to be detained in pursuance of an application for admission for treatment or by virtue of an order or direction for his admission or removal to hospital under Part III of this Act, the tribunal do not direct the discharge of the patient under subsection (1) above, the tribunal may –

(a) recommend that the responsible medical officer consider whether to make a supervision application in respect of the patient; and

(b) further consider his case in the event of no such application being made.

(4) Where application is made to a Mental Health Review Tribunal by or in respect of a patient who is subject to guardianship under this Act, the tribunal may in any case direct that the patient be discharged, and shall so direct if they are satisfied –

(a) that he is not then suffering from mental illness, psychopathic disorder, severe mental impairment or mental impairment; or

(b) that it is not necessary in the interests of the welfare of the patient, or for the protection of other persons, that the patient should remain under such guardianship.

(4A) Where application is made to a Mental Health Review Tribunal by or in respect of a patient who is subject to after-care under supervision (or, if he has not yet left hospital, is to be so subject after he leaves hospital), the tribunal may in any case direct that the patient shall cease to be so subject (or not become so subject), and shall so direct if they are satisfied –

(a) in a case where the patient has not yet left hospital, that the conditions set out in section 25A(4) above are not complied with; or

(b) in any other case, that the conditions set out in section 25G(4) above are not complied with.

(5) Where application is made to a Mental Health Review Tribunal under any provision of this Act by or in respect of a patient and the tribunal do not direct that the patient be discharged or, if he is (or is to be) subject to after-care under supervision, that he cease to be so subject (or not become so subject), the tribunal may, if satisfied that the patient is suffering from a form of mental disorder other than the form specified in the application,

order or direction relating to him, direct that that application, order or direction be amended by substituting for the form of mental disorder specified in it such other form of mental disorder as appears to the tribunal to be appropriate.

(6) Subsections (1) to (5) above apply in relation to references to a Mental Health Review Tribunal as they apply in relation to applications made to such a tribunal by or in respect of a patient.

(7) Subsection (1) above shall not apply in the case of a restricted patient except as provided in sections 73 and 74 below.

73 Power to discharge restricted patients

(1) Where an application to a Mental Health Review Tribunal is made by a restricted patient who is subject to a restriction order, or where the case of such a patient is referred to such a tribunal, the tribunal shall direct the absolute discharge of the patient if satisfied –

(a) as to the matters mentioned in paragraph (b)(i) or (ii) of section 72(1) above; and

(b) that it is not appropriate for the patient to remain liable to be recalled to hospital for further treatment.

(2) Where in the case of any such patient as is mentioned in subsection (1) above the tribunal are satisfied as to the matters referred to in paragraph (a) of that subsection but not as to the matter referred to in paragraph (b) of that subsection the tribunal shall direct the conditional discharge of the patient.

(3) Where a patient is absolutely discharged under this section he shall thereupon cease to be liable to be detained by virtue of the relevant hospital order, and the restriction order shall cease to have effect accordingly.

(4) Where a patient is conditionally discharged under this section –

(a) he may be recalled by the Secretary of State under subsection (3) of section 42 above as if he had been conditionally discharged under subsection (2) of that section; and

(b) the patient shall comply with such conditions (if any) as may be imposed at the time of discharge by the tribunal or at any subsequent time by the Secretary of State.

(5) The Secretary of State may from time to time vary any condition imposed (whether by the tribunal or by him) under subsection (4) above.

(6) Where a restriction order in respect of a patient ceases to have effect after he has been conditionally discharged under this section the patient shall, unless previously recalled, be deemed to be absolutely discharged on the date when the order ceases to have effect and shall cease to be liable to be detained by virtue of the relevant hospital order.

(7) A tribunal may defer a direction for the conditional discharge of a patient until such arrangements as appear to the tribunal to be necessary for that purpose have been made to their satisfaction; and where by virtue of any

such deferment no direction has been given on an application or reference before the time when the patient's case comes before the tribunal on a subsequent application or reference, the previous application or reference shall be treated as one on which no direction under this section can be given.

(8) This section is without prejudice to section 42 above.

References

Allan, T. R. S. (2001) *Constitutional Justice: A Liberal Theory of the Rule of Law* (Oxford: Oxford University Press).

Allison, J. W. F. (2000) *A Continental Distinction in the Common Law*, revised edn (Oxford: Oxford University Press).

Ashworth, A. (2001) 'Criminal Proceedings after the Human Rights Act', *Criminal Law Review* 855.

Baker, K. (1993) *The Turbulent Years* (London: Faber).

Barnard, E. E. (1976) 'Parole Decision-making in Britain', 4 *International Journal of Criminology and Penology* 145.

Bottomley, A. K. (1973) 'Parole Decisions in a Long-Term Closed Prison', 13 *British Journal of Criminology* 26.

Bottomley, A. K. (1984) 'Questioning Parole: Whose Discretion? What Principles?', 56 *Prison Service Journal* 21.

Bottomley, A. K. (1990) 'Parole in Transition: A Comparative Study of Origins, Developments and Prospects for the 1990s', in M. Tonry and N. Morris, (eds), *Crime and Justice* (Chicago: University of Chicago Press).

Bottoms, A. E. and Brownsword, R. (1983) 'Dangerousness and Rights', in J. Hinton (ed.), *Dangerousness: Problems of Assessment and Prediction* (London: Allen & Unwin).

Bradley, A. W. (1991) 'The Council on Tribunals: Time for a Broader Role?', *Public Law* 6.

Buchanan, A. and Leese, M. (2001) 'Detention of the ''Dangerous Severely Personality Disordered'': Some Data', *Lancet*, 358, 1955.

Bucke, T. and Brown, D. (1997) *In Police Custody: Police Powers and Suspects – Rights under the Revised PACE Codes of Practice*, HORS 174 (London: HMSO).

Carlisle, Lord (1988) *The Parole System in England and Wales. Report of the Review Committee*, Cm 532 (London: HMSO).

Clarke, D., Fisher, M. and McDougall, C. (1993) 'A New Methodology for Assessing the Level of Risk in Incarcerated Offenders', *British Journal of Criminology* 33(3) 436.

Coker, J. B. and Martin, J. P. (1985) *Licensed to Live* (Oxford: Basil Blackwell).

Craig, P. and Schonberg, S. (2001) 'Substantive Legitimate Expectations after Coughlan', *Public Law* 674.

Cross, R. and Tapper, C. (1999) *Cross and Tapper on Evidence* 9th edn (London: Butterworths).

Cullen, E. and Newell, T. (1999) *Murderers and Life Imprisonment* (Winchester: Waterside Press).

Department of Education and Skills (2000) *Skills for Life: a Strategy for Improving Adult Literacy*.

Department of Health (2000) *Reforming the Mental Health Act 1983* Cm 5016-I and II(London: HMSO).
Dworkin, R. (1977) *Taking Rights Seriously* (London: Duckworth).
Eastman, N. and Peay, J. (1999) *Law without Enforcement: Integrating Mental Health and Justice* (Oxford: Hart).
Elliott, M. (2001a) *The Constitutional Foundations of Judicial Review* (Oxford: Hart).
Elliott, M. (2001b) 'The Human Rights Act 1998 and the Standard of Substantive Review', *Cambridge Law Journal* 301.
Emmerson, B. and Ashworth, A. (2001) *Human Rights and Criminal Justice* (London: Sweet & Maxwell).
Floud, J. and Young, W. (1981) *Dangerousness and Criminal Justice* (London: Heinemann).
Forsyth, C. (2000) *Judicial Review and the Constitution* (Oxford: Hart).
Franks Committee (1957) *Report on Administrative Tribunals and Enquiries*, Cmnd 218 (London: HMSO).
Frieburg, A. and Biles, D. (1975) *The Meaning of 'Life': A Study of Life Sentences in Australia* (Australian Institute of Criminology).
Gale, M. *et al.* (1997) *A Guide to the Crime (Sentences) Act 1997* (London: Butterworths).
Galligan, D. J. (1986) *Discretionary Powers: A Legal Study of Official Discretion* (London: Clarendon Paperbacks).
Galligan, D. J. (1996) *Due Process and Fair Procedures: A Study of Administrative Procedures* (Oxford: Clarendon Press).
Gelsthorpe, L. and Padfield, N. (eds) (forthcoming) *Exercising Discretion: Decision-Making in the Criminal Justice System and Beyond* (Cullompton: Willan Publishing).
Genders, E. and Player, E. (1987a) 'Women in Prison: the Treatment, the Control and the Experience', in P. Carlen and A. Worrall (eds), *Gender, Crime and Justice* (Milton Keynes: Open University Press).
Genders, E. and Player, E. (1987b) 'Women Lifers: Assessing the Experience', in A. Morris and C. Wilkinson (eds), *Women and the Penal System*, Cropwood Conference Series No. 19, Cambridge.
Halliday, S. (2000) 'The Influence of Judicial Review on Bureaucratic Decision-Making', *Public Law* 110.
Hammond, A. H. (1998) 'Judicial Review: the Continuing Interplay between Law and Policy', *Public Law* 34.
Harlow, C. and Rawlings, R. (1997) *Law and Administration*, 2nd edn (London: Butterworths).
Harris, D. J., O'Boyle, M. and Warbrick, C. (1995) *Law of the European Convention on Human Rights* (London: Butterworths).
Hawkins, K. (1983a) 'Thinking About Legal Decision-Making', in J. Shapland (ed.) *Decision-Making in the Legal System*, Issues in Criminological and Legal Psychology No. 5, British Psychological Society.
Hawkins, K. (1983b) 'Assessing Evil: Decision Behaviour and Parole Board Justice', 23 *British Journal of Criminology* 101.
Heidensohn, F. (1997) 'Gender and Crime' in M. Maguire, R. Morgan and R. Reiner (eds), *The Oxford Handbook of Criminology* (Oxford: Clarendon Press).

Her Majesty's Chief Inspector of Prisons (1997) *Women in Prison – A Thematic Review* (London: Home Office).
Her Majesty's Chief Inspector of Prisons (2000) *Unjust Deserts: A Thematic Review of Unsentenced Prisoners* (London: Home Office).
Her Majesty's Chief Inspector of Prisons (2001) *Follow-up to Women in Prison* (London: Home Office).
Her Majesty's Inspectorates of Prison and Probation (1999) *Lifers: A Joint Thematic Review* (London: Home Office).
Her Majesty's Inspectorates of Prison and Probation (2001) *Through the Prison Gate: A Joint Thematic Review* (London: Home Office).
Holloway, K. and Grounds, A, (forthcoming) 'Mental Health Review Tribunals: the Release of Restricted Patients', in L. Gelsthorpe and N. Padfield (eds), *Exercising Discretion: Decision-Making in the Criminal Justice System and Beyond* (Cullompton: Willan Publishing).
Home Affairs Committee of the House of Commons (1995) *Murder: the Mandatory Life Sentence,* HC111 (London: HMSO).
Home Affairs Committee of the House of Commons (1996) *Murder: the Mandatory Life Sentence* (Supplementary Report) (London: HMSO).
Home Office (1990) *Crime, Justice and Protecting the Public* (London: HMSO).
Home Office (2001) *Prison Statistics England and Wales 2000* Cm 5250 (as corrected) (London: Stationery Office).
Home Office (2002) *Making Punishments Work: a Response to the Consultation* (London: Home Office).
Hood, R. and Shute, S. (1994) *Parole in Transition: Evaluating the Impact and Effects of Changes in the Parole System. Phase One: Establishing the Base-line,* Occasional Paper No. 13, Oxford Centre for Criminological Research.
Hood, R. and Shute, S. (1995) *Evaluating the Impact and Effects of Changes in the Parole System. Phase Two: Paroling with New Criteria,* Occasional Paper No. 16, Oxford Centre for Criminological Research.
Hood, R. and Shute, S. (2000) *The Parole System at Work: A Study of Risk Based Decision-Making,* Home Office Research Study No. 202.
House of Commons (1969) *Report of the Parole Board for 1967* (London: HMSO).
House of Commons (1970) *Report of the Parole Board for 1969* (London: HMSO).
House of Commons (1996) *Report of the Parole Board for 1995 and 1995–6* (London: HMSO).
House of Commons (1999) *Report of the Parole Board 1998–99* (London: Stationery Office).
House of Commons (2001) *Report of the Parole Board 2000–1* (London: Stationery Office).
House of Commons Public Accounts Committee (2001) *10th Report: Parole.*
House of Lords (1988) *Report of the Select Committee on Murder and Life Imprisonment,* Session 1988–89, HL Paper 78-I.
Hudson, B. (2001) 'Punishment, Rights and Difference: Defending Justice in the Risk Society', in K. Stenson and R. R. Sullivan (eds), *Crime Risk and Justice* (Cullompton: Willan Publishing).
Jowell, J. (2000) 'Beyond the Rule of Law: Towards Constitutional Judicial Review', *Public Law* 671.

Justice (1996) *Sentenced for Life: Reform of the Law and Procedure for Those Sentenced to Life Imprisonment* (London: Justice).
King, R. D. and Morgan, R. (1980) *The Future of the Prison System* (Aldershot: Gower).
Lester, A. and Pannick, D. (1999) *Human Rights Law and Practice* (London: Butterworths).
Lester, Lord (1998) 'UK Acceptance of the Strasbourg Jurisdiction: What Really Went on in Whitehall in 1966', *Public Law* 327.
Liebling, A. (1992) *Suicides in Prison* (London: Routledge).
Liebling, A., Muir, G., Rose, G. *et al.* (1997) *An Evaluation of Incentives and Earned Privileges: Final Report to the Prison Service* (Cambridge: Institute of Criminology).
Livingstone, S. and Owen, T. (1999) *Prison Law*, 2nd edn (Oxford: Oxford University Press).
McConville, M., Saunders, A. and Leng, R. (1991) *The Case for the Prosecution* (London: Routledge).
Mackintosh, N. J. (1998) *IQ and Human Intelligence* (Oxford: Oxford University Press).
Maden, T. (1996) *Women, Prisons and Psychiatry: Mental Disorder Behind Bars* (London: Butterworth-Heinemann).
Maguire, M., Pinter, F. and Collis, C. (1984) 'Dangerousness and the Tariff', 24 *British Journal of Criminology* 250.
Monahan, J. *et al.* (2001) *Rethinking Risk Assessment: The Macarthur Study of Mental Disorder and Violence* (Oxford: Oxford University Press).
Morgan, R. (1990) 'Less Life and More Justice', 29 *Howard Journal of Criminal Justice* 296.
Nash, M. (1999) *Police, Probation and Protecting the Public* (London: Blackstone).
Padfield, N. (1993) 'Parole and the Life Sentence', 23 *Howard Journal of Criminal Justice* 87.
Padfield, N. (1996) 'The Mandatory Life Sentence in the Balance', 146 *New Law Journal* 420.
Padfield, N. (1997) 'Fixing the Tariff and the Length of Her Majesty's Pleasure', 56 *Cambridge Law Journal* 477.
Padfield, N. (2002) 'Tariffs in Murder Cases', *Criminal Law Review* 190.
Padfield, N. and Liebling, A. with Arnold, H. (2000) *An Exploration of Decision-Making at Discretionary Lifer Panels* Home office Research Study No. 213.
Padfield, N. and Liebling, A. with Arnold, H. (forthcoming) 'Discretion and the Release of Life Sentence Prisoners', in L. Gelsthorpe and N. Padfield (eds), *Discretion in Criminal Justice* (Cullompton: Willan Publishing).
Page, J. (1998) 'The Conduct of Discretionary Lifer Panels, Discussion Paper. Unpublished Home Office paper, Lifer Unit.
Peay, J. (1989) *Tribunals on Trial: A Study of Decision Making under the Mental Health Act 1983* (Oxford: Clarendon Press).
Percy Report (1957) *Royal Commission on the Law relating to Mental Illness and Mental Deficiency 1954–7*, Cmnd 169 (London: HMSO).
Price, D. (2000) 'Security Categorization in the English Prison System' (Cambridge: unpublished PhD).

Prison Reform Trust (2000) *Justice for Women: the Need for Reform*, Report of the Committee on Women's Imprisonment chaired by Professor Dorothy Wedderburn (London: Prison Reform Trust).

Richardson, G. (1990) 'The Select Committee and the Sentencing Structure for Murder', 29 *Howard Journal of Criminal Justice* 300.

Richardson, G. (1991) 'Discretionary Life Sentences and the European Court of Human Rights', *Public Law* 34.

Richardson, G. (1993) *Law, Process and Custody: Prisoners and Patients* (London: Weidenfeld & Nicolson).

Richardson, G. and Mackin, D. (2000) 'Judicial Review and Tribunal Decision-Making: A Study of the Mental Health Review Tribunal', *Public Law* 494.

Richardson, G. and Thorold, O. (1999) 'Law as a Rights Protector: Assessing the Mental Health Act 1983', in N. Eastman and J. Peay (eds), *Law without Enforcement: Integrating Mental Health and Justice* (Oxford: Hart).

Royal Commission on Criminal Justice (chaired by Lord Runciman) (1993) *Report*, Cm 2263 (London: HMSO).

Sapsford, R. (1983) *Life Sentence Prisoners: Reaction, Response and Change* (Milton Keynes: Open University Press).

Schlanger, M. (1999) 'Beyond the Hero Judge: Institutional Reform Litigation as Litigation', 97 *Michigan LR* 1994.

Sentencing Advisory Panel (2001) *Tariffs in Murder Cases: A Consultation Paper* (Sentencing Advisory Panel).

Singleton, N. *et al.* (1997) *Psychiatric Morbidity among Prisoners: Summary Report* (Office of National Statistics).

Sparks, C. (1998) *Prisoners' Views of the Lifer System: Policy vs Reality* (London: Prison Reform Trust).

Sunkin, M. and Pick, K. (2001) 'The Changing Impact of Judicial Review: the Independent Review Service of the Social Fund', *Public Law* 736.

Thomas, D. A. (2002) 'Automatic Life Sentences after *Offen*', 3 *Archbold News* 5.

Tidmarsh, D. (1999) 'Necessary but not Sufficient: the Personal View of a Psychiatric Member of the Parole Board', in Murray Cox (ed.), *Remorse and Reparation* (London: Jessica Kingsley).

Tuddenham, R. (2000) 'Beyond Defensible Decision-Making: Towards Reflexive Assessment of Risk and Dangerousness', *Probation Service Journal* 173.

Van Zyl Smit, D. (1999) 'Life Imprisonment as the Ultimate Penalty in International Law: A Human Rights Perspective', 9 *Criminal Law Forum* 5.

Van Zyl Smit, D. (2001) 'Abolishing Life Imprisonment?', 3 *Punishment and Society* 299.

Van Zyl Smit, D. (2002) *Taking Life Imprisonment Seriously in National and International Law* (The Hague: Kluwer).

Von Hirsch, A. (1993) *Censure and Sanctions* (Oxford: Clarendon Press).

Walker, N. (1983) 'Protecting People', in J. Hinton (ed.), *Dangerousness: Problems of Assessment and Prediction* (London: Allen & Unwin).

Walker, N. (1996) *Dangerous People* (London: Blackstone Press).

Walker, N. (1997) 'Harms, Probabilities and Precautions', *Oxford Journal of Legal Studies* 611.

Whitty, N., Murphy, T. and Livingstone, S. (2001) *Civil Liberties Law: The Human Rights Era* (London: Butterworths).

Williams, D. G. T. (1984) 'The Council on Tribunals: The First Twenty Five Years', *Public Law* 73.
Windlesham, Lord (1990) 'From Tariff to Penal Sanction', 29 *Howard Journal of Criminal Justice.*
Wood, D. (1988) 'Dangerous Offenders and the Morality of Protective Sentences', *Criminal Law Review* 424.
Woolf, Lord Justice (1991) *Prison Disturbances 1990*, Cm 1456 (London: HMSO).

Index

For Product Safety Concerns and Information please contact our EU
representative GPSR@taylorandfrancis.com
Taylor & Francis Verlag GmbH, Kaufingerstraße 24, 80331 München, Germany

www.ingramcontent.com/pod-product-compliance
Ingram Content Group UK Ltd.
Pitfield, Milton Keynes, MK11 3LW, UK
UKHW022130190926
475702UK00013B/1737

9781138964648